John Edgar
HOOVER

Books by Hank Messick

John Edgar
HOOVER

An inquiry into the life and times of John Edgar
Hoover, and his relationship to the continuing
partnership of Crime, Business, and Politics

by
Hank Messick

DAVID McKAY COMPANY, INC.
New York

Author's Note

In six previous books I have documented the formation and evolution of a national crime syndicate and exposed its essential relationships to corrupt public officials and amoral businessmen.

Organized crime, as I have repeatedly attempted to illustrate, is not controlled by any one ethnic or national group. Just as businessmen and politicians have varied backgrounds, so do gangsters. Nor is the crime syndicate a formal, rigid structure in any conventional sense. In the beginning it was but a loose alliance of city and regional "combinations" working together under a board of directors to eliminate jurisdictional disputes and fix broad policy. Over the years it has changed, just as our socioeconomic system has adjusted to new conditions. It is still changing today as a new generation takes over from the old men who began as bootleggers. Decades may pass before we can fully chart the changes now occurring.

In this book I shift attention from the gangsters to a few of the public officials and businessmen who, by action or inaction in years past, have helped make organized crime powerful. Inevitably, one must begin with John Edgar Hoover.

This book is not a biography, nor even a history, of one man. It has, I hope, a broader function. I am aware of the current trend, which, under the guise of achieving "balance" and "objectivity," succeeds largely in blurring the image.

Such studies have neither "heroes" nor "villains"—just human beings. While such an approach is preferable to the one employed by Hoover—calling all lawbreakers "rats" and all civil-rights advocates "subversives"—it is not suitable for a study of this kind. I do not find it necessary, for example, to say, "*Yes*, Hoover is getting senile, *but* he did a good job rounding up kidnapers years ago." My purpose is to examine the facts, and to let them speak for themselves. That is true objectivity.

In 1971, as this book was being written, the *New York Times* disclosed the existence of a forty-seven-volume study of America's involvement in the Vietnam war. The study gives insight into the manner in which the average citizen can be brainwashed by high officials who hold his intelligence in contempt. This book demonstrates how an equally shocking hoax was perpetrated against the American people in the field of law enforcement. Tragic as the Vietnam war is, it is no more tragic than the continuing betrayal suffered in the war against organized crime. We, the so-called "squares" of this nation, have been contemptuously exploited by an alliance of respected men and the scum of our social system.

The story of this betrayal has not been locked in official files under "Top Secret" classification, however. It is very much on record in the files of newspapers, congressional committees, and investigative agencies. I have merely pulled the scattered facts together, utilizing as best I could the insight gained in many years of personal participation in the fight against organized crime and corruption.

I owe much to many in compiling such a study. I owe special thanks to Dan Catlin, an editor skilled in the art of painless surgery. But my greatest debt remains to the young sociologist I met many years ago at the University of North Carolina, and was lucky enough to marry. She has provided more than moral support. Without her active aid, this book could not have been written.

Hank Messick
Fort Lauderdale
1971

John Edgar
HOOVER

Besides, what is to be feared is not so much the immorality of the great as the fact that immorality may lead to greatness.

—Alexis de Tocqueville

Introduction

UNLIKE God, John Edgar Hoover admits to no mistakes.

God created man in His own image, and Hoover created the Federal Bureau of Investigation to preserve *his* image.

When Hoover complained that the air conditioner in his $30,000 car didn't cool sufficiently with the windows open to the Miami sun, his men took heed. Secretly, a higher-powered unit was installed in the bullet-proof vehicle.

When Hoover insisted that the television set in his office should produce a picture instantly, the staff called in an electronics expert. A special tube was installed. Burning continuously, it kept the set warm and ready. A special agent was assigned to replace the tube at frequent intervals. Years later when the electronics industry achieved some scientific breakthroughs, "instant start" TV became commonplace. But Hoover had it first.

When Hoover complained that the "cleaning people" had misplaced a paper on his desk, it became part of the evening routine to chart the desk after the director departed, in order to make certain, when cleaning chores were completed, that everything was back where the boss had left it.

When an agent spilled a cup of coffee on Hoover's rug—

1

the director was out of town—the staff, unable to remove the stain, had an exact duplicate manufactured over the weekend and installed before Hoover returned.

When a former special agent wrote an unflattering book about the FBI, arrangements were made to have the author appear on the Joe Pyne Show—a syndicated television production. Pyne, who made a career out of insulting his guests, first presented a former Russian secret agent. The Russian was permitted to make a number of wild, uncheckable statements. There was strong applause from a cooperative studio audience. The ex-FBI agent followed. Everything he said was questioned by Pyne who had been supplied with an alleged FBI "fact sheet" on the book. The studio audience booed the American. The show's climax came when the Russian reappeared to shake his finger in the face of the American, berating him for daring to question the ability of John Edgar Hoover. The show ended with Pyne declaring that he was more impressed with Hoover than ever before. The audience rose to its feet to cheer his words.

When Hoover, reviewing a lengthy report, became annoyed because the writer had not respected the margin requirements demanded for such documents, the Director scribbled at the top of the first page, "Watch the borders." The report then went its prescribed rounds. No one understood, but no one dared to ask for an explanation. Orders went out to FBI field offices to "watch the borders," and for several weeks special agents stood guard at points of entry along the Mexican and Canadian borders.

When Special Agent John F. Shaw, attending special classes at the John Jay College of Criminal Justice, wrote a private letter to his professor, the FBI reconstructed a copy from scraps in a wastebasket. Shaw, a seven-year veteran of the FBI, his wife dying of cancer, was transferred by Hoover and reprimanded.

The long letter that aroused Hoover's rage was objective.[1] Shaw, writing in confidence to his professor, assumed the right to think for himself, his fatal mistake. The organization created by Hoover does not consider independent thought a privilege of its members. Only Hoover has that right, and his thoughts are accepted without question.

Shaw, in his letter summed it up well. He wrote:

2

Basically, the Bureau pulse-beat is transmitted coast-to-coast through 55 geographically spaced field offices which operate as partially autonomous cells. A Special Agent in Charge (SAC) is *technically in command* at each of these 55 locations. Actually, a SAC is not generally known *for his independence of action or his propensity for original thought.* Operational control of the FBI is centralized in Washington, D.C.

Shaw's letter continued:

How centralized is this control? Well, woe to the Special Agent if some "independent" remark is later construed by Headquarters as out-of-line with "established Bureau policy." . . .

Rules and regulations are *amply,* if not *clearly,* spelled out, and so are the penalties. . . . Internal discipline in the Bureau is swift and harsh. Unfortunately, too, it is often quite arbitrary. Punishment is usually meted out *in direct proportion to the amount of bad publicity generated by the particular mistake or incident* . . . [Emphasis added].

. . . There is a haunting phrase that echoes throughout the Bureau: "Do not embarrass the Director." This has been so widely interpreted and liberally applied that there is some question today what action or conduct cannot be considered "embarassing," "indiscreet," "imprudent," or "ill-timed."

. . . Yes, a personality cult does extend through the echelons of management in the FBI. . . . It is certainly no "military secret," though I am sure, not widely published either, that adulation of the Director in some form or other provides the main catalyst in the process of "administrative advancement." There are some pretty funny success stories in the annals of the FBI. . . .

Inevitably, Shaw turned to the subject of crime, and it is these thoughts that are perhaps of greatest value to a proper evaluation of John Edgar Hoover. He wrote:

Only recently has the Bureau begun to develop an intelligence network for a coordinated attack on organized crime. Bank robberies and "top-ten fugitives" have always taken precedence, perhaps because they *generated headlines* in the nation's press. But now the pendulum has swung. Bank robberies are a dime-a-dozen. . . . Bank robbers are now "small apples" compared to the annual rake-in of organized crime. *For decades, the Bureau refused to believe or chose to ignore the fact that the criminal underworld had not only invaded the world of legitimate business but was operating with the efficiency and expertise of "big*

3

business." The Bureau was slow to cooperate in the organization of coordinated Federal Strike Forces which are at least a novel approach to an old stalemated problem. The Bureau generally refuses to recognize "sophisticated methods" of combatting crime which are outside its own arsenal. At the same time, the internal power structure of the FBI has been too rigidly set in its own ways to conceive or implement a novel approach involving cooperation with outside agencies.

Special Agent Shaw made no attempt in his letter to explain *why* the FBI "refused to believe or chose to ignore" the reality of organized crime. He is not alone. Yet the question is vital, the more so when it is recognized that Hoover's prestige rests largely upon the reputation of the FBI as a law-enforcement agency.

Over the decades Hoover has been far more interested in the "Red menace." In 1919 as special assistant to the attorney general, he prepared a legal brief on the doctrines of the Communist Party which concluded with these words:

"These doctrines threaten the happiness of the community, the safety of every individual, and the continuance of every home and fireside. They would destroy the peace of the country and thrust it into a condition of anarchy and lawlessness and immorality that passes imagination."

In December 1957, some thirty-eight years later, in the Foreword to his book, *Masters of Deceit*, he referred to that statement and commented:

"Today, as I write these words, my conclusions of 1919 remain the same. Communism is the major menace of our times. Today it threatens the very existence of our western civilization."[2]

This preoccupation with the Red menace is, and has been Hoover's chief source of strength. It has brought him rich and influential allies of the type described some years ago by Leo Huberman and Paul M. Sweezy in their analysis of the roots of McCarthyism. They wrote:

The American bourgeoisie has experienced a vast influx of nouveau riches and parvenus. . . . The characteristic qualities and attitudes of the nouveau riche dispose him toward fascism in the present-day capitalist environment. He tends to be aggres-

4

sive, unscrupulous, vain: he develops feelings of jealousy and even hatred for the aristocracy which refuses to accept him as an equal. Self-important, yet frustrated, craving power and prestige commensurate with his wealth, longing to emulate the snobs who don't appreciate his true value, the nouveau riche finds a natural outlet in political support of a movement which is simultaneously reactionary, brutal, vulgar—and shows signs of succeeding.[3]

But men of this type were in action long before Joseph McCarthy abandoned chicken farming for politics. John Edgar Hoover was their first hero, and has continued to be their steadfast ally. As reaction to Woodrow Wilson's idealism set in following World War I, Hoover found his spot among the bigots of that era. But, like McCarthy later, he did more than ride the tide—he helped create it. Unlike McCarthy, who was too shallow to take any cause seriously, Hoover became infected with the poison he helped to dispense. For the young man, sophisticated only in the ways of Washington bureaucracy, anti-Red sentiment became a matter of patriotism and morality. He made his mind up early and, as he has since admitted, it remained made up.

The advent of that incredible era under President Warren G. Harding found Hoover eager to take his place in the "Department of Easy Virtue," officially known as the Justice Department. His press agents and sycophants have portrayed the young man sitting by in frustrated silence as the "Ohio Gang" stole the country blind, but the facts leave no doubt that this is untrue. Hoover was selected by clever, unsentimental men to serve as assistant director of the Bureau of Investigation, and he performed ably as William J. Burns's administrative assistant while Jess Smith, Gaston B. Means, and scores of other crooks were put into office and protected by Attorney General Harry M. Daugherty. Hoover was there, working—the number-two man in the Bureau—as deals were made with bootleggers and as pardons were sold. No one has suggested that he personally profited by the corruption, but in time the Republican administration gave him the top job. He was to parlay that job into a position of power unique in American history. Reward enough.

5

More than half a century has passed since Harding was elected—one-fourth the life of this nation—and the scandals of that day are for most citizens long gone and forgotten. Yet for John Edgar Hoover it was a decisive, formative period that greatly influenced the man and the organization with which he was to become identified.

It was a time when wealth was considered proof of morality; when the ends justified the means; when the business of the country was business. It was the age when Federal laws were openly violated, when racial unrest was dismissed as the work of Communists, when "honest graft" was considered both right and natural. The "idealism" of Wilson, of La Follette, had been repudiated by a public entirely willing to leave the problems of the country and the world to the "best minds."

Hoover saw at firsthand how constitutional rights were violated under the guise of patriotism, how Federal agents were used as secret police to clobber political dissidents. He became acquainted with the real rulers of the country, the silent men who pulled the strings to which the politicians responded.

With his knowledge he developed a resistance to social changes that might threaten the status quo. But he concealed that resistance by transforming it into an exaggerated dedication to basic virtues: the flag, God, country. And in so doing he learned how to survive.

Under the New Deal, Hoover proved he was flexible. While his right-wing friends moaned about socialism, the still youthful director muted his fears and conveniently forgot about the Red menace. A new foe was found—the "criminal horde," which, according to Hoover, also threatened the American way of life. Franklin D. Roosevelt did not take Hoover very seriously. Indeed, he rather enjoyed the cops-and-robbers game played by the "G-Men" in those days of "machine-gun justice." So did the confused and disillusioned public. At the mercy of economic forces they did not comprehend, rank-and-file citizens found some relief in identifying with the "white hats" in their dramatic battles against such "bad guys"—or, to use Hoover's word, "rats"—as John Dillinger, "Creepy" Karpis, and "Pretty Boy" Floyd.

6

During World War II the FBI gained new glory as the scourge of Nazi spies. Hoover's press agents have not mentioned that Naval Intelligence considered it necessary to enlist the aid of gangsters Meyer Lansky and Lucky Luciano to protect the docks of New York City. Nor have they explained why a Japanese "fifth column" was able to operate in Hawaii under the nose of the G-Men. But they have taken credit from other agencies; for example, in the case of the German saboteurs put ashore from submarines on Long Island. The reputation of the FBI, undeserved as it was, was deliberately enhanced at the expense of the Coast Guard to boost morale at home and persuade Hitler it was useless to send more agents.

Unfortunately, while Hoover chased punks and defended the nation against bumbling saboteurs, organized crime—in league with right-wing politicians and nouveau-riche parvenus—became a major force in American life.

Postwar reaction brought "McCarthyism" and an opportunity for Hoover to return to his first hate. Blandly ignoring the shocking facts about organized crime exposed by the Kefauver Committee, Hoover concentrated once more upon the Red menace. Hysteria grew, not discouraged by Hoover and his allies—the Rosenstiels, the Murchisons. History repeated itself, the Republicans returned to power, and the FBI director played the same game he had perfected under Calvin Coolidge and Herbert Hoover. He served his masters well, restrained only by the instinct of the bureaucrat to protect his own job.

The Kennedy years were a nervous interlude for Hoover, but he proved again that he could adjust. Forced into battle against organized crime for the first time, the FBI neatly diverted national attention from Hoover's friends and allies and directed it toward the punks of the hapless Mafia. Better than anyone else he knew that his seventieth birthday on January 1, 1965, would give President Kennedy the politically acceptable excuse he needed to retire the old man.

The assassination of the President ended that threat, even as thirty-one years earlier the mysterious death of Thomas J. Walsh saved Hoover's job. Lyndon Johnson was a man with whom Hoover could work. A product of Texas politics, a spokesman for the nouveau riche, where Hoover found his basic support, Johnson waived the mandatory retirement requirements and told Hoover: "The nation cannot afford to lose you."

Richard M. Nixon was also a member of the new breed that paid lip service to the old values while clawing its way to wealth and power. Hoover had helped the young politician in the days when Nixon was known as a "white-collar McCarthy," and with him had shared the hospitality of the nouveau riche. As much as anyone, he had helped Nixon—a flexible man in his own right—to adjust to changing conditions. And, in Attorney General John Mitchell, Hoover found a nominal boss who, while perhaps more intelligent, embraced the same fears and prejudices as Harry Daugherty.

But even Hoover recognized that age was one foe that could not be diverted by references to the Red menace. He displayed an increasing shrillness, a growing irritability, a sudden grasping for new powers. Across Pennsylvania Avenue from the Justice Department, a monument fit for a Roman emperor was under construction—the future home of the FBI. Hoover wanted desperately to retain power until it was completed, until it could be dedicated to him as a permanent memorial. Were he to quit too soon, Hoover knew all too well that his confidential files might come under the scrutiny of hostile eyes. The Harding Memorial had stood undedicated for many years as scandals swirled around the name of the dead President. Hoover feared, with reason, that the same thing might happen to him if he released the reins of power too soon.

Yet more is at stake than a memorial. If Hoover can hold on until Nixon is re-elected, he can retire knowing his image will be in safe hands for four more years. Hopefully, by 1976, the public will turn to other things and the right wing will have found a new champion. The reverent memories of Hoover's greatness will be unblotched by the record that proves otherwise.

8

I

ON April 2, 1917, President Woodrow Wilson in an address to Congress called upon the American people "to dedicate our lives and fortunes, everything that we are and everything that we have, with the pride of those who know that the day has come when America is privileged to spend her blood and her might for the principles that gave her birth and happiness and the peace which she has treasured."[1]

Four days later Congress declared war on Germany.

On June 5, 1917, all men between twenty-one and thirty years of age registered for military service.

And on July 26, 1917, John Edgar Hoover—single, twenty-three, in good health—quit his job as a clerk in the Library of Congress to become a clerk in the Department of Justice.

The job paid twelve hundred dollars a year, but it carried a certain fringe benefit—draft exemption.

This became obvious a year later when the Department of Justice ordered its Bureau of Investigation (later the Federal Bureau of Investigation) to round up thousands of alleged draft evaders or "slackers." More than seventy-five thousand were seized in the New York metropolitan area alone. Later

9

it was discovered that of every two hundred men put in jail, at least a hundred ninety-nine had been mistakenly seized. Congress became aroused and demanded the names of Department of Justice employees who had been given draft-exempt status. About two-thirds of the names submitted were Bureau of Investigation agents.[2]

Hoover's press agents over the years have ignored this episode or explained that the young clerk's superiors considered his services so important "they persuaded him to spend the period of the World War at his desk."[3] No one has expounded on why Hoover's services were so valuable at that time.

The young man's sagacity in making his timely move to the haven of Justice, is explained by his background. His father had for many years been a Washington bureaucrat, and his older brother by fifteen years had followed the family pattern. A Washington boy, John Edgar Hoover knew well the security of civil service and was familiar with all the angles. More than one President has deplored his inability to reform the Federal machinery. Like the United States Senate, it is very much a private club. Thanks to his father and brother, Hoover was a member of that club from the beginning. Despite the fact that at Central High School he had been captain of a company in the school's cadet corps—and so enjoyed his rank that he wore his uniform to church, where he taught a Sunday School class—he apparently felt no need to respond to Wilson's call. Men planning a political career might find a record of war service useful—as Joe McCarthy did—but Hoover had no such ambition. It was easier, and safer, to follow family tradition. And so, while other men fought and died, Hoover won a place of power and—ironically—the reputation as a patriot as well.

Hoover did not become a significant national figure until 1934. Consequently, his activities in the earlier years received little attention at the time and we are dependent upon accounts written after his public-relations campaign was in high gear. In many cases, as Hoover himself was the source of the material, the suspicion that much of it was self-serving cannot be avoided, as with this portrait—written in 1937:

10

From the day he entered the Department, certain things marked Hoover apart from scores of other young law clerks. He dressed better than most, and a bit on the dandyish side. He had an exceptional capacity for detailed work, and he handled small chores with enthusiasm and thoroughness. He constantly sought new responsibilities to shoulder and welcomed chances to work overtime. When he was in conference with an official of his department, his manner was that of a young man who confidently expected to rise. His superiors were duly impressed. . . .[4]

The young clerk had, of course, the advantage of being unmarried and unattached. If he devoted any time to women —other than his mother—there is no mention made of it. Later, it became fashionable to explain that Hoover was "wedded" to his work, that the FBI served in lieu of wife and children. The legend builders in their zeal created an unhealthy picture of a young man, and nothing in the years that lay ahead corrected it.

A key man in Hoover's rapid rise to power was A. Mitchell Palmer. At the time Hoover joined the Justice Department, Palmer, a former Congressman from Pennsylvania, held the post of alien property custodian. He was one of those superiors who became impressed by the young clerk's zeal and his distrust of all things foreign. This distrust, combined with political expediency, caused Hoover and Palmer in 1918 to team up in an attack on Boies Penrose. Penrose, a United States senator, was also the political boss of Pennsylvania. A man of unlimited appetite—his feats as a trencherman were considered incredible—he was notorious even among the Republicans of that era. Taking advantage of the national mood, Palmer charged that Penrose received political support from the nation's brewers. The brewers, he added, were pro-German and unpatriotic. Worse, they were opposed to Prohibition which, even then, was gathering strength in Congress. The "dry" forces in Congress saw an opportunity to link their cause with patriotism and anti-German prejudice. They promptly pushed through a resolution to investigate Palmer's charges. Many of the brewers were indeed of German descent, which was considered enough basis for the accusation to justify the investigation.[5]
The probe filled three huge volumes with testimony—a

rather sad commentary on the intelligence of Congress and the public. Nothing conclusive was found, of course, and the end of the war made the entire matter utterly absurd. But the public, if it needed reassurance, could take solace in the fact that the probers did discover that the Bureau of Investigation had not neglected the problem.

Bruce Bielaski, then head of the Bureau, disclosed that his agents had already made a list of all those suspected of being pro-German. The "suspects" included such men as William Jennings Bryan, Wilson's first secretary of state. Ironically, William Randolph Hearst—later one of Hoover's most consistent supporters—was listed. Professor Albert B. Hart of Harvard was also one of the suspects. When that smear was challenged by such men as Theodore Roosevelt, Bielaski offered as proof a book by Hart. But when asked what the book showed, the Bureau chief confessed he had "not had time to examine [it] critically."

Under the circumstances, the committee decided it had better find a new angle. Bielaski, on January 9, 1919, supplied it. He suggested that the committee should investigate "radicals." A Bureau agent, Archibald E. Stevenson, provided the necessary link between "pro-German brewers" and the "radicals" by charging: "German socialism . . . is the father of the Bolsheviki movement in Russia, and consequently the radical movement which we have in this country today has its origin in Germany."[6]

In words similar to those to be used shortly by Hoover, Stevenson warned that the radicals constituted "the gravest menace in our country today." The probe that followed set the stage for Palmer's infamous "Red raids" early in 1920, and made possible Hoover's emergence as a Commie-fighter. It greatly weakened the brewers' standing and provided an opportunity for such men as Lewis S. Rosenstiel to enter the field. It also helped the "drys" immeasurably. On January 17, 1920, the Eighteenth Amendment became effective. The Bootleg era had begun—the gestation period for organized crime in America.

John Edgar Hoover was apparently too busy saving the country from the "Red menace" to worry about gangsters— then or later. It was a time of hysteria and, when someone

12

began sending bombs through the mail, it was obvious to all that the Revolution was at hand. President Wilson, fighting a losing battle for the League of Nations and desperately ill, permitted Palmer to become attorney general of the United States, and Palmer immediately tapped Hoover to be his special assistant in charge of counterrevolutionary activities.

The twenty-nine bombs sent through the mail to prominent persons injured only one person, a servant of Senator Thomas W. Hardwick of Georgia, but that did not lessen the excitement they aroused. On June 2, 1919, a bomb went off on the front porch of Palmer's house. The blast apparently killed two men who, presumably, had tossed the device and failed to get out of the way. Eight other explosions occurred that night in cities from Boston to Pittsburgh. Found near the scene of each were handbills declaring that the "class war is on."[7]

Whether the bombs were the work of dedicated Communists remains uncertain to this day. But Palmer used the incident to secure an additional five hundred thousand dollars from Congress and set up a general intelligence division in the Department of Justice, John Edgar Hoover in command.

There is reason to believe that Hoover and his colleagues played on Palmer's fear in order to enhance GID's power and prestige. To do so would be consistent with his future performance. Each time Hoover has appeared before a Congressional budget hearing he has managed to frighten those who controlled the purse strings with a new and sinister plot. As late as November 27, 1970, he created a furor by telling a Senate committee of "an incipient plot on the part of an anarchist group" to blow up underground heating tunnels in Washington and kidnap "a highly placed government official."

As Director of the General Intelligence Division, Hoover put his experience as a librarian to use. In an amazingly short time, less than four months, he set up an elaborate index system containing more than 200,000 cards. The cards contained detailed data on all known radical organizations, individuals, and publications. Palmer was later to boast that complete case histories of more than 60,000 radicals were

13

listed. The file, Palmer said, contained "a greater mass of data upon this subject than is anywhere else available." Whether it, like the earlier file on "pro-Germans," was inaccurate, there was no way to tell. Hoover had no intention of submitting it to public scrutiny—a policy he continues to follow today. The good bureaucrat learns by his mistakes; John Edgar Hoover is a master at his trade.

While the cards were being assembled, Hoover studied the new enemy—Communism. In his own words: "The amount of material was voluminous: party statements, resolutions, platforms, news accounts, manifestoes, the very documents of American Communism. I also studied the writings of Marx, Engels, and Lenin, as well as the activities of the Third International."[8]

Hoover was dazzled by his discovery. So vast was his vision, or his imagination, that almost anything could be fitted into the Communist plot. Hoover in 1919 blamed all racial unrest on the giant conspiracy he saw in the actions of the Communist Party. Reporting to Congress on November 15, 1919, he stated: "Among the more salient points to be noted in the present attitude of the Negro leaders are . . . the identification of the Negro with such radical organizations as the I.W.W. and an outspoken advocacy of the Bolsheviki or Soviet doctrine . . . The Negro is 'seeing red,' and it is the prime objective of the leading publications to induce a like quality of vision upon the part of their readers. . . ."[9] If in 1971 Hoover sometimes seems to "see Red" where Negro militants are concerned, it is traditional. He made up his mind while still a young man in 1919 when even a Negro revolt against lynching was seen as proof of Communist activity.

Negroes were not alone, of course. Labor-union leaders were depicted as unconscious tools or willing instruments of the conspiracy. College intellectuals, defenders of the League of Nations, and critics of the Ku Klux Klan could be covered with the same red blanket. Is it surprising that Hoover— emerging as champion of the anti-Communist forces—should quickly become a hero to the radical Right?

Just as the hysteria over "pro-Germanism" helped the

cause of Prohibition, so the uproar over radicals made certain the election of Warren G. Harding and the Republican Party's return to power.

Why, then, did Palmer, a Democrat, sanction the new crusade? He hoped to ride the wave of hysteria into the White House. The tool he planned to use was a sedition law, passed by Congress in October 1918 as a war measure. It provided for the deportation of aliens whose views on political and economic matters were deemed harmful to the war effort. From Palmer's point of view, deportation of aliens had the advantage that no criminal proceedings would be required. The process was administrative, requiring neither judge nor jury. Problematically, under the law, the initiative belonged to the Labor Department's Immigration Service. The Justice Department had no standing, and the Bureau of Investigation lacked arrest powers. The problems were overcome, however, in conferences between Hoover and Labor Department officials.

Using undercover informants to locate the elusive aliens— "a Herculean task," according to Palmer, "because they live in sections which are not often visited by ordinary Americans"—the Department of Labor issued a number of arrest warrants. These warrants were to be served by GID men under the direction of Hoover. The informants were urged to try to arrange meetings of their Communist friends on the night set for the raids.[10]

On December 27, 1919, a confidential letter was sent to field offices of the GID. Signed by Frank Burke, assistant director and chief, the letter began by noting that the office had previously supplied two briefs, prepared by Hoover, on the Communist Party of America and the Communist Labor Party. The letter continued:

You have submitted to me affidavits upon various individuals connected with these respective organizations, stating that these persons are aliens and members of the organizations referred to. I have transmitted to the Commissioner General of Immigration the affidavits submitted by you, with the request that warrants of arrest be issued at once. . . .

Briefly the arrangements which have been made are that the

15

warrants will be forwarded to the immigration inspector, who will at once communicate with you and advise you of the names of persons for whom he has received warrants. You should then place under surveillance, where practicable, the persons mentioned and at the appointed time you will be advised by me by wire when to take into custody all persons for whom warrants have been issued. . . .

At the time of the apprehension of these persons every effort should be made by you to definitely establish the fact that the persons arrested are members of either the Communist Party of America or the Communist Labor Party. I have been reliably informed that instructions have been issued from the headquarters of each of these organizations to their members that they are to refuse to answer any questions put to them by any Federal officers and are to destroy all evidence of membership or affiliation with their respective organizations. It is, therefore, of the utmost importance that you at once make every effort to ascertain the location of all the books and records of these organizations in your territory and that the same be secured at the time of the arrests. As soon as the subjects are apprehended you should endeavor to obtain from them, if possible, admissions that they are members of either of these parties, together with any statement concerning their citizenship status. I cannot impress upon you too strongly the necessity of obtaining documentary evidence proving membership.

Particular efforts should be made to apprehend all of the officers of these two parties if they are aliens; the residences of such officers should be searched in every instance for literature, membership cards, records, and correspondence. The meeting rooms should be thoroughly searched and an effort made to locate the charter of the Communist Party of America or the Communist Labor Party under which the local organization operates, as well as the membership and financial records which, if not found in the meeting rooms of the organization, will probably be found in the house of the recording and financial secretaries, respectively. All literature, books, papers, and anything hanging on the walls should be gathered up; the ceilings and partitions should be sounded for hiding places. . . .[5]

The letter continued giving detailed instructions as to how the evidence secured should be marked for identification, though the raiders were given a certain amount of freedom. As Burke put it:

16

I leave it entirely to your discretion as to the method by which you should gain access to such places. If, due to local conditions in your territory, you find that it is absolutely necessary for you to obtain a search warrant for the premises, you should communicate with the local authorities a few hours before the time for the arrests is set and request a warrant to search the premises.

Under no conditions are you to take into your confidence the local police authorities or the State authorities prior to the making of the arrests . . . If, however, there are taken into custody any American citizens, through error, and who are members of the Communist Party of America or the Communist Labor Party, you should immediately refer their cases to the local authorities. . . .

If possible, you should arrange with your under-cover informants to have meetings of the Communist Party and the Communist Labor Party held on the night set. I have been informed by some of the Bureau officers that such arrangements will be made. This, of course, would facilitate the making of the arrests.

On the evening of the arrests this office will be open the entire night, and I desire that you communicate by long distance to Mr. Hoover any matters of vital importance or interest which may arise during the course of the arrests. You will possibly be given from 7 o'clock in the evening until 7 o'clock in the morning to conclude the arrests and examinations. As pointed out previously, the grounds for deportation in these cases will be based solely upon membership in the Communist Party of America or the Communist Labor Party, and for that reason it will not be necessary for you to go in detail into the particular activities of the persons apprehended. It is, however, desirable that wherever possible you should obtain additional evidence upon the individuals. . . .

I desire that the morning following the arrests you should forward to this office by special delivery, marked for the "Attention of Mr. Hoover," a complete list of the names of persons arrested, with an indication of residence, organization to which they belong, and whether or not they were included in the original list of warrants. In cases where arrests are made of persons not covered by warrants, you should at once request the local immigration authorities for warrants in all such cases, and you should also communicate with this office at the same time. I desire also that the morning following the arrests that you should communicate in detail by telegram, "Attention of Mr.

Hoover," the results of the arrests made, giving the total number of persons of each organization taken into custody, together with a statement of any interesting evidence secured.[11]

The instructions given prior to the raids are reproduced here in some detail only because apologists for Hoover have attempted to deny Hoover's role. It appears obvious that the groundwork for the raids were the two briefs prepared by Hoover and sent to field offices "with instructions that these briefs be carefully examined and studied for the purpose of familiarizing yourself and the agents under your direction with the principles and tactics of these two respective organizations."

The letter from Burke also makes it plain that it was Hoover who was scheduled to remain on duty all night, available by long distance to advise an arresting officer on any matter "of vital importance or interest." Furthermore, it was to Hoover that all reports—by special delivery and telegram—were to be sent on the morning after the raid. Obviously, Hoover was actually the man in charge. Yet in 1940 Alexander Holtzoff, a Department of Justice attorney and FBI adviser wrote to the historian Mary R. Beard: "Mr. J. Edgar Hoover was not in charge of, and had nothing to do with, the manner in which the arrests were made of the so-called radicals under the administration of Attorney General A. Mitchell Palmer."

Mrs. Beard demanded to know the source of Holtzoff's information. The attorney replied: "My statement to you to the effect that he did not direct, supervise, participate in, or have any connection with the manner in which these dragnet raids were conducted was based on Mr. Hoover's personal authority to me, and therefore I am willing to vouch for it."[12]

As will be seen in subsequent portions of this book, many of the legends surrounding John Edgar Hoover can be traced back to Hoover himself.

But Hoover has not been content to let subordinates apply the whitewash. In a statement to the New York *Herald Tribune* in 1947, he said: "I deplored the manner in which the raids were executed then, and my position has remained

18

unchanged." Unfortunately for that statement, the record contains no evidence that Hoover, in 1920, was in any way dissatisfied with the raids that he inspired, and which he supervised through the lonely night. To the contrary, the record shows that in joint appearances with Palmer before two Senate committees, Hoover defended the Bureau and its agents with fervor. The record also contains a letter from Hoover to immigration officials in which he asked that no prisoner be released on bail until he had, in effect, confessed. To do otherwise, he said, "virtually defeats the ends of justice."

Approximately ten thousand persons were arrested in the widespread raids on the night of January 2, 1920. Of that total, some sixty-five hundred were released without prosecution after spending days and sometimes weeks in overcrowded jails. The vast majority of others were ultimately released. A few hundred were eventually deported. Senator Thomas J. Walsh had this comment:

> The indignities and outrages suffered by the victims, the majority of whom were released, will rankle in their breasts until their dying day, and their friends and relatives will share with them the conviction that justice "for a season bade the world farewell," when they went through the ordeal from which some of them emerged maniacal.[13]

The record shows clearly that thousands of citizens were rounded up illegally, that due process was denied them, that arrests were made without warrants in many cases, and confessions were obtained by making it the condition of their release on bail. For this sorry chapter in American history, Hoover must accept his full share of responsibility. His attempts to evade that responsibility is but another measure of the man.

At the time, Palmer was encouraged to believe that he might become President, and Hoover established himself as a foe of Reds and radicals. The hysteria continued. On September 16, 1920, at high noon, a wagon filled with dynamite blew up near Wall Street opposite the office of J. P. Morgan. Thirty persons were killed, and some three hundred injured. Palmer immediately announced that the bombing

19

was part of a huge plot to overthrow capitalism, and the GID, under Hoover, swung into action.

Giuseppe di Filipis, twenty-three, was picked up on May 17, 1921, and charged with being the driver of the wagon. The young Italian was held for two weeks incommunicado, but apparently was unwilling to confess. Some eighty days after his arrest, the charge was dismissed, and the search for the driver went on. Months later the Bureau revealed that its agents had secured a confession from a prisoner in a Warsaw jail who said that the "Third International" had put up the money for the scheme. Then, it developed, the suspect was in reality a double agent. He had not been involved in the plot but knew of it.

This was unsatisfactory, so in 1923, a murderer serving a life sentence in California said he stole the nitroglycerine used in the explosion. No proof could be found that this was so, and eventually he was dropped in favor of a man just back from Siberia. That didn't work either, and the case—like the bombings before it—remains unsolved.

If Hoover's men could not capture bombers, they at least proved their ability to gather information on the "most terrible menace since the barbarian hordes overran West Europe and opened the Dark Ages." In an August 1922 memo, Hoover noted that the Communist Party of America was holding a convention at Bridgman, Michigan. Bureau agents were watching from the woods, he said. Alas, William Z. Foster, a Communist leader, went strolling in the woods and stumbled on two agents. The alarm was given and the delegates fled. So hurried was their flight—according to Don Whitehead's account in his book *The F.B.I. Story*, a semiofficial autobiography—that they left behind "a detailed history of underground communism, including a list of all those who had been at the meeting." This "Who's Who of early American communism" was found buried in the woods in, of all things, two potato barrels.[14]

In 1922 potato barrels. In 1948 the "pumpkin papers." Do the Reds have a fondness for things agricultural? Or does a down-to-earth container make suspect documents more believable? But whereas the "pumpkin papers" helped Richard

Nixon become President, the "potato papers" were discovered too late to help Palmer reach that goal.

Attorney General Palmer's bid to win the Democratic nomination succeeded only in throwing it to James M. Cox. Between Harding and Cox there was little to choose. Or so it seemed to that old Progressive, William Allen White. In his *Autobiography* he relates: "Every time I considered voting for either of them I decided to vote for the other. I ended by thinking hard about Cox as I went into the election booth and so managed for a moment to justify a vote for Harding. I could have done it the other way quite as easily."[15]

The new era became official on March 4, 1921, when Harding was sworn into office. "Normalcy" was the word he coined to describe it.

Harding was a product of the "Ohio Gang," and the "Ohio Gang" was the product of Mark Hanna, one of the country's first political bosses, the man who introduced the concept of the "businessman in politics." As White, who greatly admired him, related: "In 1880 he learned that politics, properly controlled, prospered every business that he touched. So he set out to make a brand of politics as profitable as his mines, his ships, his railways, and his banks." Hanna was so successful that he put his own man, William McKinley, into the White House. Naturally he wanted to be close by and arranged to have himself elected to the Senate. His methods brought on an investigation. Among the witnesses called was Harry M. Daugherty—who promptly took the Fifth Amendment. Ultimately Hanna was seated. Six years later he was re-elected. Warren G. Harding ran for lieutenant governor on Hanna's ticket. Daugherty claimed the credit for Harding's victory and the others that eventually brought Harding to the White House. What then more logical than that Daugherty should become attorney general?

Immediately after Harding's inauguration, Daugherty was perhaps too busy helping the President select the "best minds" with which he planned to surround himself to pay much attention to his own domain. William J. Flynn, director of the Bureau of Investigation, put up a valiant fight to save his job. Congressmen and Federal judges wrote letters

21

supporting him, but the effort was doomed. On August 18, 1921, a terse telegram dismissed Flynn. The appointment of William J. Burns as director was announced the same day.

Burns, the head of a giant private detective agency, was a boyhood friend of Daugherty and perhaps a charter member of the Ohio Gang. His agency provided strikebreakers for industry before and after World War I. He had a lively appreciation of the economic advantages of participating in the endless battle against "radicals." Many of his "private eyes" were young men who were later to make their mark as gangsters. Ruthless, completely unscrupulous, Burns was accused by Attorney General George W. Wickersham in an official report in 1912 of rigging a jury.

Four days after taking over the Bureau of Investigation, Burns named Hoover to be assistant director at a salary of $4,000 a year. No one has explained why Hoover was offered the number-two job or why Hoover, in view of Burns's reputation, accepted it. Certain conclusions are inescapable. Obviously, Burns believed that Hoover would be a member of his team—and a man to rely upon. Just as obviously, Hoover, then twenty-six years old and no novice, was willing to cooperate. Thus any picture of an idealist Hoover striving to "clean up" the mess caused by the Ohio Gang is misleading. By his decision to accept the job as Burns's chief aide, he made himself a part of the gang's operations.

The story of the Teapot Dome scandal, the Veterans Administration scandal, the Alien Property scandal—all have been told many times and need no repetition here. They cost the nation literally billions of dollars. It was not for nothing that when the scandals were revealed during the Coolidge administration the Justice Department became known as "the Department of Easy Virtue" and the Bureau of Investigation as "government by blackmail." And John Edgar Hoover was the assistant director of that Bureau.

II

OHN Edgar Hoover's record as a crusader against the Red menace began to be useful to his new Republican bosses early in 1922. As rumors about wholesale graft in the Harding administration began circulating in Washington, Attorney General Daugherty decided it was time to find a scapegoat in order to divert public attention.

In an address to the American Bar Association in August, Daugherty warned: "The enemies of law and order are more active than ever before in sowing the poisons of lawlessness and unsound and experimental theories of government."

What was worse, according to Daugherty, the "enemies" were "casting unjustifiable reflections on men holding public office with the intent to undermine the confidence of the people in them."[1]

This refrain is sounded at intervals by corrupt men under attack. Hoover has made repeated use of the gambit. So did Senator Joseph McCarthy. And in every gangster-controlled city from Newport, Kentucky, to Miami Beach, Florida, reformers over the years have been accused of attempting to destroy faith in local law enforcement. It is no coincidence that the John Birch Society asks its followers to "Support

23

Local Law Enforcement," regardless of how corrupt local law enforcement might be.

Daugherty eventually blamed all his subsequent misfortunes on a Red plot. In support of his thesis he pointed to the presence of Hoover in the Bureau of Investigation. Reason enough, so went Daugherty's logic, that the radicals would be out to discredit him and his good friend, Warren Harding.[2] Hoover, in fact, did use the GID to supply Daugherty and Burns with "proof" of the continuing Red effort. The coal strike of 1922 was a good example. As Burns testified to a Congressional committee:

There the Third Internationale sent a great many instructions to their representatives in this country, and, among other things, we found statements from them and instructions stating that they were to do everything possible to arouse the striking miners to the point of armed insurrection."[3]

Miners were only one target, if the Bureau could be believed. Radical propaganda, it said, was being aimed at colleges, churches, labor unions, Negroes, and even women's clubs. The army and navy were being infiltrated by the Reds. Most of the work was being done, of course, by undercover agents, so, naturally, the Bureau had to fight fire with fire and increase its use of counterspies. This presented problems. The Bureau told Congress: "You can imagine the great difficulty we have in getting men who can do that character of work whom we can trust, and, of course, we check them up very, very closely."[4]

All the Department of Justice's overt and covert activity failed, however, to stop the gossip about payoffs, shakedowns, and high-level graft. Eventually, word reached Harding and spoiled some of his poker parties at the White House. Not even the bootleg liquor with which he was supplied or the infrequent sessions with Nan Britton in the White House cloakroom, could keep him from worrying. He complained to William Allen White: "My God, this is a hell of a job! I have no trouble with my enemies. I can take care of my enemies all right. But my damn friends, my God-damn friends, White, they're the ones that keep me walking the floor nights."[5]

For some reason, Harding centered his wrath on Jess Smith who was Daugherty's flunky, a court jester, deeply devoted to the scheming attorney general, with whom he shared an apartment in Washington and a fishing camp in Ohio. Smith was no great villain despite his role in graft collection. But Harding, seeking perhaps to warn Daugherty and others indirectly, locked Smith out of the White House and suggested he leave Washington. Smith, brokenhearted and bewildered, obeyed, but soon returned. Shortly after his return, he was dead.

Gaston B. Means, a close friend of, and former detective for, Bureau chief Burns, and others have suggested that Smith was murdered to stop him from talking. Still others have dismissed the allegation as just one of many bizarre rumors surrounding the entire Harding saga. Herbert Hoover, in his memoirs, written in 1952, tells of a conversation with Harding aboard ship en route to Alaska. Harding called Hoover, his secretary of commerce, to his cabin, and explained that he had heard "rumors of irregularities centering around Smith in connection with cases in the Department of Justice." According to Hoover, Harding then disclosed that he had sent for Smith and "after a painful session he told Smith he would be arrested in the morning. Smith went home, burned all his papers, and committed suicide."[6] This confidential information, from a President of the United States to a cabinet officer and future President, makes Gaston B. Means's story more credible. Smith was indeed trapped; he faced arrest. He knew too much and he was weak. For the Ohio Gang it was a moment of crisis.

Attorney General Daugherty, who must have known of Harding's showdown with Smith, spent that same night at the White House. He assigned Warren F. Martin, a member of the Ohio Gang and one of the Bureau of Investigation's notorious "dollar-a-year" men to stay with Smith. According to the official record, Martin himself found Smith's body the next morning. He was dressed in pajamas, and his head was in a metal wastebasket, along with the ashes of his papers. A revolver was in his hand. Agent Martin immediately summoned Burns, who managed to "misplace" the pistol. Getting the Bureau chief to the scene was no problem; he lived on the floor below. There is no way of knowing what else Burns "misplaced" before the police arrived. As Samuel Hopkins Adams was to write: "There were circumstances in connection with the death that were dubious. No autopsy was performed. The Department of Justice took efficient charge and all was hushed up as soon as possible."[7]

Smith's body was sent back to Ohio for burial. Accompanying it—as if the Department of Justice wanted Smith guarded in death—was Rush Holland, another "dollar-a-year" man, who held the title of assistant attorney general. Holland carried a sealed package to Mally Daugherty, the attorney general's brother. He took one look at the papers the package contained and burned them in his bank's furnace.[8]

Attorney General Daugherty was still waiting at the White House when news of the "suicide" arrived. By all accounts, it was a tense and gloomy day. Both Harding and Daugherty had lost an old friend—and both men, whether murder or suicide was involved, had to feel a degree of responsibility. Yet they both knew Jess Smith dead was infinitely preferable to Jess Smith alive and talking.

If Daugherty, Burns, and the Bureau of Investigation itself were above reproach, it would be easy to accept the official version of events and assume that Smith cracked under the strain. But given the character of the men who investigated the death, and the size of the stakes involved, such acceptance is naive. The stakes were more than the political jobs of a few grafters; they included the reputation of the President of the United States and the Republican Party itself. The ashes found in Smith's wastebasket included more than his personal papers, as Daugherty himself later admitted in testimony before a Senate committee.[9]

Where was John Edgar Hoover, the number-two man in the Bureau of Investigation, while all this was going on? Don Whitehead would have us believe that Hoover was battling the Ku Klux Klan in Louisiana. "Ironically," writes Whitehead in his *F.B.I. Story*, "while Bureau agents were being used to protect civil rights in Louisiana and other places, William J. Burns and Jess Smith were sending men to spy on members of Congress who were then demanding investigations of reported corruption in the Harding Administration."[10]

Ironical, indeed, and more than a little misleading. The "shadowing" of Congressmen and their demands for investigation did not begin until after Smith's death. Even more misleading, perhaps, is the implicit suggestion that Hoover somehow managed to remain apart, untouched and pure, while all the sordid things were happening. Was a man who, above all things, has placed a premium on loyalty from his underlings, less than loyal to his superiors?

Adding to Harding's headaches in 1923 was a potential rival for office. Henry Ford, maker of the Model T, was rated far ahead of the President in a poll conducted by *Colliers'*. So concerned did Harding become that he took the "pledge" to abstain from liquor in an effort to win the dry vote. The sacrifice was unnecessary as Ford's boom ended abruptly, and the man described as "one of the most illiterate and inane millionaires in the land" resumed his hobby of publishing anti-Semitic articles.[11] One of his targets was Aaron Sapiro, a Chicago attorney, who filed a million-dollar suit against Ford. Eventually it was settled out of court.[12] Sapiro went on to help form the Molaska Corporation, one of the first joint ventures by New York and Cleveland gangsters. Molaska operated the largest illicit distilleries in the nation long after Prohibition ended. The partnership of such men as Meyer Lansky and Moe Dalitz in Molaska prepared the way for a national crime syndicate and joint ventures that continue to the present day. Ford, meanwhile, became involved with gangsters through his security chief, Harry Bennett, who allegedly had to be on good terms with the hoods in order to protect his employer. Such Lansky associates as Joe Adonis were to make profitable deals with the Ford Motor Company during Bennett's long employment there.

All of which helps illustrate the nature of our free-enterprise system and its relation to organized crime. John Edgar Hoover, while able to unravel the international Communist conspiracy, has never been able to comprehend—on the record, anyway—the economic forces that bind crime, business, and politics. Perhaps he is too close to it.

Less than a month after Smith's death, President Harding

27

departed from Washington by special train. It was May 20, 1923, and the harried Chief Executive hoped to escape his troubles and do some fence mending at the same time. He billed his trip, which was to carry him across the nation and by boat to Alaska, as a "voyage of understanding." Before leaving he called in Harry Daugherty and made his will. It proved to be a timely action. Only days before he had sold his newspaper, the *Marion Star*. Did he have a premonition?

But it was not easy to escape the past. William Allen White has described what happened at a hotel room in Kansas City where the Presidential party stayed for the night. White and Harding were talking when "Mrs. Fall, the wife of the Secretary of the Interior, came to the door. He [Harding] excused himself a minute, took her into an adjoining room, and did not return. Finally I made my excuses to Mrs. Harding and to Senator Capper and went on my way. Senator Capper told me afterwards that Mrs. Fall and the President stayed closeted in that room until the very moment he went to make his speech, and that he came out obviously frustrated, worried and excited."[13]

Mrs. Fall was married to Albert B. Fall, who leased the Teapot Dome oil reserve to Harry F. Sinclair. Some rumbles of the impending scandal had leaked out in 1922, and Fall had offered to resign. Harding asked him to stay on and promised to appoint him later to the Supreme Court. At the end of his second year of service, however, Fall quit.

That Mrs. Fall, "veiled and furtive", brought Harding bad news that night cannot be doubted, especially in view of the converstions Herbert Hoover had with the President en route to Alaska. According to the future President, Harding asked him a blunt question: "If you knew of a great scandal in our administration, would you for the good of the country and the party expose it publicly or would you bury it?" Hoover advised the President to "publish it." Harding "abruptly dried up and never raised the question again."[14]

The trip to Alaska was by all accounts a dismal affair. Harding was in poor spirits and worse health. By the time he got back to Seattle, "a feeling of strain and apprehension was beginning to pervade the entire company."[15] After an exhausting day of parades and speeches there, Harding became ill with what was called "acute indigestion." Speaking dates were canceled, and the President moved on by special train to San Francisco. At 7:35 P.M., August 3, 1923, he died.

Much mystery surrounded his death. When any President dies in office, rumor takes wing. In Harding's case there was no official investigation. No autopsy was performed. Mrs. Harding would not even permit a death mask to be made. Later, she destroyed many of the President's papers. There were other curious circumstances that have been well documented elsewhere.[16] One can only be sure that the entire truth—whatever it is—remains hidden.

Most of the questions were raised long after Harding's death when the extent of the corruption in his administration had become known. At the time, however, the President was still popular and was given a hero's farewell by the American people.

There were, of course, more immediate results from Harding's death. Senator Thomas J. Walsh had been quietly investigating the Teapot Dome situation—a fact that certainly contributed nothing to Harding's peace of mind during his last months in office. On October 22, shortly after the late President's coffin was placed in a twenty-six-hundred-pound sarcophagus in his tomb at Marion, Ohio, the Senate Committee on Public Lands began hearings. Senator Walsh was effectively in charge. The witness on the second day was Albert B. Fall, ex-secretary of the interior. The image of Harding quickly began to tarnish.

More was to come. The Senate authorized an investigation of Daugherty. Roxy Stinson, former wife of the late Jess Smith, was the first witness. Shortly thereafter, Gaston B. Means took the stand.

Many writers have assumed that the congressional hearings were inevitable, that the entire sordid truth about Teapot Dome and the "Department of Easy Virtue" somehow demanded to become known and did so almost automatically. Would that politics was so simple. A closer examination is warranted.

The party leadership sought desperately to conceal the graft and corruption from public view. Party security demanded no less. Since this was being made impossible, thanks to the determination of Walsh and his colleague Senator Burton K. Wheeler, it seemed best to find a scapegoat to take the blame. Daugherty was the obvious choice.

As the scandals became known, Secretary of Commerce Herbert Hoover and Secretary of State Charles Evans Hughes "went to the President [Calvin Coolidge] and urged Daugherty's removal. Coolidge had a high sense of justice," so Hoover wrote, "and asserted that he had no definite knowledge of wrongdoings by Daugherty and would not remove him on rumors."[17] But the pressure increased, and when Daugherty refused to furnish the Wheeler Committee with some files of the Bureau of Investigation, President Coolidge on March 28, 1924, demanded that his attorney general resign. Harding had been dead not quite eight months.

Harry M. Daugherty, stubborn and bitter, did quit, but he was not ready to act as a penitent scapegoat. Months before, using all the resources of the Justice Department, he had begun a counterattack against Walsh and Wheeler. Assisted by friends, he continued the battle in private life. Concurrently, his successor, Harlan Fiske Stone, carried on the official investigations begun by Daugherty.

Stone was a good choice to replace Daugherty. In 1921 he had protested the excesses of the Red scare and commented on "the violation of constitutional safeguards and statutes by the agents of the Department of Justice."[18] He was now in a position to make his opinions felt. One of his first acts was to fire Burns as director of the Bureau of Investigation. It was May 9, 1924.

Over the decades, press agents for John Edgar Hoover have erroneously dated the Hoover legend from the following day when the twenty-nine-year-old Hoover became acting director of the Bureau. A lot of nonsense has been written about the Hoover-Stone interview that preceded the appointment. This is how it is told in Whitehead's *F.B.I. Story:*

Hoover took a seat. Stone peered at him over his glasses and the two men looked at each other across the desk. Then Stone said abruptly, "Young man, I want you to be Acting Director of the Bureau of Investigation."

Hoover realized the magnitude of the compliment. He knew in that instant that Attorney General Stone had rejected the arguments that he was too young for the job. Far more important, he knew that Stone did not hold him responsible for the policies, mistakes and corrupt actions of those who had directed the Department of Justice and the Bureau of Investigation in the past.

Finally Hoover said, "I'll take the job, Mr. Stone, on certain conditions."

"What are they?"

"The Bureau must be divorced from politics and not be a catch-all for political hacks. Appointments must be based on merit. Second, promotions will be made on proved ability and the Bureau will be responsible only to the Attorney General."

The Attorney General scowled and said, "I wouldn't give it to you under any other conditions. That's all. Good day."[19]

Whitehead's account, of course, is based on information supplied by Hoover. Stone never confirmed it.[20]

Hoover was a professional civil servant, like his father and his older brother. Nothing anywhere in his record indicates that when offered a promotion he would make any conditions before accepting it. He had already played ball with two attorney generals—Palmer and Daugherty—without setting any conditions. Surely he was prepared to accept a promotion to, from his point of view, the ultimate position in the bureaucratic structure. Certainly he was prepared to adjust to please his new boss.

Nor did the appointment necessarily mean, as some have claimed, that Stone considered Hoover untouched by corruption. As assistant director, Hoover was the logical choice to take over the machinery when Burns was fired. Stone, in office little more than a month, needed someone familiar with the personnel, the procedures, and the investigations pending in the Bureau. To have brought in an outsider would have been politically dangerous.

Too few have noticed that before making the appointment Stone sought some advice. According to Alpheus Thomas Mason, Stone's biographer, Mrs. Mabel Willebrandt, an assistant attorney general, was questioned about Hoover.[21] And Herbert Hoover in his memoirs states that Stone asked him for a recommendation. According to the former President: "Lawrence Richey, one of my secretaries who had at one time been in the Bureau, suggested he consider J. Edgar Hoover (no relation), who was an able young lawyer already in the Department of Justice."[22]

In view of what happened later, there is reason to believe that Richey—if not Herbert Hoover and Stone—was thinking of politics as much as professional police work. Richey's recommendation should be considered in the light of a diary entry made some years later by Harold Ickes. On May 2, 1933, he wrote:

> The Attorney General [Homer Cummings] said at the Cabinet meeting today that he was informed that a strict espionage was being maintained of Cabinet members and other officials high in the Government Service. This work is under the charge of Lawrence Richey, one of the secretaries to former President Hoover, and is supposed to be in the interests of Hoover particularly and of the Republican Party in general. Richey is maintaining elaborate offices in the Shoreham Building. He [Cummings] warned all of us to be on our guard and he said that the same precaution should be taken by our wives and members of our families. His information is that some women are being employed to worm themselves into the confidences of our wives.[23]

On the basis of this reported political intrigue nine years later, it seems a bit naive to assume that Richey in 1924—at a time when the Republicans faced a grave crisis of confidence —was not thinking of the investigations of Senators Walsh and Wheeler then under way in the Bureau of Investigation. From his previous experience in the Bureau, Richey would have known that John Edgar Hoover could be depended upon to carry on the probes. And that, of course, is just what John Edgar did.

During the probes, Walsh's office was ransacked by the Bureau agents, his telephone was tapped, his mail was opened. His daughter was accosted on the street while pushing her child in a baby carriage and warned that her father should drop his probe. A Bureau agent, Blair Coan, was sent to Montana to muckrake Walsh's past. Coan did not find anything useful on Walsh but he stumbled on some allegations about Wheeler, allegedly uncovered by postal inspectors. To this Coan added some affidavits, then, according to his book *The Red Web,*

. . . went to the federal district attorney, John L. Slattery, at Great Falls, Montana, with the evidence I had obtained. . . . The evidence was placed before a grand jury, the witnesses I had discovered were heard, and the result of it was that Wheeler was indicted. The indictment was obtained after Attorney General Daugherty's enforced resignation from the Attorney Generalship, and the entire preparation of the case took place, not under the Daugherty regime, but under that of Attorney General Harlan F. Stone.[24]

Not content with one indictment, the Justice Department under Stone sought a second one in Washington. In *his* book, *Yankee From The West*, Wheeler charges that the second indictment was nothing less than political blackmail in an election year.[25]

The counterattack was led by Walsh, who charged that Stone—and Hoover—had failed to clean up the Justice Department. Walsh "ran through an elaborate listing of all the important officials appointed by Daugherty and retained by Stone." Hoover was one of those named. Ultimately Wheeler was tried in Montana. Unfortunately for the Republicans, the home-town jury required only one vote to acquit Wheeler. Later, a Federal judge in Washington threw out the second indictment. A Senate investigation also vindicated Wheeler.

Despite the politics and the counterpressure, Walsh and Wheeler painfully continued to extract details of graft and corruption from scores of witnesses. The Teapot Dome scandal in all its shame and complexity was documented beyond all reasonable doubt. The participation of cabinet-rank officers in sordid alliance with "respectable" Republican oil millionaires was fully established. The story needs no repetition here. Walsh and Wheeler left no one able to believe that the Justice Department and its Bureau of Investigation were not a disgrace to the nation.

A few days after Hoover was appointed acting director, he was called as a witness. He gave his name as John Edgar Hoover—it had yet to be shortened to J. Edgar—and his profession as "lawyer." Attorney General Stone, he said, had ordered him "to initiate no investigations except upon his specific approval." The examination brought out the additional information that "prior to the war, most of the men in the Bureau were young lawyers." Over the years, Hoover's press agents have credited him with beginning the policy that special agents shall have either law or accounting degrees. He has received much praise for the policy. In reality, however, as Hoover admitted, the policy had been in effect since the Bureau was organized in 1909. It had lapsed during the war years and been ignored under Palmer and Daugherty. At Stone's suggestion, it was reinstated. "We are making no recommendations for appointments except of persons with legal training," Hoover told the committee.

He was asked: "The policy, then, will be to get rid of those professional, double-crossing detectives?"

"Most positively," said Hoover. "We do not intend to have anybody in the service of that character."

Hoover also disclosed that Stone had given him a six-point memorandum to guide him in the operation of the Bureau. In effect, it relegated the Bureau to the role of "a fact-gathering organization," with decisions as to investigations and personnel firmly in the hands of the attorney general. Item five provided that "all the 'dollar-a-year' men, 'honorary' agents and others not regularly employed would be cut from the rolls."

The "dollar-a-year" men had become especially notorious under Daugherty, and the Wheeler committee was anxious to get a list of them. At the conclusion of Hoover's testimony, such a list was put into the committee's record. Included among the names was "Hoover, J. E."

When the list was presented, it was titled: "List of Persons Holding Credentials of the Bureau of Investigation but not regular per diem special agents thereof." A note added: "All of these except those who are not officials of the Department of Justice have been dropped on orders of Attorney General Stone."

The names were given one below the other, but a careful examination shows that there were six groups. The first grouping of ten names contained one judge, George A. Car-

34

penter. The second group of six names was distinguished by the presence of D. M. Daugherty, the alcoholic son of Harry Daugherty and close friend of Gaston B. Means. Also in the group was Edward "Ned" McLean, millionaire and close friend of the Ohio Gang. McLean played an important role in the Teapot Dome scandal. Hoover was in the third grouping, along with Rush Holland, the man who accompanied Jess Smith's body back to Ohio. Eight others were in that grouping. Fred Upham, treasurer of the Republican National Committee, was one of seven names in the next group. When Burns, who was later called to testify, was asked why, he explained: "He [Upham] was going to Europe and with our commissions and badges a man can save himself a great deal of time and annoyance."

Below Upham's name was that of Cornelius Vanderbilt, Jr., who wrote a magazine article appearing in *Liberty* on October 17, 1931. The article concerned an alleged interview with Al Capone and quoted the Chicago gangster as saying: "Graft is a byword in American life today. It is law where no other law is obeyed. It is undermining this country. The honest lawmakers of any city can be counted on your fingers. I could count Chicago's on one hand." Vanderbilt also quotes Capone as saying: "Bolshevism is knocking at our gates. We can't afford to let it in. We've got to organize ourselves against it, and put our shoulders together and hold fast." Whether Capone actually made that statement is perhaps immaterial. It remains the excuse for an alliance of organized crime, right-wing politicians, and business leaders that did evolve in this country. When it comes to fighting the Red menace and to maintaining the status quo, the Hoovers and the Joseph McCarthys, and the Capones and Lanskys, are in agreement.

The fifth group of "dollar-a-year" men included Irwin "Ike" Hoover, chief usher at the White House. Was his cooperation required in keeping Harding happy by smuggling Nan Britton into the cloakroom at frequent intervals? In the last group were such names as W. F. Martin, the man who found Jess Smith's body and called Burns upstairs to take charge of the investigation. Also listed was W. H. Votaw, Harding's brother-in-law, who had served as superintendent of Federal prisons and been up to his neck in scandal. All together there were forty-eight names, a weird combination of rich men, politicians, grafters, and plain crooks. No one has explained when John Edgar Hoover's name got on the list, or why. But it was there. The legend makers can ignore it, but they can't erase the record.

The records of the Wheeler committee also include an episode that perhaps illustrates Hoover's loyalty to his ex-boss. Mrs. Jesse V. Duckstein, former confidential secretary to Burns, was subpoenaed before the committee and questioned. Among other things she gave validity to Gaston B. Means's account of his various roles. Shortly after Mrs. Duckstein testified she received the following letter:

Department of Justice
Bureau of Investigation
Washington, D.C.

May 26, 1924

Mrs. J. B. Duckstein
Care of E. R. Bohner,
Hurley-Wright Building,
Washington, D.C.

Dear Madam:

At the direction of the Attorney General, I am hereby requesting your resignation as special agent, Bureau of Investigation, Department of Justice, to take effect at the expiration of such accrued leave of absence as you may be entitled to.

Very truly yours,
J. E. Hoover, Acting Director

Senator Wheeler, upon hearing of the affair, commented: "When they did tell the truth, why, they fired them."[26]

In the decades that followed, the pattern was repeated again and again. Any special agent who told the truth—if the truth reflected in any way on the legend of John Edgar Hoover—was fired or banished. Obviously Hoover, who had been loyal to his superiors, expected his men to be loyal to him.

It seems only logical to assume, therefore, that Hoover's

contempt for Gaston B. Means stemmed not from Means's wheeling and dealing but from the fact that the agile Means —sensing the way the wind was blowing—consented to be a witness against Daugherty and Burns.

During his career in Justice, Means had been suspended, given work as an undercover agent, officially reinstated, and ultimately fired again. Records of the Wheeler committee show that Bureau agents—under Hoover's direction—began "tailing" Means on March 18, 1924. Then the Bureau of Investigation prosecuted and sent him to jail.

Putting Means in jail, however justified, was an act of revenge and more. It was part of the campaign to discredit Senator Wheeler's witnesses. Ironically, Means used the time in prison to think out a book that did more to discredit the Harding administration than anything he said from the witness chair. *The Strange Death of President Harding* became an immediate best-seller.

Later, in 1932, the slippery Means conned the wife of "Ned" McLean, millionaire owner of two newspapers and friend of the Ohio Gang, into believing he could solve the Lindbergh kidnaping, and extracted $100,000 from her to ransom the baby. When Mrs. McLean eventually became suspicious, the Bureau of Investigation arrested Means, but was unable to find the money. They dug up half of Washington looking for it. As late as 1936, Hoover wrote: "This bureau has searched diligently for the money and will continue to do so throughout the years. We have hopes of finding it."

According to a 1965 *Saturday Evening Post* article, Hoover visited Means in prison and demanded to know where the money was hidden.

"Dammit, Gaston," Hoover was reported to have said. "You stop lying about it."

Means looked up at his old associate, clutched his heart piteously, and replied:

"This is the last straw, Edgar. You've lost faith in me."

Means died in prison. The money was never found.

IN a moment of unusual modesty, John Edgar Hoover in 1946 credited Harlan Fiske Stone with being "the real father of the Federal Bureau of Investigation as we know it today."[1]

Modest, perhaps, but hardly accurate. The FBI in 1946, as in 1971, bears little resemblance to the agency Stone left in Hoover's hands in 1925. Certainly, many lasting improvements were made under Stone. The policy of employing men with legal training was reinstated. Two venerable fingerprint files were consolidated in the Bureau of Investigation, and other approaches to scientific law enforcement were begun. Hoover was smart enough to recognize good ideas and to implement them.

But the Bureau of Investigation during the eleven months Stone served as attorney general was basically a "fact-gathering organization" firmly under the control of the attorney general. Hoover as acting director and, after seven months, director, was essentially an administrator assigned to carry out the policies of his boss. Stone was a man of firm convictions. Not only did he know what he wanted the Bureau to be, he also knew what he did not want it to be. On the day he appointed Hoover acting director he told the *New York Times*:

There is always the possibility that a secret police may become a menace to free government and free institutions because it carries with it the possibility of abuses of power which are not always quickly apprehended or understood. It is important that its agents themselves be not above the law or beyond its reach.[2]

If Stone's warning was directed at Hoover, it was ignored. Over the decades he has built a secret organization subject to his will, or whim, alone. Neither Congress nor President has dared demand a review of FBI activities. Consequently Hoover has not only been above the law but able to put his agency above it too. Mistakes, abuses of power, and special privileges have been concealed behind a curtain of one-way glass while an active propaganda machine created a popular legend about Hoover and the "G-men."

Stone was the last attorney general to exercise complete control over Hoover. Even Robert Kennedy, brother of a President, postponed a showdown with Hoover until it was tragically too late. And Stone's period of control was less than a year.

There is reason to believe that Stone was "kicked upstairs to the Supreme Court," because he went too far in cleaning up the Bureau of Investigation. Mrs. Mabel Willebrandt, an assistant attorney general, had no doubts about it. She commented: "Justice Stone *was* kicked upstairs to the Supreme Court. I feel confident that he thought so too. When he told me of the offer, it was with a sense of regret, because, as he said, 'I like doing this job. It needs to be done and I've only just gotten started.' "[3]

Despite his reservations, Stone was elevated to higher office, and Hoover was left to build an organization devoted primarily to keeping the Reds under control and making banks safe from robbers. Stone and Wheeler eventually became friendly, and Wheeler said he received a semi-apology from the jurist who went on to become Chief Justice. "They lied to me," he quotes Stone as saying.[4]

Who lied? Assistant Attorney General William Donovan,

who recommended that the investigation of Wheeler continue, or Hoover, who conducted it? Or both? Like so many other unanswered questions from that era, today only Hoover knows the truth. And he isn't talking.

The build-up for Hoover started immediately. The *Literary Digest*, that bastion of Republican principles, devoted an article to Hoover on January 24, 1925. It noted:

> A young lawyer has succeeded William J. Burns, the prominent and much discussed detective, as the head of the U.S. sleuthing business. So the days of the "old sleuth," the man of "shadows" and "frame-ups" and "get the goods anyway you can" are past. . . . The new chief detective, John Edgar Hoover, is a scholar, a gentleman, and a scientist. It is an interesting experiment that the just-promoted Attorney General Stone started. . . . Young Mr. Hoover, of the new school of crime detection, has no entangling alliances. Among his friends, he is known to be as clean as a hound's tooth. He looks at detective work from a new angle. He sees the evidence side. Instead of merely "getting the goods" he is concerned with making the "goods" stick in court. And with all his scarcity of years and legal training, he is no novice at the detecting game. . . . It was he who worked up the cases and obtained the deportation of the leading Reds of their day. . . . As an assistant to Burns, young Hoover got some education in the arts of the old school. But most of these he is casting aside. He is striking out along new and clean lines. He is not going on wild-goose chases. . . .[5]

And so on. Overnight, Hoover had become not only a scholar and a gentleman, but a scientist as well. On this foundation, Hoover's press agents were to build. Grace notes were added over the years, but the melody remained the same. By sheer dint of repetition, the image created by the magazine became accepted as fact. As one reporter put it: "When Hoover went into law enforcement, Madison Avenue lost a genius."[6]

Stone was replaced as attorney general by John G. Sargent, a native and former attorney general of Vermont. Apparently he gave Hoover no trouble. Sargent's successor was William D. Mitchell, Herbert Hoover's attorney general. Mitchell, it seems, permitted Hoover to tap telephones. Or, to put it more correctly, he gave official sanction to the practice.

Forty years later another Attorney General Mitchell felt the same way.

In the months after Stone was promoted, Hoover was busy with a rather curious investigation of corruption in Cincinnati. Corrupt cities were the rule rather than the exception in those days. Certainly there was more corruption in such cities as New York, Boston, Atlantic City, Chicago, St. Louis, Kansas City, and Miami—to mention but a few—than in Cincinnati. The question thus arises—why was the "Queen City" selected? And why was the Bureau so late in hearing about conditions in Cincinnati?

As early as 1920, William J. Mellin, a pioneer wiretapper for the special intelligence unit of the Bureau of Internal Revenue, was sent to Cincinnati to "bug" the hotel room of one George Remus. The recorded conversations largely concerned corruption. On one day alone, forty-four men came by the hotel suite for pay-offs averaging $1,000 each. City police were well represented, but there were Federal agents as well.[7]

Mellin took his stenographer's notes—he did not use a tape recorder—to a Federal official in Cincinnati. He had been told, he said, that the official was honest. Perhaps so, but that official was also acutely aware of the impending election of Harding. He told Mellin: "Son, there's times when a man has to be practical in this business. It's only a few weeks to election and the information you've dug up is political dynamite. Go back to New York and forget it."

Disgusted, Mellin went to Washington and complained to Elmer Irey, head of the special intelligence unit. Irey demanded action. Despite Remus's pay-offs to Jess Smith, unbribed Prohibition agents from another state were sent in and Remus's headquarters in "Death Valley," near Cincinnati, was raided. At his trial in 1922, Remus was defended by James M. Linton—a special assistant U.S. attorney attached to Daugherty's office. Remus was sent to the Federal prison in Atlanta for two years.

Shortly thereafter, Remus was called as a witness before the Senate committee investigating Daugherty. He not only admitted bribing Smith, he also revealed the state of corruption existing inside the Atlanta prison. Remus's testimony

41

embarrassed W. H. Votaw, one of the "dollar-a-year" men, and Harding's brother-in-law, who was director of Federal prisons, and it forced Stone to order a probe of the prison that resulted in its warden going behind bars as a prisoner.

Retaliation against Remus began immediately. A probe was launched into the looting of the Jack Daniel's Distillery at St. Louis. In that caper, Remus had arranged with a syndicate of local politicians to pump out thirty-one thousand gallons of bonded whiskey stored in warehouses and replace the liquor with water. One of the Bureau investigators, Franklin L. Dodge, a tall, flashy agent, made Mrs. Remus, who lived in a fantastically luxurious house on Price Hill, his personal project. From his cell in Atlanta, Mr. Remus began to wonder if Imogene would be waiting outside the prison gate as promised.

Meanwhile, four years after the action began and with the 1924 elections out of the way, Hoover's agents swept into Cincinnati to interview witnesses and collect affidavits. Let Whitehead tell the tale:

In less than three months' time, the FBI [BI to be correct] agents were ready to act. A special federal grand jury was called and sealed indictments were brought against forty-eight Cincinnati police and twenty-three village "dry" agents charging conspiracies in violation of federal Prohibition and narcotics laws.... Of the seventy-one indicted, seventy were tried and sixty-two convicted.

This investigation opened the way for a reform movement in Cincinnati which swept the old city hall gang out of office along with the crooked police, who, according to the evidence, had received some three hundred and forty-eight thousand dollars in graft over a three-year period.[8]

The probe had another result—it destroyed the personal empire of George Remus, the man who had talked too much. Remus was to have his revenge.

When he got out of prison in July 1925, a United States marshal arrested him on an indictment returned in the St. Louis whiskey theft case. Fifteen St. Louis politicians were also indicted. Some of them went to prison. Remus finally made bail on the new charge and rushed home. Not only was his wife missing, but his house had been stripped. Even the solid-gold door knobs were gone. Neighbors told him his wife had left with the handsome Bureau agent.

Before Remus could look for her, he was forced to serve a year in state prison. The St. Louis indictment was squashed when Remus turned Federal witness. Then, on the morning of October 6, 1927, Remus's heavy touring car forced a cab to the curb. Mrs. Remus leaped from the cab and fled. Remus fired once. His wife died an hour later. The ex-king of the bootleggers was charged with murder. He pleaded insanity and was acquitted. Sent to the State Hospital for the Criminally Insane, Remus quickly proved his sanity and was released. But, thanks to the Bureau investigation, his empire was gone. Remus didn't mind—his wealth was estimated at twenty million dollars. Gangsters had taken over his business and were busy killing each other off in futile efforts to gain a monopoly. His lieutenants, such as Buck Brady and Glenn Smith, had established themselves across the Ohio River in Newport and Covington, Kentucky, and created what was to be in the years to come the largest illegal gambling center in the nation—a place where Federal and state laws did not apply. The Cleveland syndicate moved into the area in 1940, quickly becoming the principal power.

Thus the Bureau's well-publicized probe only scattered corruption over a general area. The Cleveland syndicate ruled Newport until 1961 when Attorney General Robert Kennedy ordered a massive probe that closed the plush casinos. The shuttering of the casinos, bust-out joints, and brothels had an immediate impact on Cincinnati across the river—its convention business nosedived.[9]

During Newport's heyday, the FBI was well acquainted with the sin-city's facilities. Every year a census was taken of all prostitutes. The girls and their madams posed willingly for pictures which, alledgedly, were needed to check out possible violations of the Mann Act.[10] But Hoover saw no need to repeat the investigation of 1925. The syndicate, which had local and state officials in its pocket, didn't worry about "the Feds" until Attorney General Kennedy launched his "coordinated war on crime."

The breakup of Remus's liquor empire provided busi-

43

nessmen as well as gangsters with new opportunities. Among the first to seize the chance was Lewis S. Rosenstiel, who in time would become even more wealthy than Remus. Rosenstiel was a Cincinnati native, born July 21, 1891. His father, Solon, was in the textile business, but an uncle on his mother's side of the family was an executive with a distilling company in Milton, Kentucky, across the Ohio River. According to Rosenstiel's legend builders, the boy quickly recognized the advantages of his uncle's business and at the age of fifteen began working in the distillery. Eleven years later he became assistant superintendent of the plant.[11]

Nineteen seventeen was a key year for Rosenstiel, who at twenty-eight was ready to make his move. He married the first of five wives (if his disputed last marriage is counted), and in the process acquired a brother-in-law with financial connections, Herbert C. Heller, an investment broker. In the same year, the Eighteenth Amendment to the United States Constitution was submitted to the states for ratification. Prohibition was clearly coming, and there was a sudden rush among distillers to dispose of their whiskey inventories. Aiding the panic was pressure on the brewing industry resulting from a right-wing attempt to label it pro-German. Rosenstiel swiftly took advantage of the fluid situation. With other investors, he formed the Cincinnati Distribution Corporation, whose business was to buy and sell whiskey warehouse receipts. This activity eventually put Rosenstiel's company into direct competition with Remus, who during the twenties was doing the same thing on a bigger scale. Following Remus's fall in 1927, and with Prohibition the law of the land, Rosenstiel and others formed the Schenley Products Company. They then purchased the Joseph S. Finch distillery, which owned four thousand barrels of whiskey in four warehouses. A little later, in December 1927, Schenley bought five-year options on warehouse receipts covering two hundred forty thousand cases of Old Overholt whiskey. In 1930 Schenley purchased receipts covering over one hundred thousand cases of Large whiskey.[12] Unlike Schenley, other distillers were giving up hope that Repeal would come within a reasonable period. They were wrong. When Repeal came in 1933, Schenley was ready indeed; it

44

owned stocks of aged and well-known whiskeys that represented an estimated one-fifth of the total national inventory of domestically produced whiskey.[13] Gangster Johnnie Torrio was eager to help Rosenstiel dispose of it. Profits were enormous.

For Rosenstiel, the long waiting period had not been unprofitable or uneventful. Among other things he had been indicted in a case that well illustrates the fringe benefits of organized crime. The indictment, returned in the Eastern District of New York, charged a huge conspiracy involving distillers, glass companies, cork companies, label manufacturers, and dozens of individuals with conspiracy to violate the National Prohibition Act. Overholt Distilling Corporation and Sherwood Distilling Company, Inc., were accused of storing large amounts of whiskey in barrels and then failing to treat the barrels as required by law when their contents were sold for "medicinal purposes." Instead, the liquor-soaked barrels were used in the conspiracy. The insides were shaved, and the "chips" were sold for use in flavoring illegally manufactured liquor. The Schenley Products Company and Lewis S. Rosteniel were accused of buying the empty barrels "and did distribute and sell the said barrels above described for the purpose hereinbefore set forth" to the Sukonik Cooperage Company in Philadelphia.

The several glass companies that were indicted were charged with manufacturing forged whiskey bottles to contain the illegal liquor. The bottles were in the shape and form of several popular brands of whiskey. A printing firm produced counterfeit labels, wrappers, cartons, containers, and stamps to increase the illusion that high-priced whiskey was in the bottles, the stamps "being in similitude, likeness, resemblance and general appearance of Internal Revenue Stamps required by law," as the indictment noted. Another company supplied wooden crates to resemble those used by John Walker & Sons, Haig & Haig, Ltd., Peter Dawson, Ltd., and many others. The cork companies manufactured "certain corks on which were printed and stamped by means of dyes, the names and wording of certain well-known whiskey brands." Another firm, Glickstein and Terner, Inc., allegedly supplied a kit known as "Test-Ur-Own," which permitted the busy bootlegger to test the proof of his rot gut. The final products, combining all the elements, were sold as "outfits," although the liquor-flavored chips were also sold separately as "units."

Operators of illicit stills up and down the East coast bought both the "outfits" and the "units." By letting the "chips" soak in his newly made, second-rate booze for awhile, an operator could improve both the flavor and coloring. Then he would pour the cheap liquor into the counterfeit bottles, insert the counterfeit corks, apply the counterfeit labels and stamps, pack the bottles in the counterfeit cartons, and load the cartons into counterfeit crates, and sell the final packages as expensive, imported liquor supposedly just off the boat. How many naive citizens died from drinking rot gut they thought was good whiskey will never be known. They are simply dead.

As far as the big distilleries were concerned, this packaging activity cited in the indictment was only a sideline operation. Nevertheless, it illustrates how the businessmen of booze never missed a trick to increase their profits. Rosenstiel, of course, denied knowing anything about the part his two companies played in the conspiracy. An underling took full responsibility, pleaded guilty, and was given a fine. The charges against his boss were dismissed.[14]

Around the country, as in Cincinnati, the shape of things to come was visible. The process known as the "survival of the fittest" was shaking down the underworld. All ethnic groups were involved. In city after city what became known as the "Combination" developed. As yet there was little intercity cooperation, but that would come as local situations stabilized and as rumrunning became the principal source of liquor.

A loose, largely autonomous organization did exist on a national basis. Imported from Sicily, it was known to its members as the "Honored Society." The public knew it under a variety of names, the most common being the Mafia. Nicola Gentile, who came to this country in 1903 as a stowaway, is the only one of its members to have written about it at length. Here is his version of its history and purpose:

The organization had originated many, many years ago in antiquity and it gives the right to defend the honor, the weak,

46

and to respect the human law. With these principles as its guide, it still operates.

All the organizations are born with principles and humanitarian goals—but in their midst the opportunists are never missing and will try to make a profit. With this I don't want to make an apology for the Honored Society or Mafia, as it is commonly called; it would be just as if I would admit a state within a state. The Honored Society I could compare, for its assistance to the associates, to the Masons. But, the Masons' philosophical teachings are mystical or theological. The Honored Society finds its reason for existence in force and terror. However, it was started by land owners as a disciplinary force in the community. It was started in the least developed part of Sicily and was brought to America in the sections of the country where Sicilians, Calabrians and Neapolitans lived.

Their associates are called "fratellos," and they obey a Capo elected by them. The Capo afterwards picks the consigliari that help him to work out justice and make judgments. When one of them finds himself in difficulty of any kind, the association tries to help and assist him.

With the passing of time in every city of America these associations were formed. Between the heads of the various "Borgate" or families they select the overall capo whom they call the Capo di Capi Re. That means the re, or king, of the Honored Society. At New York and Brooklyn among the five Borgate, there are two thousand associates.

My temperament was bringing me a life of adventure. The courage which nature had endowed me with, my intrepid spirit and imperious nature, and my code which I thought was right, made me join the Honored Society.[15]

Gentile served as a capo in various cities and became something of a troubleshooter. The account of his travels makes it clear that—in the twenties—there was little central control. Local capos, using fear and terror, could organize the first-generation Americans in the ghettos with some degree of economic efficiency. In each city men sought to achieve Capo status by murdering the incumbent. Vendettas were common. The second stage of Prohibition, when rot-gut liquor was manufactured in thousands of small stills, gave the Mafia its real start. It expanded from an organization which preyed primarily on its own people to become a force in American life. But when rumrunning—the third stage—began, the

Mafia lost much of its power and became part of the various "combinations." Even then, the Mafia's violent ways kept it in turmoil and often prevented it from getting its fair share of the loot.

For example, the Cleveland syndicate took over from the Mayfield Road mob, as the Mafia organization was known, and organized liquor smuggling across Lake Erie from Detroit to Buffalo. In Detroit, the Purple Gang—a Jewish outfit —clashed with "The Little Jewish Navy" and imported the Licavoli brothers from St. Louis to serve as its gunmen. In Minneapolis-St. Paul, the Kid Cann Gang emerged to dominate the rackets. Boston was controlled by Charles "King" Solomon. And so it went. In every city one organization eventually emerged as the supreme power.

Nevertheless, national attention centered on only two cities: Chicago and New York. In both of them, the same man—John "the Fox" Torrio—played decisive roles.

Torrio, a native of Naples, never joined the Honored Society. He grew up in Brooklyn, managed prizefighters for a while, and in 1910 accepted an invitation from his uncle, Big Jim Colosimo, to come to Chicago. He took charge of his uncle's brothels, added card rooms in back, and expanded so rapidly that he decided to send East for an assistant. "Scarface" Al Capone heeded the call and was quickly made manager of the Four Deuces, one of Torrio's combination brothel and gambling joints. Instantly recognizing the possibilities of Prohibition, Torrio decided that his uncle was too old-fashioned and arranged his murder. But, by and large, Torrio preferred reason to violence, a trait Capone did not share. By 1924, the liquor business was booming. Competition cut down the profits, however, and the endless gang warfare was giving the city a bad name. Although Torrio called a peace conference and proposed that Chicago be divided into territories, the idea was too intelligent to be accepted. And there were too many ambitious men.

Eventually, Torrio abandoned Chicago and left his organization to Capone. The warfare continued. Capone at one point was forced to retreat to the suburbs. Earlier, under Torrio's direction, he had captured such cities as Cicero, which some thirty years later was described as "a walled city of the syndicate." At best, Capone bossed only one-fourth of Chicago and was never able to eliminate such rivals as George "Bugs" Moran. Thanks, however, to the press, and his own bloody ways, he became the nation's most famous gangster.

The Mafia had little part in Capone's success. The Capone gang was a true combination, including Italian, Jewish, and Irish elements. The Mafia, as such, cooperated more or less, but did not pretend to dominate. In time, Capone was accepted into the organization and achieved the rank of capo decina—head of ten.

After leaving Chicago, Torrio took a long cruise, spent some months in Hawaii, and returned to his old home in New York. There he put his organization plans to work. The gangs along the East coast were more sophisticated than those in Chicago—thanks to the pioneering work of Meyer Lansky—and were willing to listen to reason. At Torrio's urging they joined into the "Big Seven"—the forerunner of the national crime syndicate.

John Edgar Hoover in the course of his career has shown great wisdom in his choice of targets. The international Communist conspiracy has, of course, been his favorite, but he has gone after bankrobbers and kidnapers with equal zeal. In doing so he stepped on no important toes, made enemies of no important segment of the financial or political establishment. Occasionally a few people might express concern about civil rights, but they could be dismissed as left-wingers, "fuzzy thinkers," or naive tools of the Reds. It is not surprising, therefore, that Hoover not only ignored the existence of the Mafia for forty years, but denied it existed. In exactly the same fashion, he avoided a clash with the organized crime syndicates that began evolving during Prohibition and grew to full flower in the next decade.

When Prohibition began, a special enforcement unit was set up in the Treasury Department. Elmer Irey, head of Treasury's special intelligence unit, objected violently, arguing it belonged in the Department of Justice. As Justice under Palmer was too busy investigating the Red menace to bother with liquor law enforcement, Irey's men were assigned to police Prohibition agents. Irey's men did a good job, considering the impossible nature of their mission. From 1920 to 1928, they were responsible for firing seven hundred and six Prohibition agents and prosecuting two hundred and seven more. One of their first assignments was to probe a delicate situation involving high officials. As Irey commented: "It then became the Intelligence Unit's unpleasant duty not only to arrest a Congressman [John Langley of Kentucky] but to indict our own boss." The boss was Millard West, appointed by Harding to serve as acting commissioner of internal revenue.

One can see why Hoover did not want to venture into such dangerous waters. Investigations in New York, Milwaukee, Cleveland, and other cities resulted in the indictment of high officials, but so complete was the corruption that little else was achieved. Irey had less than a hundred men, and he was literally combating an army of many thousands. Furthermore, he could not attack the rumrunning gangsters directly, since his authority extended only to corrupt activity of Prohibition agents, although the situation changed on May 10, 1927, when the Supreme Court ruled that profits from illegal business were subject to taxation. With that ruling in his briefcase, Irey turned to Chicago and Al Capone.

Perhaps alarmed by Irey's activities, the Republicans in 1928 shifted the Prohibition enforcement unit out of the Treasury Department and into Justice. The responsibility for policing the Prohibition agents—formerly done by Irey's men—was assigned to the Bureau. Nothing happened. Later, in 1933 when President Roosevelt ordered the Prohibition Bureau consolidated with the Bureau of Investigation, Hoover protested loudly and successfully, despite the fact that the Prohibition unit was being phased out with the coming of Repeal. After Repeal, the task of enforcing liquor laws was shifted back to Treasury. Presumably, Hoover was happy to see it go. He seemed to have no desire to step on the toes of such men as liquor baron Lewis Rosenstiel or, for that matter, John Torrio and Meyer Lansky.[16]

Hoover's caution in dealing with the liquor barons has done nothing to tarnish his image, perhaps because his busy press agents have managed to dip into the past and steal some of the credit due other agencies. Many books leave the impression, for example, that the FBI "got" Capone.[17] They did—for contempt of court. Or the books tell of five thousand indictments for bootlegging hurriedly secured by the Bureau on the eve of Capone's trial for income-tax evasion. That all were promptly dismissed is seldom mentioned. In actual fact, it was Irey's men in the Treasury Department who provided the evidence that sent Capone to prison and ended his career. In passing, they and not Hoover also convicted such lieutenants as Frank Nitti and Jake Guzik. But in the minds of the public today, the FBI gets the credit.

Another example of stolen glory is that of the Lindbergh kidnaping, generally considered "the crime of the century." The infant son of the "Lone Eagle," Charles A. Lindbergh, was stolen from his crib near Hopewell, New Jersey, on the night of March 1, 1932. The kidnaping created a sensation, and everyone from Capone to the local police chief tried to get into the act.

Arthur Brisbane, the influential columnist of the Hearst Press, brought Capone into the picture by informing the world on March 10, that Capone, if freed, could find the missing child. Ironically, his announcement didn't help Scarface Al, but it did call out the men who eventually contributed most to solving the case—the special agents of the intelligence unit of the Bureau of Internal Revenue. Brisbane's theory was based on a misconception shared by John Edgar Hoover and much exploited by him—that with the coming of Repeal, organized crime would turn to kidnaping as its major field of operation.

Kidnaping became common during Prohibition, but the victims were almost always rival gangsters. Men like Daniel Walsh, rumrunner of Providence, Rhode Island, were seized, and huge ransoms collected. In many cases the victim was then killed. It was a profitable sideline for the gangsters of that era, who knew there was small chance of being caught. But these same gangsters, the smart ones who survived, had better sense than to kidnap respectable citizens who, if rich enough to pay ransoms, would be rich enough to have suf-

51

ficient prestige and political power to involve the public and law-enforcement agencies. Thus kidnaping never became an organized racket.

Nevertheless, Brisbane's story caused Lindbergh to call Secretary of the Treasury Ogden Mills to discuss Capone's offer. Irey was sent to Hopewell and persuaded Lindbergh that Capone had no information of value. Although Lindbergh agreed, Irey assigned two special agents to the case at Lindbergh's request.

On May 11, 1932, the country was shocked when a body identified as that of the Lindbergh baby was found in a shallow grave. President Hoover responded by ordering all Federal agencies to cooperate with New Jersey authorities in the search for the killer. John Edgar Hoover and the Bureau of Investigation were made responsible for "coordinating the activities of the Federal services."

The assignment was a hot potato—and Hoover felt he might be burned. At a May 19 conference of all cooperating agencies, he stated that the actual direction of the probe should be left to New Jersey officials. A special agent of the Bureau would be sent to New Jersey to act as liaison officer, he said, and all other Federal men would be withdrawn. Irey obeyed, ordering his two agents already working on the case to return to Chicago. Six days later, Lindbergh again asked Secretary Mills for assistance. Mills conferred with President Hoover, who ordered Irey to confer with the Bureau chief "in the most diplomatic manner" to work out a solution.

There was no real problem. John Edgar Hoover had already heard of Lindbergh's request to Mills and had ordered his liaison man home. Irey suggested tactfully that the Treasury agents be assigned to work under Hoover and be "practically divorced" from the intelligence unit while so serving. Hoover would have none of that. He told Irey to carry on as before. The special agents of the intelligence unit went back to work. At their insistence, gold certificates were included in the ransom payment and their serial numbers recorded. Eventually one of the certificates, used to buy five gallons of gasoline, led to the arrest of Bruno Hauptmann. And it was a special agent who proved that Hauptmann owned or spent exactly forty-nine thousand, nine hundred and fifty dollars and forty-four cents more than he had earned since coming to America, just forty dollars and fifty-six cents less than the fifty-thousand-dollar ransom paid in the case.[18]

The withdrawal of Hoover from the investigation did not, of course, prevent future press agents with crediting the FBI with solving the case. Even today, it is presented as one of the major feathers in Hoover's war bonnet. But there were more immediate benefits. Three months after the kidnaping, Congress passed the so-called "Lindbergh Law" which, as later amended, provided the death penalty for transporting a kidnap victim across state lines. Responsibility for enforcing the law was given to the Bureau of Investigation.

Isolated kidnapings continued and continue today, but when kidnaping didn't develop into the racket Hoover had predicted, President Herbert Hoover was later able to write: "The efficiency and courage of the FBI under J. Edgar Hoover finally stamped out this particular crime wave. The fears in the hearts of millions of mothers were lifted."[19]

Of such sentimental nonsense is the legend of John Edgar Hoover composed. Lindbergh was more realistic. During the trial of Hauptmann, he told Irey, "If it had not been for your Service being in the case, Hauptmann would not now be on trial and your organization deserves the full credit for his apprehension."[20]

Herbert Hoover can be pardoned for his praise of John Edgar Hoover. Any credit given the Bureau chief reflects on the man who claimed responsibility for his appointment in 1924. And certainly by 1932, Herbert Hoover needed all the credit he could salvage.

Much has been written about the stockmarket crash and the Great Depression, but little attention has been played to one of its more important and far-reaching aspects—its influence on organized crime. Bootleggers made plenty of money in the days before the crash; so did a lot of other people. The respectable citizen put his money into banks or invested it in the stockmarket; the bootlegger kept his wealth liquid. After the Supreme Court ruling making illegal profits taxable, thousands of gangsters paid token income taxes and moved their money from banks to secret hiding places. Even small grafters kept their unreported cash incomes in "little tin boxes" buried in back yards. So when the banks failed, when businesses went bankrupt, when investments soured, when credit became as scarce as cash, the gangsters had money to spend. Although there is no record of how much they had, it amounted to billions.

Irving Wexler, better known as Waxey Gordon, had an income-tax liability of eight hundred and twenty-one thousand, one hundred thirty-six dollars for the years 1930 and 1931. Morris Kleinman, charter member of the Cleveland syndicate, banked one million, six hundred and seventy-three thousand, five hundred fifty-four dollars in a two-year period, 1929–1930, and paid no taxes on any of it. José Miro, New York numbers racketeer, deposited one million, eighty-three thousand, one hundred fifty-four dollars in ten bank accounts in a three-year period. Frank "the Enforcer" Nitti was convicted of neglecting to pay taxes on an income of seven hundred fifty thousand dollars over a three-year period, and he was only one of Al Capone's lieutenants.[21] Most of these men were young. So were such lucky colleagues as Meyer Lansky, Frank Costello, Moe Dalitz, Charles "Lucky" Luciano, Abner "Longie" Zwillman, Charles Polizzi—their names were legion—who avoided income-tax raps. They had wealth, which only whetted their appetite for more. And they recognized their unique opportunity.

During the depression organized crime first penetrated legitimate business. Comparatively speaking, it was a small penetration, but the beachhead expanded and mushroomed over the next two decades. Some respectable executives jumped out of their office windows when their companies collapsed. Others turned to gangsters for the cash they had to have to survive.

The restaurant-nightclub industry had long been a favorite field for gangsters; now they added hotels. Entertainment was a logical next step, especially the new movie industry. Liquor was, of course, already allied to the mob; after Repeal it became even more of a crime-controlled business. Service industries, food chains, radio, and newspapers—all were penetrated.

Of course, organized crime needed the help of parvenus— amoral men with great greed who needed only cash to get

54

started. They became the respectable fronts for underworld cash. The gray area between the legal and the illegal steadily widened. These parvenus became millionaires in less than a generation as they changed the tone of the business world by dropping many of the pretensions originally inspired by the Puritan ethic.

Politics changed too. Until the depression, the politician had been the boss. Now he had to consider the gangster who decided which candidate would get his support and the support of his ally in business. An invisible government developed that achieved full control of many cities, some states, and influenced the make-up of Congress. At the 1932 Democratic convention in Chicago, gangsters attended the meetings in the smoke-filled rooms.[22]

Where was John Edgar Hoover as organized crime got organized? Perhaps he was thinking about his own future. The election of Franklin D. Roosevelt confronted Hoover with a personal crisis. For Roosevelt's attorney general was slated to be Hoover's old enemy, Thomas J. Walsh.

IV

FRANKLIN D. Roosevelt was President-elect, but four months would pass before he took office and he steadily refused to become involved in any of the last-minute emergency measures of the dying, discredited Hoover administration. Banks were closing, breadlines grew longer. The so-called Bonus Expeditionary Force, a hungry, ragged army of some fifteen thousand men, had been dispersed by troops under the command of Douglas MacArthur.

The crisis made the troubles of 1919–1920 that produced the Red scare seem like a college panty raid, but this time there was no hysteria. Roosevelt had promised a "new deal for the American people," and patiently the people waited.

Where was John Edgar Hoover at this critical moment when the very life of the American economic and political system hung in the balance? Where was the man who, according to legend, had refused the job of acting FBI director unless he could have it on his own nonpolitical terms? He was scurrying around Washington, applying pressure, cashing in on past favors, desperately attempting to hang on to his job. He did not talk now of "conditions," did not mention the international Communist conspiracy, did not fear that the promised "new deal" would steer the country to the left. No, Hoover, like many another Washington bureaucrat, was using all the influence, all the skills he had developed in a lifetime in government, just to survive the change in administration. Hat in hand, he even went to Senator Wheeler, the man he had openly branded as a Red only a few years before. The record contains only Wheeler's version of the interview, which was written many years later after Wheeler had turned reactionary and become fond of Hoover. His statement that Hoover convinced him he had no part of the reprisals of 1924–1925 conflicts with his earlier remarks, but it does confirm the desperate measures Hoover was forced to take.[1]

Wheeler was not the main danger, of course. The man Hoover feared, and with reason, was Thomas J. Walsh. As late as 1929, Senator Walsh blocked a proposal to make William Donovan attorney general. Donovan had been an assistant attorney general under Stone and had recommended the prosecution of Wheeler. But the investigation had been carried out under the direction of Hoover, and Walsh knew it. Hoover must have hoped that Walsh was ready to retire. It was public knowledge that he could be attorney general if he desired, but he was seventy-three years old. Moreover, he was becoming senile—or so his critics said, pointing to his infatuation with a much younger Cuban widow. In late February Walsh confided to his colleague Wheeler that he was going out of town for a few days. He didn't say where he was going, and Wheeler was astonished to read a day or two later that Walsh had married Senora Perez Chaumont in Havana. By February 28, Walsh and his bride were in Daytona Beach en route to Washington. And on that day Roosevelt made it official—the new bridegroom was his choice for attorney genera. Word had it that Walsh—who had been chairman of the Democratic convention at Chicago—would be the elder statesman of the Roosevelt cabinet. A *New York Times* dispatch from Daytona Beach made it plain, however, that the senator intended to be more than a symbol or an advisor. The story quoted Walsh as saying, "he would reorganize the Department of Justice when he assumed office, probably with an almost completely new personnel." He added that his appointment came as no surprise—he had known of it for days.[2]

John Edgar Hoover must have shivered when he read those words. Walsh left no doubt that he considered the Justice Department still infected with men appointed in the Daugherty-Burns days, among them Hoover.

What followed next must be classed with some of those strange events that still cloud the Harding era. Walsh and his bride were aboard a train streaking through the night toward Washington and the inauguration which was only two days away. As the train neared Rocky Mount, North Carolina, Mrs. Walsh awoke to find her husband on the floor of the compartment, barely alive. She called a porter, who located a doctor on the train. Walsh was dead by the time the doctor reached him.

The news shocked Washington. According to the *New York Times*, Walsh had been in "vigorous health." Recently, in Daytona Beach, he had complained of pain. A doctor examined him. "The doctor assured me," Mrs. Walsh said, "the Senator did not have heart trouble. I think he did that to spare me." Doctor Harry L. Merryday told reporters "he found M. Walsh suffering from a mild angina pectoria and intestinal disorder." The death certificate, signed by Dr. M. A. Pittman of Wilson, North Carolina, said about the death: "Cause unknown, possibly coronary thrombosis." In retrospect, the whole affair reminds one of the "tainted crabmeat" that was blamed for President Harding's illness prior to his death. Interestingly enough, a Bureau of Investigation agent boarded the train at Rocky Mount and guarded Mrs. Walsh during the long ride to Washington with the body. As the *New York Times* put it, the agent, Edward E. Conroy, "kept watch outside her drawing room."[3]

In the excitement of the inauguration, and the hundred days that followed, the Walsh death was forgotten. Homer Cummings was quickly named attorney general in lieu of Walsh, and was sworn in with the entire cabinet. On March 6, the President and the cabinet took time out to attend Walsh's funeral and then hurried back to the White House to attend a conference of governors. The nation's economic crisis left few moments to wonder about a fallen warrior.

Walsh's unexpected death gave Hoover a reprieve, and time to mount a new offensive. News stories in June noted that "powerful political pressure" was being employed to keep him at his job. Some of that pressure came from J. Bruce Kremer, a former lobbyist for the Anaconda Copper Company. Kremer, who had been a bitter foe of Walsh and Wheeler, was close to Cummings, the new attorney general. A long-time Democratic politician, Cummings served as chairman of the Democratic National Committee in 1919–1920, when Palmer was attorney general and Hoover was his special assistant. Cummings had also been a prosecutor in Fairfield County, Connecticut, from 1914 to 1924, and had adopted a hard-nosed policy toward crime. Somehow, Kremer was able to convince Cummings that Hoover would be as rough on criminals as he had been on Reds.

Another source of support that has received little attention was the National Crime Commission, a private group organized in 1925 by leading businessmen, who felt that most criminal acts were the work of aliens. Mark O. Prentiss, was the prime mover in the organization, which was formed in the board room of the United States Steel Corporation. The group advocated a national police force and was easily persuaded that Hoover was the man to head it. After all, he had proved his patriotism in going after Reds and deporting them. It was Hoover's good fortune that President Roosevelt had been a member of the executive committee of the commission for several years.[4]

Hoover, who was later to oppose loudly all talk of a national police or, for that matter, a national crime commission, welcomed the support of Prentiss and his friends. Hoover was also assisted by the storm of public concern aroused by the Lindbergh kidnaping. The press and the public demanded that something be done, and Roosevelt and Cummings were willing to oblige.

One June 10, 1933, by executive order, a division of investigation was set up in the Justice Department. Hoover was placed in charge. The following year, the division was given new, expanded powers: the right to carry weapons and the right to make an arrest. Jurisdiction was broadened as well. Robbing a national bank became a Federal crime. Flight across state lines to avoid prosecution, racketeering in interstate commerce, transporting stolen property across state lines—all these and many more became Federal crimes that the division of Investigation could investigate. With the phasing out of Prohibition, as previously noted, the setup was reorganized once more, and on July 1, 1935, the Federal Bureau of Investigation came into being.

Hoover showed wisdom in his choice of names. The Federal Bureau of Investigation had an all-inclusive sound, which helped convince citizens that the FBI was the only government investigative agency, and helped Hoover's press agents credit the FBI with work done by other agencies such as the Secret Service, the Postal Inspection Service, the Alcohol Tax Unit, and the intelligence unit of the Bureau of Internal Revenue.

Roosevelt also ordered a similar consolidation for Treasury agencies. Although Elmer Irey was given the job of "coordinator," he was satisfied to get an interchange of intelligence data between agencies while leaving each to pursue its own specialty. He made no effort to create a superorganization.

Many students of Roosevelt have commented on his practice of playing one bureaucrat off against another, deliberately leaving jurisdictional lines vague. While this approach caused confusion and overlapping, it also enabled a busy President to maintain better control over the ambitious men who served themselves while serving him. Only a man of great self-confidence could get away with such procedures and still achieve results. Thus, he enjoyed the feud between Irey and Hoover as well as its counterpart on the cabinet level between Secretary of the Treasury Henry Morgenthau and Attorney General Cummings.

The big jobs, the investigations of political bosses such as Huey Long and Tom Pendergast, and the fight against organized crime, were left to Irey's men while the FBI chased bankrobbers, kidnapers, and car thieves. Thanks to the new legislation, the FBI was no longer the "fact-collecting organization" envisioned by Stone. It had become, in fact, if not in name, a law-enforcement agency, a Federal police force. And, in its haste to achieve a reputation, it sometimes played the role of judge, jury, and executioner as well.

John Edgar Hoover, by instinct and training, knew that it was time to find a new menace, easily identifiable, easily impressed on the public mind. The collapse of the old order, the changing economic and political situation dictated the nature of the new foe. Law and order had always been popular, so the Red menace was put aside. Hoover adopted the role of the tough cop. More than adoption was needed, however. The American people had to be sold by a masterful public relations campaign. At the Washington branch of the YMCA, Hoover found an expert salesman.

Louis B. Nichols had served as assistant business manager of the YMCA for three years when he quit to become an assistant director of the FBI. During his years at the YMCA, he had become well acquainted with congressmen, cabinet officers, and bureaucrats of every level of government. Like Hoover, he had attended George Washington University, getting his LL.B degree in 1934, the year he joined the FBI. Most observers credit Nichols with the amazing public relations campaign that in a few short years made Hoover and the "G-Men" household words. Every communications device then in use was employed: newspapers, radio, magazine articles, books, even comic strips. Mistakes, and there were many, were ignored or blurred; victories, however petty, were exaggerated to heroic proportions.

The public, ground down by the depression and made cynical by the scandals of the past, was ready for new heroes. The FBI filled the bill perfectly, the more so since Hoover simplified the war on crime to the old game of good guys versus bad guys, white hats against black hats. When the Director spoke of "scum," of "rats," of "craven beasts," of "vermin" and "vultures," the public could understand and applaud. No mumbo jumbo about environment, social conditions, broken homes, no talk of job opportunities and rehabilitation—the only good punk was a dead one. It was a return to the code of the old West with the FBI serving as a national posse and, occasionally, as a lynching party. If a

61

bank robber was shot down without cause, so what? The G-Men had saved the government the expense of a trial.

Hoover opposed parole and called for more and stronger prisons. The underworld became a "criminal horde," which if not checked would destroy the nation. He cited figures. If sometimes they conflicted, few noticed. In 1936, for example, he said that the "armed forces of crime" numbered more than three million. Three months later he said that the "criminal standing army" numbered "a whole half million armed thugs, murderers, thieves, firebugs, assassins, robbers, and holdup men." A few months later the total "criminal population" was back to three million, five hundred thousand, and several months after that he claimed that four million, three hundred thousand persons were engaged in the commission of felonies.[5]

Perhaps the coining of the term, "G-Men," was the single most important coup of the public relations campaign. In later years, the FBI sought vainly to repeat that triumph by requesting that "LCN" be used as a suitable headline substitute for La Cosa Nostra. It never caught on, however, since the word "Mafia" was almost as short and certainly more familiar—to everyone but the FBI.

Over the years an occasional writer has attempted to debunk some part of the FBI legend, but it is a hopeless task. The truth, plain, unexciting, and unmotivated, never catches up with the colorful, dramatic half-truth or outright lie. So it is with the "G-Men." According to the legend, Machinegun Kelly—one of the more notorious punks of the day—when surrounded, went down on his knees and begged: "Don't shoot, G-Men; don't shoot." When asked what "G-Men" meant, Kelly explained it was short for "Government men." In the past, gangsters had used the term "Feds" to distinguish between local and Federal officers. Obviously that had become old hat. Today they still use "Feds," but that fact has escaped general attention.

Did it really happen? In a 1936 article in *Harper's*, Howard McLellan gave quite another version. Kelly, he maintained, was captured by Detective Sergeant W. J. Raney of the Memphis Police Department, which was cooperating with the FBI in the hunt. Raney shoved a shotgun barrel into Kelly's stomach and ordered him to drop his gun. Kelly obeyed, and that was all.[6]

Perhaps the capture of Alvin "Creepy" Karpis was even more important to Hoover's legend. Karpis was a bank robber who occasionally worked with the "Ma Barker" gang. The FBI mowed down Ma and her son, Fred, in 1935, again saving the government the cost of a trial, but Karpis continued to elude them. Hoover proclaimed him "Public Rat Number One," and vowed to eliminate the rodent. Meanwhile, Senator Kenneth D. McKellar, chairman of the Senate Appropriations Committee got a little tired of the endless publicity. When Hoover appeared for a hearing, McKellar seized his chance and made Hoover admit he had never arrested anyone. The Director left the hearing room "boiling mad." Just in time, Karpis was located in New Orleans. Hoover assembled a raiding party and flew south. Plans were made to surround and storm Karpis's hideout, an apartment on Canal Street.

According to the approved version, and it has been repeated in books and countless articles, Karpis saved everyone some trouble—and perhaps even his own life—by sauntering to a car on the street. A small boy on a bicycle rode by, forcing the FBI agents to hold their fire. Other versions have it that a man rode by on a white horse. Take your choice. In any case, Karpis was seated in the car when John Edgar Hoover—in person—came running up to arrest him. The FBI had neglected to bring along handcuffs—an indication perhaps that they had not planned to take Karpis alive—and they had to tie him up with an agent's necktie. It made a good story, and it presumably answered McKellar and other critics. Since the FBI had neglected to inform the local police, the only witness to the capture who might have spoiled the story was Karpis himself. It wasn't until 1971, however, that Karpis—released on parole in 1968—talked. According to Karpis, Hoover stayed safely under cover until his men had the situation under control. Then he rushed forward to claim the glory. "I have nothing but contempt for J. Edgar Hoover," said Karpis in his autobiography.[7]

Ordinarily, one would hesitate to accept the word of an ex-convict and disbelieve a respectable public official. But too often the legend makers have so exaggerated the FBI exploits and their consequences that they have opened a credibility gap for all but the indifferent and the naive.

Journalists—and most of those who have written about the FBI began as journalists at least—are not really naive, but a newspaperman, be he reporter or editor, likes what he would call a "good" story. A "good" story has action. It may be dramatic action or emotional action, but it has punch. Unfortunately, such stories are infrequent. Ethics prevent most reporters from inventing details that would change a routine tale into a "good" story, but they don't prevent a reporter from writing a story he suspects is too "good" to be true if he can attribute it to a respectable source.

The FBI was a respectable source. And Hoover, or at least some of his public relations people, decided to supply the hero worshippers of America with a whale of a lot of "good" stories. The kidnaping of five-year-old James Bailey Cash is one example.

In point of fact, the FBI had no business being involved in the case at all since the drama was confined to Dade County, Florida. But it had become customary in kidnaping cases to assume that if twenty-four hours passed without word from the victim, he or she had been spirited out of the state. The FBI then automatically went into action. As often as not, it did not even wait twenty-four hours.

The Cash boy was kidnaped from his bed in Princeton, Florida, some miles south of Miami on the edge of the Everglades, on Saturday, May 28, 1938. The next afternoon Hoover was in Miami at the head of a small army of agents. He immediately asked the press to say nothing about the crime until the ransom had been paid and the child recovered. The newspapers agreed, on condition that their reporters could follow the progress of the investigation in order to prepare stories for future publication. Hoover was willing.

When no stories appeared in the Monday edition of the *Miami Herald,* hundreds of people called to tip off the editors. How did the public know? The FBI had turned the hunt into a three-ring circus, complete with searchlights to aid in beating the bushes of the Everglades. As many as forty "G-Men" were dashing about interviewing everyone in sight. As Quentin Reynolds was later to write in *Collier's,* "there

64

were more men working on the Cash kidnaping last month in Florida than on the Lindbergh case."[8] That was not surprising, of course, in view of Hoover's withdrawal from the Lindbergh affair, but apparently Reynolds didn't know the background. His source, after all, was Hoover.

Forty-eight hours after the kidnaping, John Pennekamp, the city editor of the *Miami Herald*, ordered the story to press. Tuesday's front page was full of it. On the same morning, too late to make the paper, the ransom was delivered. Hoover hit the ceiling. He told reporter Steve Trumbull that if the child was found dead, the *Herald* would be responsible.

Meanwhile, Sheriff D. C. Coleman, who was being ignored by the FBI, arrested Franklin McCall, a local youth, who had been acting mysteriously and failed to answer the sheriff's questions. He turned McCall over to Hoover, who promptly released him. McCall was the son of a preacher, clean cut and intelligent. The investigation continued. The FBI arrested several other "suspects" and hauled them into Miami for questioning. No results. Meanwhile, Sheriff Coleman kept his eye on McCall and again arrested the youth. Questioning him, he caught him in an obvious lie. Again McCall was turned over to Hoover. This time a confession was obtained, and McCall led the FBI to the grave. When the *Miami Herald* reporters followed, Hoover ordered them to stop. Reynolds quotes the Director as saying, "You men are obstructing justice by following us. If you don't turn around and go back, you will be arrested for interference with Federal officers in the performance of their duty." Allegedly, Hoover feared McCall might be lynched if the news got out.

It turned out that the boy had been killed the night of the kidnaping. That didn't prevent Hoover—through Reynolds —from blasting the newspapers and implying they were responsible. Hoover's announcement of the arrest of McCall, by the way, made no mention of Sheriff Coleman.

The FBI's manner of taking over, excluding local authorities, and hogging all the credit angered police officials from one end of the country to the other. The case of Harry Brunette and Merle Vandenbush in 1936 annoyed both the New Jersey state police and the cops of New York City.

Brunette and Vandenbush were wanted for bank robbery

and the kidnaping of a New Jersey state trooper. The New Jersey officers, by some good detective work, traced a car used by the pair to New York. New York police joined in the hunt. Although the FBI was notified that a good lead had been developed, the search was continued on the local level. Eventually, it was discovered that Brunette and his new bride were living in an apartment at 304 West 102nd Street. A conference was held. The police wanted to delay action in the hope that Vandenbush would visit the Brunettes. The FBI did not want to wait. Finally, an agreement was reached to raid the apartment on a given Tuesday afternoon. Some fourteen hours before zero hour, Hoover appeared and personally led his men in a spectacular assault on the apartment. Brunette shot back, and a battle royal raged for thirty minutes as other apartment occupants in the building cowered under their beds for safety. Tear-gas bombs were tossed. The building caught fire. Firemen arrived only to be caught in a crossfire. Luckily none were hit. The fire forced the occupants out. Mrs. Brunette had been shot in the thigh; her husband was unhurt.

Two months later Vandenbush and two associates were captured by village police in Armonk, New York, who did not have to fire a shot. Vandenbush revealed that he had come to 102nd Street on the night of the big raid—as New York police had anticipated—and got so close to Hoover he could have touched his shoulder. He watched the excitement for awhile and strolled off.[9] Criticism was strong, but Hoover, by now enthroned as chief "G-Man," could shrug his shoulders and dismiss it all as "kindergarten stuff."

Despite his double-crossing the New York police, Hoover had no desire for bad relations with local police agencies. As early as 1936 he had written to the *Daily Capital* in Topeka, Kansas, stating:

The Federal Bureau of Investigation believes that the secret of crime eradication lies not in a national police force but in solidarity and the combined linking of all law enforcement agencies. It believes in close-knit cooperation, each unit capable of handling its peculiar problems but capable also, when necessary, of mobilizing its efforts in a concerted drive against the criminal element. . . .

There were two major reasons for this attitude. Hoover knew that any drive against regional vice centers, for example, would annoy local politicians. He also recognized that if an attack was made on such centers, his men would be exposed to temptation and thus perhaps give the FBI a bad reputation. As previously noted, organized crime was not involved in kidnaping or bank robberies, which were the safe targets. If the FBI sometimes annoyed local authorities, it was not serious, since such pursuit of bank robbers and kidnapers posed no threat to the crime syndicates who paid many local and state officials for permission to operate undisturbed.

To improve relations with the police, Hoover instituted the FBI National Academy, which admitted its first class on July 29, 1935. In theory, the top men from police departments around the country have been selected to attend the academy, where they get specialized information on crime techniques and are "brainwashed" on the virtues of the FBI and its director. In practice, however, since the nomination is made by the police chief, a lot of flunkies, and even crooks, have had the privilege of a two-week vacation and the prestige of being an academy graduate.

Miami Beach, for example, for many years had one of the most corrupt police departments in the nation. Its men served primarily as bodyguards to visiting gangsters or "moonlighted" as bouncers in the plush if illegal casinos that dotted the area until the Kefauver Committee came to town. Yet a number of these corrupt officers attended the academy, and they were not always selected by their chief.

Jesse Weiss, for many years the owner of Joe's Stone Crabs, the favorite seafood restaurant of countless gangsters, became a friend of John Edgar Hoover when the director—in town for the races—became a regular customer. Weiss regularly employed Miami Beach officers as "doormen"—the tips made it a lucrative position—and when such an officer showed promise of rising in Miami Beach politics, Weiss would recommend him to Hoover as a candidate for the academy. Invariably he received an invitation to attend.

In its first twenty-one years, more than thirty-two hundred law officers attended the FBI National Academy, thus forming a hard-core knot of avid FBI admirers in almost every city. Many of the men were capable, of course, and went on to achieve high rank legitimately. The academy became, in time, a tremendous source of strength for Hoover.

The FBI Laboratory also lived up to its promise and helped countless amateur detectives in police departments across the nation look like professionals. With the coming of World War II, much of the old conflict between the FBI and the locals vanished. The FBI turned to spies and saboteurs, and police no longer had to worry about being upstaged by John Edgar Hoover in person. Moreover, by 1940, a steady stream of ex-FBI agents—all still personally devoted to "the Chief"—had entered private employment to cash in on the prestige of their former job. Many of them had been special agents in charge of local offices, and had learned to do favors for the local establishment. Such men seemed ideal for the job of police commissioner in many cities. Others were given responsible positions in business, having, presumably, proven they were solid thinkers, opposed to Reds and radical ideas. Many opened private detective agencies, often recruiting strikebreakers and industrial spies. More and more, as the years passed, they contributed to the growing FBI legend and to the power of their former boss.

As Hoover's power increased, it should be noted, so did organized crime. And there was a reason. Both were supported by the same people—right-wing politicians and right-wing businessmen, many of them building new fortunes. The leaders of the old order still had their accumulated wealth, but much of their energy was spent in denouncing Roosevelt and the New Deal. The Liberty League was organized in 1934 "to offer shelter to those who believed that Roosevelt was embarked on a revolution subtly designed to carry out the same functions as the Bolshevik model in Russia."[10] John Edgar Hoover, while perhaps privately agreeing with them, had enough political sense to know that they were fighting a hopeless battle. In any case, he was not about to risk his job by openly agreeing with them. As far as Hoover was concerned, the Red menace was on the shelf until the political climate changed. He looked for allies among men who had amassed new fortunes but who had not attained the respectability of the old rich. Such men needed Hoover's prestige, and to get it they were willing to flatter him and pick up the tab. Organized crime, meanwhile, was equally useful to the new breed in many ways. Both shared one goal—to make as many fast bucks as possible.

Consider the case of Prendergast-Davies and Johnny Torrio.

When he returned from Honolulu in 1928, John "the Fox" Torrio settled down in the New York area. Shortly afterward, as we have seen, the "Big Seven", a loose alliance of rumrunners along the East Coast from Baltimore to Boston, was formed. Central headquarters were set up in New York, quotas were established, prices fixed. Participating in the organization were men whose names would later be infamous: Meyer Lansky, "Bugsy" Siegel, Joe Adonis, Frank Costello, "Longie" Zwillman, "King" Solomon, and others, many others. Out of this cooperation, and other ventures, ultimately developed the national crime syndicate. Their achievements over the decades would make such men as John Dillinger and Alvin Karpis look like the small-time punks they were. But if John Edgar Hoover knew of these men's existence, or even of the existence of the "Big Seven," he said nothing, and did nothing, about it.

With the approach of Repeal, Torrio decided to "go legit" as far as the liquor business was concerned. But because of his reputation, he had to work through others. He selected his brother-in-law, William Slockbower, to represent him. Also playing an important role in the formation of the legal liquor distribution company known as Prendergast-Davies was the brother-in-law of Lewis S. Rosenstiel, Herbert Heller. He operated a municipal bond house in Cincinnati with which Rosenstiel had long been associated. Rosenstiel himself was preparing for Repeal. His old company, Schenley Products, became Schenley Distillers, Inc., and Grover Whalen, former police commissioner of New York, was elected chairman and general manager.

Prendergast-Davies—the name was taken from employees of Heller—was incorporated on November 14, 1933, just a month before Repeal. Associated with Heller were Jerry Baum, who dabbled in various businesses, and Allen N.

69

Bernstein, another investment broker. Three days after Repeal, the partners had a disagreement, and Bernstein bought out Baum. The money to do so came from Slockbower, Torrio's brother-in-law. Bernstein and Heller remained until March 14, 1934. By then the company was a growing concern, thanks in part to Schenley's willingness to fill huge orders on credit. Schenley's credit enabled the new company to beat other less lucky competitors on the retail market.

Credit was sometimes arranged in strange ways. For example, Herbert Heller & Company, the bond house, bought ten thousand dollars' worth of Cook County, Illinois, bonds from—officially—Slockbower, for sixty-two hundred, and made the check payable to Prendergast-Davies. Thus, the two brothers-in-law dealt with each other while their principals, Rosenstiel and Torrio, remained discreetly on the sidelines.[11]

In 1939 the Government tried Torrio for income-tax evasion. The files of the Internal Revenue Service contain much intriguing information about Torrio's associations. They show that Torrio—perhaps following Rosenstiel's example—wanted to employ a New York politician as liquor czar. His candidate was Jimmy Walker, the former playboy mayor of New York, who had resigned under fire in 1932. Walker's friendship with underworld figures was well known, but he was still very popular. Torrio, according to testimony, believed Walker "could satisfy all interests and types in the wholesale liquor business."[12]

The probe of Torrio began in 1935, started by agents of the Alcohol Tax Unit, one of the several Treasury agencies under the command of Elmer Irey. Progress was slow, but in April, 1936, a rumor reached Irey that Torrio was planning to leave the country. It was decided to arrest "the Fox," although the case was far from complete. Torrio was lured to his neighborhood post office in White Plains, New York, on April 22. Here is the way a Treasury agent—obviously thinking of some of the FBI's many shootouts—described what happened:

There were no dramatics when Torrio was arrested. No agents were lurking behind half open doors with submachine guns and

70

automatic rifles in their hands ready to shoot down the man if he reached for a cigarette. Two members of the Alcohol Tax Unit walked up to Torrio, asked him if he was John Torrio and when he acknowledged that fact, informed him they were placing him under arrest on a Commissioner's warrant. The overlord of gangdom walked out of the White Plains Post Office between the two government men, got into a car and was whisked off to New York where he was arraigned before Commissioner Platt and held under $100,000 bail for alleged conspiracy to violate the internal revenue laws.[13]

It soon developed that the Alcohol Tax Unit could not make a case under its regulations, and the investigation was turned over to the intelligence unit of IRS. A long and tedious probe followed, the records of Prendergast-Davies were seized, and the history of Torrio from his departure from Chicago to the present was reconstructed. Indictments were secured. In the middle of the trial, as evidence piled up, Torrio changed his plea to guilty and went off to prison.

Before his conviction, however, he sold Prendergast-Davies to Boston interests closely associated with Joe Linsey, a former bootlegger who had worked with King Solomon in the "Big Seven." In later years Linsey became a Schenley distributor, a close friend of Rosenstiel, and a power in Boston's economic and political life. With Rosenstiel, he gave huge sums to Brandeis University, and even persuaded his old friend Meyer Lansky to contribute. Known in Boston as a "philanthropist," Linsey invested in race tracks from Boston to Denver, and in real estate and motels in the Miami area. Like Rosenstiel and Torrio, Linsey made use of his brother-in-law, David Yaffe, in his business dealings. Strangely, when Lansky was arrested in Miami in 1970, the brother-in-law's phone number was found in his pocket.

Even before the Torrio investigation began, Irey's boss, Secretary of the Treasury Henry Morgenthau, had been curious about the new, legitimate liquor industry that had emerged after Repeal. He was aware that at Repeal, domestic bootleggers still had forty or fifty million gallons of illicit liquor, much of it smuggled in from Canada, and he was curious as to how this liquor would be disposed of on the legitimate market. In June, 1934, a group of respectable

71

New York attorneys proposed to Morgenthau on behalf of the bootleggers that they be permitted to pay the excise tax on the smuggled liquor in order to get it legally on the market. Morgenthau conferred with President Roosevelt, who agreed that nothing should be done to legalize Prohibition activities. The Prendergast-Davies case seemed to indicate that the exbootleggers had found another way to achieve their goal—by setting up their own distribution companies.

Morgenthau authorized Samuel Klaus, an assistant, to make an investigation of an alleged "whiskey trust." Klaus reported on November 26, 1934, that there was indeed "an effective entente cordiale" involving fourteen distillers who produced ninety-five percent of all U.S. liquor. They had international connections as well, and ties to manufacturers of industrial alcohol, bottles, corks, and barrels.[14] Klaus's findings were presented to the Justice Department for possible antitrust action, but Justice refused to act. As late as 1952, a Senate subcommittee probed allegations that liquor barons, by means of effective political contributions, had foiled possible investigations by Justice into the liquor business. One of the witnesses at the 1952 hearing was Rosenstiel, but he denied that his contributions were made with that objective in mind.[15]

The gangsters, of course, formed other companies after Repeal. One of the most notorious was the Capitol Wine and Spirits Company. The front man was Louis I. Prokass, who managed to conceal his record as a bootlegger. Prominent in the firm were members of the old Broadway mob who had joined in the "Big Seven": Lansky, Costello, and Adonis.

In 1942 the Alcohol Tax Unit caught up with Prokass and fined him one hundred thousand dollars. The basic permits of the company to do business were revoked; the assets of the company were sold and later invested in the syndicate's first venture on the Las Vegas Strip, the Flamingo Hotel and Casino, constructed by Bugsy Siegel. Prokass became a vice-president of the Flamingo, though Lansky remained the boss for decades.

The Reinfeld syndicate, which allegedly collected some sixty million dollars during Prohibition by supplying Canadian liquor to rum rows off the East Coast, emerged as Distillers Corporation-Seagrams, Ltd. In time it became Rosenstiel's chief rival.

Prendergast-Davies was only one of several post-Prohibition liquor companies used by Rosenstiel to distribute the liquor stocks he had built up during the dry years. One of the most important was Gold Seal Liquors, Inc. of Chicago, which was organized in 1934 by William Gamble, Louis Alpern, and Marion Hicks, who many years later turned up in Las Vegas as a front for Meyer Lansky in the Thunderbird Hotel and Casino. The key man in Gold Seal was, however, Joseph Fusco, who over the years was a frequent guest aboard Rosenstiel's yacht, where business was combined with fishing. Fusco admitted to the Kefauver Committee in 1950 that from 1924 until Repeal his "sole business" was bootlegging.[16] Al Capone arranged for him to "get some beer," he admitted, and he was on friendly terms with such Capone lieutenants as Louis Campagna, John Roselli, Charles Fischetti. Fusco said that when he joined Gold Seal Liquors, Inc. it was doing very little wholesale business, so he set out to remedy that deficiency. "The first line I thought I could get was Schenley," he said.

In 1970, Louis Nichols, then a Schenley executive, told the New York Joint Legislative Committee on Crime that Fusco did not become a Schenley distributor until 1955. Fusco told the Kefauver Committee in 1950 he began handling the Schenley line in "possibly 1935 or 1936." There was a brief interruption, however, at about the time World War II, when Schenley gave an exclusive distributorship in the Chicago area to Lou Golan. The arrangement didn't work out and, according to Fusco, after two years Schenley reversed itself. The bitter rivalry between Samuel Bronfman of Seagram's and Rosenstiel of Schenley was involved. As Fusco told the Kefauver Committee:

Schenley wanted to get back in our house, and I wouldn't talk to them. I told them after all the years I gave them and handled their whiskey for twenty-five and thirty cents a case and knocked my brains out for many years, that overnight they put us practically out of business. Seagram's was good enough to take us on after they [Schenley] threw us out, let us stay in business, and Schenley is back now trying to get into our door.

73

I said, "What is your deal?"

They said, "Well, we'll give you about eight thousand cases a month."

This was at the break of the war. I think it was around 1944 or 1945.

So I went to Seagram's and said, "What are you going to do for me? Here you guys are giving me twenty-three hundred or twenty-five hundred cases. I have a chance to get nine thousand."

He [Seagram's] said, "Don't take it because after all they are trying to break our setup all over the country."

I said, "Listen, we are in business to try to make a buck and try to stay in business. Either you are going to give us more whiskey or we are going to take on Schenley."

He said, "If you do, I have to take you off the line."

So I went back to Schenley and I said, "Well, you made a deal for eight thousand cases and I lost twenty-five hundred cases [of Seagram's]. What are you going to do for me? You have to replace it."

"He [Schenley] said, "We are going to replace what you lost from Seagram's."

I said, "Okay, then, that is ten thousand, five hundred cases a month I get."

They said, "That is right."[17]

In further testimony Fusco revealed details of business deals with a number of exbootleggers and gangsters. He admitted knowing John Torrio: "I had some business with Johnnie Torrio in New York. I purchased some whiskey from the company he was supposed to have been connected with."

Prendergast-Davies.

So it went all around the country: old names, new companies, old associations in new corporate guise. Presumably the FBI was too busy to bother the liquor industry. As the FBI chased punks, organized crime achieved respectability— and vast economic and political power.

V

*O*N September 11, 1931, the guns of the Bugs and Meyer mob cut down Salvatore Maranzano, the latest and last Capo di Capi Re of the Honored Society. Meyer Lansky, head of the Bugs and Meyer mob, had been a secret ally of Charles "Lucky" Luciano for several years, and it was on Luciano's behalf that the execution was conducted. When word was passed that Maranzano was dead, Luciano ordered a nationwide purge of the Mafia. Around the country the "Mustache Petes" were eliminated, and the ancient Sicilian society was effectively Americanized.

At the time no police agency, Federal or state, added up the score or even related one murder to another. Ramsey Clark, former Attorney General and bitter foe of John Edgar Hoover, places the total killed at forty.[1] Nicola Gentile, the old Mafia troubleshooter, tells of the aftermath:

> No sooner did news of the death of Maranzano reach Cleveland than I and Bazzano thought of eliminating Siracuse of Pittsburgh, who, in his time at Chicago during the famous assembly convened for general peace, had done everything possible to have me killed. Even Toto LoVerde deserved the same, in that during that famous assembly he was associated fraudulently with Maranzano and his associates.

75

In the meantime, the Castellammaresi (the faction composed of men originating from Castellammare del Golfo, Sicily) asked for a truce because they wanted to know the motive for the execution of Maranzano. Because of that request, a new general assembly was held at Chicago, and, on that occasion, thanks to the testimony of Ciccio Scalisi there were revealed actions and crimes committed by Maranzano during the period of his dictatorship. Then tired and enlightened by experience, this time it was decided to place as Capo di Capi Re of Mafia a commission of six persons.

The idea, which was suggested by me at that time, was placed in effect. In fact, a commission was appointed whose duty it was to govern the destiny of all the Mafia of the United States. This resulted in the commission being composed of:

"Lucky" Luciano—because he was the representative of the ex-borgata of Joe Masseria; Vincenzo Mangano—capo of the famous borgata of D'Aquila; Joe Profaci—capo of a borgata of Brooklyn and nicknamed the Olive Oil King; Peppino Bonanno —capo of another borgata of Brooklyn; Al Capone of Chicago; Masi Gagliano, native of Coreone, Sicily; Ciccio Milano, of Cleveland.

With the administration of the commission, a more confident air was breathed. Peace returned and everybody could peacefully perform their individual labors. Everybody remained satisfied because justice had been done. The administration, or governing body so composed, gave assurances of confidence because each person was able to turn to them without being coerced as to their own ideas and free to be able to ask them for their proper rights.[2]

In effect, this meant that such men as Gentile could pursue their private quarrels without being involved in a larger conflict for control of the Mafia. Feuds and vendettas continued, but full scale civil war ended for the first time in five years. Luciano, while technically only one of several, was in reality first among equals, and—in cooperation with Lansky— he directed the energies of the Honored Society toward more modern methods.

The settlement of the Mafia civil war made possible close cooperation between all ethnic groups and led directly to the formation of the national crime syndicate in 1934. This was not, of course, a tightly organized, close-knit organization. Crime had become too big, and certainly too scattered, for such a rigid structure. It remains so today. Originally, at a meeting in New York, the leaders of city "combinations" and regional syndicates got together and agreed on a loose alliance which began by confirming existing arrangements. Provisions were made for joint ventures, for a board of arbitration to resolve disagreements, and for an enforcement arm to handle murder on a professional basis. This was later to become famous as "Murder, Incorporated."[3] The Mafia was represented in the new association, but leadership came largely from Lansky, Torrio, and Luciano. Thanks to Luciano, the Mafia accepted the situation, but thirty years later Mafia punks grumbled because they couldn't kill Jews without permission and because those same Jews had effective control of gambling centers such as Las Vegas.

John Edgar Hoover's FBI has never adknowledged the existence of the national crime syndicate. In fact, Hoover did not admit there was a Mafia until 1963, and then the FBI had to give it a new name—La Cosa Nostra.

If Hoover ignored the new developments in crime, two of his rivals did not. Elmer Irey avidly pursued the trails of gangster cash and convicted many of the top crooks for income-tax evasion. And in New York City, Thomas E. Dewey achieved a reputation that for a time eclipsed Hoover's. Organized crime, though still deeply involved in the liquor business, began to turn to other things. Organized gambling became a gold mine, more profitable even than rumrunning.

Irey's case against Moses Annenberg tells much of the expanding nature of organized crime and of the society which tolerated it. Born in East Prussia in 1877, Annenberg was brought to Chicago by his father, a junk dealer, in 1884. The boy quit school at the age of twelve and worked at a variety of jobs. He became a subscription solicitor for a Chicago newspaper in 1895. Quickly proving his worth in the bitter newspaper circulation wars of the period, when hired goons battled with iron pipes and steel knives for choice locations, he worked his way up to become circulation manager of one of William Randolph Hearst's Chicago papers.

Not content to work solely for others, Annenberg branched out with borrowed money into real estate and publishing ventures, and was approaching millionaire status by the time he was appointed circulation manager of all Hearst newspapers and magazines in the country. In 1922 he bought the *Daily Racing Form*, the horseplayer's bible, and a little later took control of the *Morning Telegram*, a New York publication devoted to theatrical and sporting news. In 1926 he resigned from Hearst to devote himself to his own empire. His next major step involved getting control of the vital wire services, the data-dissemination network without which bookies could not operate. He gathered together, in one way or another, all existing services and greatly expanded them until he had a nationwide network which, logically, he called Nationwide News Service. Some muscle from Chicago and Cleveland gangsters was necessary, but organized crime saw the advantages Annenberg could offer and cooperated willingly enough. In no time leased wires carried race results to more than fifteen thousand bookies around the country, and they paid Annenberg twenty million dollars in a three-year period. This was just the beginning. He expanded into related fields as fast as he could. At its peak Annenberg's empire had several divisions. The wire-service business was divided into fourteen corporations controlling thirty-six branches, and operating in two hundred and twenty-three cities. Twenty corporations controlled his publishing business, which included such newspapers as the *Philadelphia Inquirer*. The wall-sheet business—printed lists of each day's races for use in the better handbooks—was handled by five corporations and countless partnerships. Sixteen corporations took care of magazine and newspaper distributorships. Fourteen corporations were necessary to oversee his real-estate, insurance, liquor, and laundry companies. Seven corporations handled his affairs in foreign companies. One investigator, digging into the affairs of the *Philadelphia Inquirer*, commented on "the extent to which payments of bank loans growing out of the purchase of the *Philadelphia Inquirer* are dependent upon the continued operation of gambling establishments throughout the United States."

Irey's men had quite a job when they began to untangle Annenberg's corporate affairs. After years of digging, Annenberg was indicted on charges of evading three million, two hundred and fifty-eight thousand, eight hundred nine dollars in taxes. And that was just the beginning. Rather than face a jury on the tax charges, Annenberg agreed to pay a fine of eight million dollars, over a five-year period at six percent interest. He was also *sentenced* to three years in prison. Shortly after his release, he died.

Before going to prison in 1939, Annenberg turned over his wire-service business to Mickey McBride of Cleveland. Not a dollar changed hands. Annenberg stepped out one day, and McBride took over the next. The name was changed to Continental Press—that was the only difference. The wire-service under any name was too important to organized crime to permit interruptions. The Chicago syndicate did make an abortive effort to grab the service, but the attempt was soon squashed. It remained for the Kefauver Committee to break up the empire Annenberg had built by sponsoring restrictive legislation.

The remainder of Annenberg's vast business enterprises, including the *Philadelphia Inquirer*, was taken over by Walter Annenberg, the founder's son. Walter had been indicted with his father in 1932 on charges of sending obscene literature—one of his magazines—through the mail, but charges were dropped after some associates took the rap.[4]

In 1969 President Richard Nixon rewarded Annenberg for political contributions by appointing him ambassador to England. There the Annenbergs became famous for their parties—especially those given for Frank Sinatra after the Democrats snubbed the singer because of his alleged mob connections. In two generations, the Annenbergs had achieved vast wealth—and respectability—thanks largely to the American sucker who makes illegal bets on horses while voting for "law and order" candidates.

During Irey's long investigation of Annenberg, Dewey was making headlines in New York as "the fighting district attorney." That he had his eyes on the governor's chair at Albany and perhaps the White House from the beginning is now clear. Like John Edgar Hoover, Dewey was not particular as to the means used to achieve results. His most famous case, the conviction of Luciano on vice charges, may have been nothing more than a frame-up. Certainly many gangsters who have absolutely no reason to lie, insist that it was, and there is even some hard evidence to confirm it.[5] In any case, Louis Buchalter, better known as "Lepke," was a more immediate target. Dewey pursued him and in the process clashed with John Edgar Hoover.

It seems that Lepke, who had his hand in a dozen rackets, foolishly continued smuggling narcotics after the more cautious Lansky withdrew. In November 1937 the Federal Narcotics Bureau secured an indictment. Lepke went into hiding and the "big heat" began in New York. Dewey, who hoped to nab Lepke in connection with baking industry shakedowns, spread a net. Not to be outdone, Hoover branded Lepke "the most dangerous criminal in America" and launched a nationwide search for him. New York police were also eager to find the elusive little man, and the hunt became the biggest national sensation since the Lindbergh kidnaping. Eventually a conference was set up to work out a coordinated approach. Hoover attended. So did Narcotics Bureau Chief Harry J. Anslinger, Dewey, and New York Police Commissioner Lewis J. Valentine. The four men agreed to pool information at the top level while continuing their individual efforts.

Meanwhile, the top leaders of the national crime syndicate were debating what they should do. The hunt for Lepke was interfering with business. Thanks largely to Lansky, who saw a chance to rid himself of a dangerous rival, they decided to force Lepke to surrender. An elaborate plot was arranged, and Lepke was convinced that by cooperating he would escape with a light sentence. Walter Winchell, one of the many radio and newspaper personalities who helped build Hoover's legend, was the contact man. The syndicate, working through Winchell, arranged to turn Lepke over to Hoover on a dark street in New York. Lepke, as it developed, had never left the city so Hoover's warrant charging him with unlawful flight across state lines did not mean a thing.

The FBI, while enjoying the immense publicity that followed Lepke's surrender, has become a bit self-conscious about the affair in subsequent years. Extended discussion would, presumably, require an acknowledgement that there was indeed a crime syndicate and that, when the chips were down, its leaders preferred to deal with John Edgar Hoover,

80

not with Anslinger, Dewey, or Valentine. Someone might ask why.

The Narcotics Bureau, not the FBI, made the first case against Lepke. Dewey, enraged at taking second billing in the middle of a political campaign, tacked on an additional conviction. Then Burton Turkis, assistant district attorney in Brooklyn, sent Lepke to the electric chair for his part in Murder, Inc.[6]

Dewey, and for that matter Valentine and Anslinger, remained angry at Hoover for some time. Once again, they charged, he had violated his promises to cooperate. Eventually, however, better relations were established. Dewey, his reputation as a crime-buster made, was elected governor and began campaigning for the Presidency. Hoover, who had no political ambitions of his own—he had achieved the position he wanted—gave him a hand. Helping to heal the breach and bring the old rivals together, was Lewis S. Rosenstiel, a friend of both men who believed all good right-wingers should stand together.

Anslinger was not so easily mollified. As head of the one Federal agency that insisted there was a Mafia, he resented Hoover's ability to ignore the facts and get away with it. Years later Anslinger wrote:

> We revealed the existence of the Mafia when many officials insisted that the organization, its rituals and rules and punishments, were largely myths, and that I, personally, was building this distorted picture of conspiracy largely to make an attack on Italians and those of Italian-American descent.[7]

Ironically, a few years after Anslinger wrote those words, Hoover and the FBI came under attack from Italian-Americans on the same grounds. Anslinger was not only far ahead of the FBI chief in recognizing the existence of the Mafia, but he also put it into better perspective. He wrote: " 'Syndicate' in America is a loosely used phrase. In underworld parlance, it may have several interpretations. Nationally, it refers to what others call the 'organization,' a term that takes in not only the Mafia itself but other related groups."[8]

When the FBI "discovered" La Cosa Nostra in 1963, it refused to admit the existence of "other related groups."

Blithely, and without any documentation or other basis in fact, it assigned to such men as Lansky the special status of "associate member" of LCN. In short, everything that conflicted with the picture as conceived by Hoover, was either ignored or distorted to fit.

In the 1930s, of course, when the national crime syndicate was being organized, when it was most vunerable, the FBI had much on its mind besides gangsters. Supposedly, as early as 1936 Hoover was called to the White House to discuss the problem of subversives. Supposedly, the FBI was assigned to collect intelligence information on "Communists, Fascists, and representatives or advocates of other organizations or groups advocating the overthrow or replacement of the Government of the United States by illegal methods."

If Hoover did have a green light from Roosevelt, he didn't get the funds to do the job. On January 5, 1940, he appeared before the House Appropriations Committee and asked for more money. Currently, he said, there were thirteen hundred and seven "espionage matters," three hundred eleven "treason matters," sixteen "sabotage matters," a hundred ninety-six "defense plant protection matters," for which he lacked special agents to assign. This, he explained, represented forty-one percent of "national-defense matters." In addition, thirty-five percent of the total cases were "delinquent" because of the lack of manpower. Congress, as usual, supplied the funds. Hoover then announced that in order to do the assigned counterespionage work, he was reviving the old General Investigation Division. The statement created a national uproar. Among other things, he said, it would investigate persons "in movements detrimental to the internal security." The GID, it will be remembered, was originally set up by Palmer in 1919 to investigate radicals. It had received much criticism then, and it drew more when reincarnated in 1940. A series of raids conducted by the FBI in February against veterans who had fought against Franco in the Spanish Civil War fueled the flames.

Adding to the excitement was another raid by the FBI. Miami Beach, that glittering sin city on the edge of the Gulf Stream, was the target. The strike had nothing to do with national defense—it was a last effort to enforce the ancient

Mann Act, the law forbidding interstate transportation of women for immoral purposes. Several gambling joints were hit, and twenty-one persons—ten of them women—were arrested. The *St. Louis Post-Dispatch*, one of many newspapers to protest, recalled Hoover's earlier testimony about his manpower shortage and wondered why "raids on gambling dens and pleasure palaces" couldn't be left to local authorities while the FBI concentrated on more serious matters.

Local authorities, of course, had no intention of doing anything about the glittering syndicate casinos and plush brothels operated by such folks as Madame Sherry, who numbered among her guests the likes of Alvin Karpis and Prince Alfonso of Sweden. That vice was essential to the tourist industry had been well sold to state and local officials, and Hoover's raid, coming as it did near the end of the winter season, annoyed a good many people.

Despite the FBI claims, the raid made scarcely a dent in the greater Miami vice situation. The crime syndicate was too deeply entrenched to be bothered, and Hoover must have known it. Why, when he was allegedly shorthanded in his battle against subversion, did he take a crew of special agents on a futile crusade?

An answer has been supplied by a former FBI supervisor, head of the hoodlum squad at the Miami office. Hoover, it seems, had become a horse fan. Each winter, when the bangtails were running at syndicate-owned tracks in Florida, he came down for a session in the sun. Gangsters appreciated the humor of the situation, and began taking advantage of Hoover's ignorance by getting themselves invited to his box at the track and posing with him for pictures. It became something of a game. Eventually someone tipped off the Director that the friendly horseplayers who posed with him were not exactly his fans. Enraged, Hoover ordered the raid. It was intended as a warning, although some agents insist that in his vanity Hoover actually believed that the disapproval implicit in his reaction would topple the crime structure along the Gold Coast.

It didn't happen, of course, so Hoover set up the so-called "Hoodlum Squad" in the Miami office. It functioned for years, its only purpose to identify the various gangsters in the area so that Hoover could be shielded during his annual visit to the tracks. Since almost every gangster of importance spent as much time as he could afford in the Miami area, the squad, in time, put together quite an intelligence file. In 1963 when Hoover launched his battle against organized crime, the file proved useful. The Hoodlum Squad finally came into its own. It was assigned to investigate the men it had watched so long in futile silence.

Hoover's desire to avoid embarrassment did not prevent him from occasionally seeking good racing tips from gangsters, if a former agent is to be believed. He described how Phil "the Stick" Kovolick, a life-long lieutenant of Meyer Lansky, boasted about being asked by Hoover at the Hialeah racetrack for a tip on the upcoming races. Asked if he obliged, Kovolick replied, "Hell no, I didn't give him nothing. Wouldn't give him the sweat off my ass. That guy's got a lotta nerve."

The uproar over Hoover's ill-timed Miami raid had another effect. Aware that he had annoyed some wealthy businessmen and politicians in the area, Hoover, thereafter, took a hands-off attitude. Despite some harsh words directed at Miami Beach during his Kefauver Committee appearance in 1950, Hoover ordered his men to "go along" with local sentiment. In 1965 when the *Miami Herald* decided to do a little crusading, a reporter went to the FBI office and solicited aid. The FBI was cautious. The request would have to be cleared with Washington. It was not until some six weeks later, after the newspaper published a series of front-page stories, that the reporter was called back and promised full cooperation. Thereafter, until the *Herald* lost interest, the files of the FBI were available to the press. What's more, the FBI conducted several brilliant raids against leading gamblers. When, however, the newspaper turned to other things, the FBI immediately halted its own campaign.[9] No one could say that John Edgar Hoover did not profit by his mistakes—even if he never admitted making one.

The more serious uproar over the revival of the GID was dismissed by Hoover and his apologists as a Red plot to "get" Hoover. Nevertheless, the GID was dropped as the critics demanded. Presidential pressure was not required. The instinct for self-preservation was sufficient.

As a matter of fact Roosevelt recognized in Hoover the civil-servant mentality with its lack of political ambitions. And he didn't take Hoover or the FBI too seriously. When in 1941 Hoover's men spied on Harry Hopkins, Roosevelt's most trusted aide, at a confidential press dinner in London, the President was amused. As Robert Sherwood commented: "It delighted Roosevelt to know the 'G-Men' were checking up on his personal representative."[10]

Francis B. Biddle describes how, after he had become Roosevelt's attorney general and gained Hoover's confidence, the FBI director began

sharing some of his extraordinarily broad knowledge of the intimate details of what my associates in the cabinet did or said . . . Edgar was not above relishing a story derogatory to an occupant of one of the seats of the mighty, particularly if the little great man was pompous or stuffy. And I confess that, within limits, I enjoyed hearing it.[11]

Hoover, of course, made it his business to collect such data on all occupants of "the seats of the mighty." It was good insurance to know about a cabinet officer's indiscretions, whether they involved sex, liquor, or gambling. Similar information about congressmen could pay off any time additional appropriations were needed or the "Red" launched an attack upon the activities of the FBI.

It is perhaps a measure of Roosevelt's confidence in his ability to manage men that he never worried about Hoover's internal spy system. Instead of regarding Hoover as a potential menace, the President found him, and his agency, amusing. Of course, on occasion, the Director's jealous zeal caused problems. Upon learning that Scotland Yard had picked up two British deserters at a Baltimore bar and driven them back to their ship in New York, Hoover threatened to arrest the agents for kidnaping. A high-level meeting with Lord Halifax was necessary to soothe Hoover's feelings. Biddle reported that Lord Halifax was "shocked," but he promised to see it wouldn't happen again. Hoover wanted no secret agents operating independently, even if they were allies. But of course he didn't hesitate to spy on Hopkins in England.

Late in 1939 the FBI wasted much time investigating Dr. Adam von Trott, a foe of Hitler and close friend of Associate Justice Felix Frankfurter. Trott came to this country with the full knowledge of Roosevelt, and his full confidence, but the FBI believed he was dangerous and submitted a voluminous report on his alleged activities. Amused, Roosevelt sent Frankfurter the following memo:

The White House

January 17, 1940

For Heaven's sake! Surely you did not let your Trott friend get trotted out of the country without having him searched by Edgar Hoover. Think of the battleship plans and other secrets he may be carrying back. This is the height of indiscretion and carelessness on your part.

F.D.R.[12]

Unhappily, Hoover was no more successful in his pursuit of Dr. Trott than he was with Japanese agents at Pearl Harbor. Prior to 1939, Naval Intelligence was responsible for investigating foreign activity, but then the FBI took over and established an office. Primary responsibility for investigation of matters connected with the civil population was also given to the FBI.

Nevertheless, when bombs fell on Pearl Harbor, Hoover was off on a Sunday jaunt to New York. Other top FBI officials were attending a professional football game at Griffin Stadium. Certainly, the FBI was as surprised as the rest of the country on that "day of infamy," as Roosevelt labeled it. And, later, Secretary of the Navy Frank Knox was to call the Japanese fifth column in Hawaii second only to the "Quislings" who made possible the Nazi takeover of Norway earlier in the war.

Perhaps it was the disaster at Pearl Harbor that influenced Naval Intelligence to bypass the FBI and turned to the national crime syndicate for help in safeguarding the docks of New York and New Jersey.

While much mystery still surrounds "Operation Underworld," it is clear that in April 1942 Naval Intelligence became concerned about the number of Italian-Americans working in key positions on the waterfront. Even assuming the loyalty of most of them, the possibility that Italian or German agents could infiltrate the docks seemed very real. Across the Atlantic, Russia and England depended for their lives on a steady and increasing flow of supplies. Nothing could be permitted to interrupt that flow.

Someone got the idea that the Mafia—an organization Hoover still didn't recognize—could be used to keep an eye on the longshoremen and spot suspicious strangers. The district attorney's office was contacted. Dewey had moved up to governor, but Frank Hogan, his old assistant, now in charge, was willing to help. Ultimately, it was decided to contact Lucky Luciano in the prison cell where Dewey had put him. To talk to Luciano, it was necessary to get the cooperation of Meyer Lansky, Luciano's close friend who had helped "Americanize" the Mafia by killing Maranzano. Lansky was willing. He had promised to get Lucky out of jail, and the project proposed seemed to be a good way to do it.[13]

On Lansky's recommendation, Luciano ordered the Mafia to cooperate with the navy. And not a single case of sabotoge was reported during the war. Luciano supposedly provided the navy with additional aid in the invasion of Sicily, and at war's end he was rewarded for his alleged contributions to the war effort. Paroled by Dewey, he was deported to Italy. Lansky became his "regent," the one non-Sicilian, non-Italian, who could give orders to the jealous members of the Honored Society.[14]

Logically enough, Hoover has never mentioned this episode, nor have any of his apologists. Nevertheless, the FBI is given full credit for protecting America's industrial machine from Nazi spies. That they had help from the national crime syndicate and the Mafia is highly ironic.

The case of the Nazi saboteurs landed by submarine on Long Island is even more ironic. The Germans were hardly ashore when a young seaman, John Cullen, on beach patrol for the coast guard, stumbled upon them. The Nazis, perhaps believing all they had heard about the greed of Americans, gave Cullen a bribe of two hundred and sixty dollars to keep quiet. The seaman raced back to the coast guard station and reported the incident. When the sun came up, the footprints of the Germans were found. Their tracks led to boxes buried in the sand. The boxes contained equipment and the German uniforms the Nazis had worn ashore. It was twelve hours before the FBI was notified. An angry Hoover complained to the admiral commanding the coast guard and asked that he reprimand his men for intruding into matters assigned to the FBI. What the admiral replied is not a matter of record.

One day after the landing, the Nazi agent who had tried to bribe Cullen decided the whole expedition was a fool's errand. He took a brief holiday in New York, went down to Washington and called the FBI. When they arrived, he gave them full information about the assignment, including a handkerchief on which was written in invisible ink the names of all those he was supposed to contact in this country.

It was then a routine matter to round up the other agents who were proceeding to their targets not knowing they had already been betrayed. The story of the capture was released without mentioning the betrayal, allegedly to impress Hitler with the idea the FBI had discovered the caper without help. Whether Hitler was impressed or not, the U.S. public thought the affair was sensational. Hoover's prestige went up tremendously. As Attorney General Biddle described it:

> It was generally concluded that a particularly brilliant FBI agent, probably attending the school in sabotage where the eight had been trained, had been able to get on the inside and make regular reports to America. Mr. Hoover, as the United Press put it, declined to comment on whether or not FBI agents had infiltrated into not only the Gestapo but also the High Command, or whether he had watched the saboteurs land. . . .[15]

Of such is the Hoover image made. The draft-exempt bureaucrat of 1917 had become the spy catcher of 1942. The legend had been made essential to the war effort, and it survived the war when at last the facts leaked out.

The war, of course, was good not only for Hoover; certain

right-wing businessmen were doing all right too. Not the least of these was Lewis S. Rosenstiel.

In addition to such former bootleggers as Joe Fusco in Chicago and Joe Linsey in Boston, Rosenstiel added to his payroll others who stood in that gray area between the legal and the illicit. Such a man was Arthur Samish, the so-called "Secret Boss of California."

Basically, Samish, who admitted friendship with mobster Frank Costello, was a lobbyist, but the word hardly describes his business. He was a political boss, a man who could make or unmake legislators, even governors, and he used his power to further the special interests of those businessmen who could afford his services. In 1936, for example, there was an opening in a Los Angeles district when a popular assembly-man decided not to seek re-election. Samish selected a candidate but, ten days before the election, he changed his mind for reasons of his own. It was necessary to find another man. Someone advised him to take a look at Jack Tenney, the author of the famous song, "Mexicali Rose." Tenney was not a serious candidate—but having just been admitted to the bar he was seeking publicity. Samish gives this account of the interview:

> "What did you do before you studied for the law?" I asked him.
> "I played piano in a whorehouse in Mexicali," he admitted.
> I had to laugh. "Jack, you'll make a good legislator," I told him.[15]

Thanks to Samish, Tenney won easily. Later he got himself elected chairman of the California Legislature's un-American activities committee and, as Samish put it, "he made Martin Dies and Joe McCarthy seem like pinkos." The *San Francisco Chronicle* described his technique, which was to become all too familiar:

> Anyone who was in favor of overthrowing Tenney, as distinguished from overthrowing the Government, was likely to be hauled up and smeared by inquisition and innuendo. His methods have done more damage to the cause of intelligently combatting Communism than almost any other influence in California.

According to Samish, he was minding his own business when, one day, Rosenstiel called him from New York and asked him to try to change a law that hurt Schenley profits in California. Samish did, and went on the Schenley payroll at fifty-four thousand dollars a year. When Senator Estes Kefauver asked Samish what he did to earn the money, he replied: "I am 'callable' when they want me."[16]

Kefauver later gave his impression of Samith:

In both personality and physique, Samish is a remarkable figure. Physically, he stands over six-feet, two inches, in height, with a monk's tonsure of gray fringe, and his face has the bland innocence of an *enfant terrible* about to light a giant firecracker under his nurse's chair. In manner, he is a combination of Falstaff, Little Boy Blue, Machiavelli, crossed with an eel.[17]

Rosenstiel entered into a business arrangement with this man. "But it was more than a business arrangement," wrote Samish, "Lewis Rosenstiel and I became close friends. I mean close. So close that he sent me the key to his house and said it was open to me at all times. I staged birthday parties for him. I knew all four of his wives"—including the one who later married Walter Annenberg.

Thanks to Samish, Rosenstiel was able to penetrate the California wine market in 1940. Increasing whiskey taxes, plus the shadow of impending war, made it essential that Rosenstiel enter other enterprises. Samish arranged for him to buy the "old, picturesque Cresta Blanca Wine Company," as Fortune magazine put it, with its eight gold medals for excellence. The company cost two hundred and eighty thousand dollars, a bargain only Samish could have arranged. The purchase of Cresta Blanca was only the opening wedge. During the war years, Schenley bought still other wine companies and began a campaign to make wine the national beverage.[18]

Other Samish services included what Samish called the "10 High caper." According to Samish, he was summoned to New York—he was "callable", remember—and told to do something to Harry Hatch, the president of Hiram Walker, one of Schenley's liquor competitors. "He's a mean man," said Rosenstiel. It turned out that Hatch had a whiskey called "10 High", which was a best-seller in California, despite the fact that it was aged only thirty-six months. That was all Samish needed to know. He returned to California and pushed a bill through the legislature requiring that all whiskies sold in the state had to be at least four years old. Blends had to be at least twenty percent four years old. It was no coincidence that Schenley owned the great bulk of four-year old whiskey at that time. "10 High" was run out of California.[19] Like his friend, John Edgar Hoover, Rosenstiel tended to see the world in absolute terms. His business enemies were not only competitors but "mean men" or, as Hoover would put it, "rats." And, of course, the reverse was true.

One of Samish's particular pals—"a wonderful man, a real sweetheart"—was movie man Joe Schenck. "Whatever Joe Schenck wanted, I got for him," said Samish. Schenck, it should be noted, played a major role in one of the crime syndicate's most profitable ventures—the movie extortion case.

It all began in 1934 in Louisville when the crime syndicate got control of the International Alliance of Theatrical Stage Employees and Moving Picture Machine Operators of the United States and Canada at the union's annual convention. Involved in the takeover were the top leaders of the Chicago mob— still referred to as the "Capone syndicate"—and Lepke, representing the Eastern executives of crime. Two small-time punks, Willie Bioff and George Browne, who had conceived the racket on a small scale in Chicago, were allowed to front for the mob. Browne was installed as president of the union.

Movie-house operators in Chicago and New York were shaken down for huge pay-offs in order to avoid strikes that would have closed their business. Then in 1935 the syndicate moved in on Hollywood. The studios there were in bad shape, thanks to the depression, and needed a steady supply of cash from movie houses around the country to stay in the picture-making business. The situation was made to order for the gangsters. The pressure began when some twelve thousand studio employees were told to sign up with the union or lose their jobs. They were promised a ten-percent raise if they cooperated. The film moguls were then ordered to pay two million dollars in cash, or face a strike that would ruin them. The movie men had made too many gangster films—they were victims of their own exaggerations.

Joe Schenck, Samish's buddy, was told to work out a deal with the gangsters. With help from Samish—who had close relationships with many top gangsters—a compromise was reached. The large companies would pay fifty thousand dollars a year in tribute, the smaller companies only twenty-five thousand. Shortly thereafter, Schenck delivered several bundles, each containing fifty thousand dollars in cash to Bioff at the union.

Bugsy Siegel, Lansky's long-time associate in the Bugs and Meyer mob, was sent to the West coast to keep an eye on Bioff and Browne and to organize other rackets. Lansky, in addition, ordered him to develop neighboring Nevada— where gambling was legal. Eventually, Siegel turned Las Vegas into a high-roller's heaven, and Lansky skimmed millions off the top of the casinos' handle.

One favor Schenck did for Bioff led to disaster. Willie, it seems, wanted to be like all his new movie friends and buy a ranch, but all he had was racket money. He gave a hundred thousand dollars to Schenck, who wrote a respectable check for the same amount to Bioff, who used it to buy his ranch. Word of the check reached Robert Montgomery, president of the Screen Actor's Guild. Suspecting a pay-off, Montgomery created an uproar that brought the special agents of Elmer Irey's intelligence unit to the scene. Bioff's attempt to "laundry" his unreported cash in an effort to escape the eyes of the IRS, had boomeranged. The resulting probe led to the conviction of Schenck for income-tax evasion in March, 1941. Joe was shocked at being sentenced to three years and, after thinking about it, decided to talk. As a result, Bioff, Browne, and Nick Circella of Chicago were indicted and convicted for income-tax evasion.

Once the income-tax angles were out of the way, the case belonged to the FBI. John Edgar Hoover pleaded, however, that he was too busy "ferreting out Jap and Nazi spies," as Irey noted, and after much pulling and hauling it was decided the intelligence unit would continue the probe. Nev-

92

ertheless, the FBI kept its hand in. FBI Special Agent John P. Gleason sat in on some of the intelligence unit's interviews and obtained access to the confidential memorandums prepared by the intelligence unit. He promptly reported all the information to Hoover, implying that he had personally dug up the information. This led to some bitterness on the part of the intelligence men who, in turn, got possession of Gleason's reports. On July 27, 1942, intelligence agent Alf Oftedal sent Irey a copy of one of Gleason's reports to Hoover and commented:

The writer, Special Agent John P. Gleason of the Federal Bureau of Investigation, was never present when any of the secret informers to whom he refers were interviewed . . . All of the information contained in the report of Agent Gleason was developed by agents of the Intelligence Unit in Cooperation with Assistant United States Attorney [Boris] Kostelanetz.

Why Hoover was even interested in view of his preoccupation with espionage matters is, on the surface, inexplicable. There is no question, however, that he tried to keep informed on the probe he had declined to undertake. What he did with the information after getting it isn't known either. If Art Samish knew, it was one of several secrets he did not disclose.

After Nick Circella's girl friend was murdered and her house set afire to conceal the crime, Bioff and Browne decided to talk. Their "song" put the finger on the top men of the Chicago syndicate: Frank "the Enforcer" Nitti, Paul "the Waiter" Ricca, Frank Mariote, Charles "Cherry Nose" Gioe, Louis "Little New York" Compagna, Phil D'Andrea, John Roselli, and Louis "Potatoes" Kaufman. All were indicted, all were convicted except Nitti, who killed himself, and all were quickly paroled from prison after serving a fraction of their sentences.[20]

Bioff also mentioned Murray Garsson, a former friend of Hoover's who had helped hunt Reds. It seems that Schenck paid Garsson two hundred thousand dollars *not* to investigate him. Garsson had become a munitions manufacturer with a little help from Representative Andrew Jackson May of Kentucky. May happened to be chairman of the House

Military Affairs Committee. Starting with a letter to the War Department on borrowed stationary and on behalf of a non-existent firm, Garsson obtained seventy-eight million dollars in war contracts. May received better than fifty thousand dollars in bribes. Eventually, both May and Garsson were convicted. Another Red-hunter bit the dust. Garsson died in 1957 in poverty at the home of another Commie-fighter, Dr. Emmanuel M. Josephson of New York. Death apparently resulted from a fall down the stairs. In his last days, Garsson regaled Dr. Josephson with "inside" stories about his past associations with such men at John Edgar Hoover.[21]

As a final footnote to the movie-extortion case, it should be noted that Bioff, after serving his sentence, appeared in Phoenix, Arizona, where he became a good friend of Gus Greenbaum and Barry Goldwater. Greenbaum, long a syndicate figure, gave Bioff a job at the new Riviera Hotel and Casino in Las Vegas. Later someone cut the throats of Mr. and Mrs. Greenbaum in their Phoenix home. Goldwater, who later won some distinction as a right-wing candidate for President of the United States, considered Bioff an expert on labor relations. He enjoyed flying Willie to and from Las Vegas, where the Goldwaters owned a clothing store in the Cleveland syndicate's Desert Inn. On November 5, 1955, two weeks after Goldwater flew Willie back to Phoenix for a vacation, the syndicate caught up with Bioff. When he started his car that morning, a bomb blew Willie all over the neighborhood. The Goldwaters attended that funeral as well as the Greenbaums' when they, too, went to their reward.

It is dangerous, of course, to generalize. Guilt by association is a tricky business. Yet a pattern emerges. John Edgar Hoover has received support, as well as more tangible rewards, from right-wing businessmen who, in turn, have dealt directly and indirectly with organized-crime figures who were not disturbed by John Edgar Hoover. The movie-extortion case is but one example. Another is supplied by Robert Gould who, in the tradition of George Remus, became black-market liquor boss during World War II. His headquarters, logically enough, was in Cincinnati, where both Remus and Rosenstiel got their starts.

Gould was a Schenley distributor, and a close personal

friend and frequent fishing companion of Rosenstiel. Gould was also a whiskey broker with a controlling interest in several distilleries. Born in 1897, he lived on Signal Hill in Cincinnati, where Remus had built a palace for Imogene. He was highly respected in the Cincinnati area, which, of course, included Newport and Covington, Kentucky, just across the river. Insight into Gould's black-market activities comes from Sam Stein, a Cleveland syndicate associate who gained prestige by becoming Moe Dalitz's brother-in-law—or one of them, since Moe shed wives as easily as Rosenstiel. Stein took part in a unique liquor-smuggling operation in 1939 when, for a brief time, there was money to be made in shipping liquor to Canada, a reversal of the old procedure. This caper led him into a gold-smuggling operation, this time from Canada into the United States. He was finally caught in 1943 and convicted. Before going to prison, however, he moved into the black-market liquor business. It was a syndicate operation, of course, as Federal agents trailing Stein discovered.

In a long statement, Stein revealed that he was told to contact Gould. The procedure was to buy "warehouse receipts" at prices in excess of the ceiling set by the OPA—Office of Price Administration—and ship the liquor to a qualified dealer who would bottle it and sell it to bars and taverns, which were having trouble under wartime regulations in getting enough liquor to satisfy the demand. Gould, after checking Stein out, offered receipts for a thousand barrels of whiskey at four dollars per gallon. The OPA ceiling price was a dollar and fifteen cents per gallon.

Stein, who thought he was a sharp trader, objected. Gould told him "if I left the office without closing the deal the price would be four twenty-five when I returned." Stein left anyway, conferred with his gangster associates, and was told to pay four dollars. However, he discovered the price had indeed gone up. Again he hesitated, and was told it would be four fifty the next time. Stein still thought it necessary to check with his friends. Upon coming back, he was told the deal was off. He had been "fooling around" too long. Stein persuaded Gould he was sincere; the liquor was offered at four dollars and fifty cents a gallon, but he was warned that if the deal was delayed, the price would be five dollars a gallon.

"I just held out my hand and asked him to shake on the deal," said Stein, who by now was convinced he was no match for Gould.[22]

Top gangsters such as Peter Licavoli, "Big Al" Polizzi, and Morris Margolis, were involved. The liquor went to syndicate-controlled bars all over Ohio. Stein was just one of Gould's customers. In 1943 alone, Alex Joasselson and Edward Baumer, liquor dealers of Ashaland and Newport, Kentucky, paid one million, one hundred thirty-nine thousand, six hundred sixty dollars to Gould. This sum was five hundred and forty-seven thousand and twenty-nine dollars in excess of the OPA's ceiling price. Much of the whiskey sold by Gould involved Schenley brands. Great use was made of Fairfield Distillery, Inc., at Bardstown, and Pebbleford Distillery Company at Wilder, a suburb of Newport, Kentucky. Gould owned half interest in Pebbleford.

Two Treasury agencies, the alcohol tax unit and the intelligence unit, cooperated in the investigation that brought Gould's 1945 indictment on forty-eight counts. He was sentenced to prison for six years and fined four hundred and eighty thousand dollars, for violating the OPA regulations, and he settled the income-tax case by agreeing to pay two million, five hundred thousand dollars in a lump sum. Schenley, meanwhile, bought control of Fairfield Distillery, and soon acquired Pebbleford as well. Gould and Rosenstiel remained good friends.

It was October 1946 before Gould's appeals were exhausted. Meantime Rosenstiel began to woo the Catholic Church in the interests of the wine companies he had acquired with the help of Art Samish. A letter dated March 12, 1946, to a Schenley official gives details:

> Since Schenley's best interests were served at two very important affairs in Chicago for Samuel Cardinal Stritch, I would like briefly to tell you about them.
> On Thursday, March 7, at the Drake Hotel, our company sponsored a cocktail party at a luncheon for over 2,000 of the clergy in Cardinal Stritch's archdiocese.
> A gift of $1,500,000 was presented to His Eminence.

96

It would be difficult to describe the tremendous table covered with fancy hors d'oeuvres which were flanked by two Schenley bars. Our two large bars, one 50 feet long, were manned by 14 bartenders who were kept busy dispensing drinks made of Schenley products. There was no mistake about it being a Schenley party since the array of exclusively Schenley bottles the full length of the back bar made an imposing sight.

I arrived early so all the bartenders and the Drake personnel received my usual Schenley pep talk.

If the host was unknown and hadn't been spotted during the cocktail hour, I took care of that situation before luncheon when I unobtrusively approached the Cardinal to congratulate him.

The press photographers in front of the dais started snapping since I was the only personage outside of the important clergy on the platform with whom the Cardinal posed.

On Friday I received the enclosed medal, blessed by the Pope and brought from Rome by the Cardinal. I want you to have it and enjoy the blessings that were bestowed with the award.

On Sunday, March 11, the grand ballroom of the Stevens Hotel was filled to overflowing with 1,700 of Chicago's most important citizenry—leaders in all walks of life paying homage to the great man, Cardinal Stritch.

And in the North Ballroom, preceding the banquet for His Eminence, it was like old home week as I greeted old friends at a cocktail party sponsored by Schenley for his honor Mayor Kelly and the City of Chicago.

Here again, we had two large bars set up the full length of the room.

The Mayor and City Hall at large were profoundly pleased with Schenley's gesture.

If our management sees fit to manufacture "Kosher Wine", Bishop "Shapiro" Lewis will proceed to sell same for altar wine.

Respectfully submitted,[23]

On November 19, 1946, Schenley was back in action with a cocktail party "during The Silver Jubilee of the Consecration of His Eminence Samuel A. Cardinal Stritch." A list of all Catholic bishops was obtained, and each was sent a Christmas package containing one bottle each of Aurora Port and Cresta Blanca Triple Cream Sherry.

A scrapbook was needed to contain all the "thank-you

notes" received from the bishops. Many signed the notes with the words, "Yours in Christ." Perhaps they were part of the reason Rosenstiel converted to Catholicism, thus forging another bond between the liquor baron and the forces opposing "Godless Communism."

One month before the Silver Jubilee party, Gould went to prison. Twenty-six months later he was released. The episode became one of the "Truman scandals" when it was discovered that Gould's attorney had made a political contribution through Major General Harry H. Vaughan, military aide to President Truman.[24] Gould took his millions to Miami Beach, where he bought a shipyard-marina. Among those docking his yacht there in 1971 was Rosenstiel.

VI

DAILY casualty lists had become a routine item in many American newspapers, of interest only to those next of kin who had already been notified of a loved one's death on the battlefields of a world war.

On April 13, 1945 the daily casuality list in some newspapers was headed by this entry under "Army-Navy Dead":

ROOSEVELT, Franklin D., Commander-in-Chief. Wife, Mrs. Anna Eleanor Roosevelt, the White House.

Roosevelt died on a sunny afternoon, with the smell of honeysuckle in the air at his beloved Warm Springs, Georgia, whose waters he credited with restoring him to health and limited mobility. Not many months before, a suggestion that facilities for Negro victims of poliomyelitis be provided at Warm Springs was made to Roosevelt. The war had brought Negroes out of their isolation and intensified a demand to end segregation. Roosevelt, ever sensitive to human needs, knew the problem was a serious one, despite a statement from John Edgar Hoover that "a good proportion of unrest as regards race relationships results from Communist activities.[1]

Roosevelt may have wished that the social evils dating

back to the slave trade could be attributed to a Red plot, but he had no time to waste on Hoover's fantasies. On his last day, with American and Russian armies a hundred miles apart in stricken Germany, he was looking ahead to San Francisco and the new era of international cooperation he hoped would arrive with the birth of the United Nations there. A confident, optimistic man by nature, Roosevelt expected to succeed where Woodrow Wilson had failed. Had he lived to serve his fourth term, the nation might have been spared the "cold war" and "McCarthyism." His death unleashed the forces of reaction.

Those forces had been building for years, representing as they did not only the money and prestige of the old guard, but the new wealth and the new politics created by the alliance of organized crime and big business. Ironically, Roosevelt had aided their cause by destroying—with the notable exception of Chicago—the big-city political machines. By directing the national government to take over such things as social welfare programs, and by sending intelligence-unit investigators into New Orleans, Kansas City, Atlantic City, and elsewhere, to probe the big-city bosses, he made it possible for the crime syndicate to increase its political power on every level.

To cite one example, Thomas J. Pendergast had ruled Kansas City and much of Missouri in alliance with the mob until Irey's men sent him to prison in 1939 on income-tax charges. But before he was convicted he launched Harry S. Truman on his political career. Truman, according to Irey, was "a creature of Pendergast." Beginning as a county judge in Kansas City, Truman was elected to the United States Senate in 1934 and reelected, despite the fall of "the Boss," in 1940. During the war as head of the "Truman Committee," investigating war contracts, he did a creditable job and received national attention. Robert Hannegan, another graduate of the Pendergast school of politics, became commissioner of internal revenue in 1943, and a year later, chairman of the Democratic National Committee. He was thus in a perfect position to advance Truman's cause when Roosevelt, preparing to run for his fourth term, looked about for a Vice-President to replace Henry Wallace. As one politician put it: He [Truman] just dropped into the slot."[2] Thus, on April 12, 1945, Truman became President of the United States.

Since he left the White House in 1952, Truman's reputation has steadily improved. Today, some consider him a great President. His rehabilitation is based largely on his conduct of foreign affairs. The "Truman scandals" have receded into the background. Most critics agree that Truman did not personally profit from the graft and corruption that plagued his days in the White House. Like Harding, he was victimized by his political friends and business allies. In a real sense, he gave the country the kind of government it wanted—and deserved. Nothing comparable to Teapot Dome occurred—the scale of pay-offs was correctly illustrated by mink coats and deep-freeze units.

Much of the scandal was inevitable. The Republicans, long out of power, were hungry and not only exploited the corruption but helped create it. Moreover, the postwar reaction to idealism and sacrifice followed the traditional course, and was aggravated by the cold war. Freed of wartime restrictions, U.S. citizens wanted to travel, to spend, to enjoy themselves. It was the era of the big fix. Leaders of the Chicago syndicate were paroled and sent home to resume their rule. Lucky Luciano, paroled by Dewey, was deported to Italy; Robert Gould won his freedom. The day of the casino, of the regional gambling center, arrived. The Cleveland syndicate developed its holdings in Newport and Covington, Kentucky, expanded into West Virginia at Huntington and White Sulphur Springs, moved into Indiana, and operated joint ventures with Meyer Lansky in Miami and Las Vegas. Hot Springs, Arkansas, despite the boasts of the FBI, flowered under the cautious rule of Owney "the Killer" Madden, attracting the oil-rich suckers of Texas by the thousands. Lansky, forced out of Havana by the 1944 election defeat of his friend, Batista, built a new empire on the Gold Coast of Florida. Broward County, where Sheriff Walter Clark was his ally, became Lansky's home and headquarters, although he was equally busy in and around New Orleans, in Saratoga,

New York, and in Las Vegas, where his old partner Bugsy Siegel had built the Flamingo using black-market materials and syndicate money.[3]

The ancient and honorable Reconstruction Finance Corporation, originally sponsored by Herbert Hoover, became a source of funds for syndicate figures who had learned long before to operate on other people's money. Loans were obtained for such things as the Maples Hotel and Casino in Reno. It got nine hundred seventy-five thousand dollars to add two stories and install up-to-date gambling equipment. Supposedly people who went to Nevada for divorces needed a good hotel. Another RFC loan went to the Ribbonwriter Corporation of America to develop a typewriter attachment that would turn out five copies without the use of carbon paper. Sheriff Clark of Broward County was one of the promoters. The RFC was told in a letter of August 26, 1949, that Clark was "a very close personal friend of the President." Other loans went to Miami Beach hotels controlled by the mob, and to syndicate interests in Cleveland, Detroit, and other cities.[4] Flo Bratten, confidential secretary to Vice-President Alben Barkley, was made an honorary deputy sheriff of Campbell County, Kentucky—home of Newport—for her aid in helping gangsters get RFC loans. She became a personal friend of Red "the Enforcer" Masterson and other Newport hoods.[5] In other words, the RFC served the same purpose as the pension funds of the Teamsters Union in the next decade.

The most important influence peddler of the period was perhaps the mysterious "Dutchman," Henry W. Grunewald, although there were several others of nearly equal distinction. Born in South Africa in 1892, Grunewald came to this country in 1907. After a term in the navy, he joined the Bureau of Investigation after the first World War when John Edgar Hoover was beating the bushes for Reds. Seeing the possibilities in alcohol, Grunewald switched to the Prohibition unit, where he got into trouble issuing fake permits to remove champagne from the U.S. Custom's bonded warehouse in New York. Turning to private enterprise, Grunewald became confidential secretary to Henry Marsh, a wealthy businessman of Washington, D.C., a job that gave him much insight into public and private business. In 1943, after Marsh died, leaving him fifty thousand dollars, Grunewald set himself up as a private eye in Washington. He made himself useful to men in and out of government, and won a reputation as a strikebreaker. The money flowed in, and Grunewald followed the example of other successful hoods by buying a home in Florida. It cost him ten thousand dollars to install private telephone lines for long-distance calls in the rooms he maintained there for his guests. His customers included everyone from the Chinese government, which wanted his aid in buying airplanes, to liquor companies, for whom he helped arrange black-market deals. Eventually he specialized in fixing tax cases. To obtain influence, he was generous with his campaign contributions. He passed five thousand dollars to a young Congressman named Richard M. Nixon. The money was used to help Nixon move up to the Senate. Nixon admitted receiving the cash, though he denied knowing it came from Grunewald.[6] "You never get enough," was Grunewald's motto, and it perhaps expressed the spirit of the times.

Another man who attracted much attention in the Truman era was Theron Lamar Caudle, a North Carolinian who became assistant attorney general in charge of the criminal division of the Justice Department. Caudle had served as a U.S. attorney in Charlotte, N.C., before his appointment. He credited Senator Robert Rice Reynolds, a rabid right-wing admirer of John Edgar Hoover, for the job that got him started, but from his own testimony it is obvious that as a prosecutor he was gifted with unusual tact. "I always dread to slip up on somebody," he explained. "I do not want to take advantage of them."[7] Plenty of people were willing to take advantage of Caudle's tact after he got to Washington. In return his wife received mink coats; he got new cars, expense-paid trips to Florida and Europe, and other small favors.

The trip to Europe was paid for by Carmen d'Agastino, president of the Renault Champagne Company, who also "loaned" the traveling Tar Heel two thousand dollars. The alleged purpose of the expedition was to investigate—what else?—Communism.

Caudle got into real trouble when he took five thousand

103

dollars from Larry "the Fixer" Knohl, a syndicate money-man, later Meyer Lansky's partner in a plush resort on the Florida keys. Knohl was convicted of attempting to fix a grand jury investigating the disappearance of Mafia boss Joe "Bananas" Bonanno, and still later he was convicted of illegal possession of three hundred thousand dollars in stolen Treasury notes. Larry Knohl was quite an operator until 1971, when a stroke paralyzed the right side of his body.[8]

Where was John Edgar Hoover in this period of unprecedented syndicate expansion and complete laxity within the national government? Hoover became very concerned about juvenile delinquency. The FBI set up a juvenile-delinquency instructors' school to equip special agents with the expertise needed to lecture police groups on the problem. In an article for the *Syracuse Law Review*, Hoover warned: "Criminal behavior is learned behavior. The child and the adolescent are impressionable, and their active minds develop codes of morality no higher than those to which they are exposed."

Obviously it was far safer to worry about delinquency than to try to stem the tide of syndicate development or step on the toes of corrupt officials in Washington. Hoover, the professional civil servant, had to play it safe with the change in administration until he could be sure his own position was not threatened. Luckily, Tom Clark, Truman's first attorney general, had his heart set on the Supreme Court and made no move to upset any of Hoover's friends in Congress. Before long, however, the Red menace had come alive once more, and Hoover—old enemy of radicals—was safe in the saddle once more.

Meanwhile, organized crime gave the FBI director a strange vote of confidence. Impressed, no doubt, by his concern over the juvenile-delinquency problem, they gave generously to the J. Edgar Hoover Foundation, which was set up to finance research on the sociological aspects of juvenile delinquency. The most famous contribution was five thousand dollars given by Yonnie Licovoli, a former hired gun of the Purple Gang of Detroit who later headed his own organization of kill-crazy gangsters.

104

Born in 1904 to honest, hard-working parents of Sicilian descent, Yonnie and his brothers grew up in St. Louis, where they learned to speak Yiddish as well as English. As a boy he earned pennies by lighting lamps on the Jewish Sabbath in the nearby synagogue. Such contacts proved useful later. As a tough kid, he found he could earn a quarter carrying beer to the local gang, known as Eagen's Rats. School was eight blocks away, and Yonnie had to fight his way to reach it. A good student, Yonnie was class valedictorian, and his parents —hoping he would become a priest—sent him to Christian Brothers College. He stayed a few months, but, as he put it, "I was too lively. I wanted to travel and see things." Promptly, he got into trouble. His parents paid the fine, and Yonnie joined the navy, only to jump ship in San Francisco. Luckily, President Harding signed a general amnesty for all deserters. After wandering around for a time, the youth found himself in Detroit working for the Purple Gang. He received up to six dollars a case for liquor smuggled in from Canada, and all he had to do was guard the shipments from hijackers. "When you bring over a thousand cases a night, you are making money," he once explained.

Impressed, Yonnie sent for his brother Peter and other relatives. When the Purple Gang scattered after a particularly sensational massacre of its rivals, Licavoli took over. The name was too colorful to die, and the press applied it to Yonnie's outfit. In time the gang graduated to the status of a Mafia "family."

In 1959 Licavoli told Todd Simon of the *Cleveland Plain Dealer* that there was no such thing as the Mafia in his world. "When I was a kid they'd threaten, 'I'll get the Mafiaosa after you.' Mafiaosa meant a tough guy, or a guy who thought he was tough." Yonnie conceded, however, that "there is such a thing as certain people cooperating with each other in different cities."[9]

Licavoli was a tough guy and he formed his gang from friends and relatives he trusted. This is the way most gangs develop—along ethnic lines. In some areas having a heavy Sicilian-Italian population, there was, apparently, a direct relationship to the old-world Mafia, but Yonnie Licavoli

105

began his organization in a city far from his birth, and he started from scratch. In the same fashion, men like Moe Dalitz—who also worked with the Purple Gang—created the Cleveland syndicate. Its hard-core base was Jewish, but in time its leaders directed a "combination" that included men of all ethnic backgrounds. Peter Licavoli eventually became one of them.[10]

Yonnie also expressed very well the motivating force that drove such men: "I became known as a big spender. I went nightclubbing, cabareting. I had good clothes, a big car. I lived in the best hotels. I had been a poor kid; I wanted to have the best things. I wanted them, and I fought for them."

The murder of Jerry Buckley, a pioneer radio crusader in Detroit, caused a tremendous commotion and forced many gangsters under cover. The heat drove Licavoli to Toledo, where he clashed with beer baron Jackie Kennedy. When Kennedy was murdered in 1933, Yonnie was convicted of masterminding the job and was sentenced to prison for life. The jury recommended that he never be paroled. Following Yonnie's departure, Peter Licavoli took over the gang. In cooperation with the Cleveland syndicate, he built a huge empire in crime and helped exploit the Tuscon, Arizona, area where he bought a large ranch. Yet he remained loyal to his brother, and used all his wealth and political influence in a futile effort to spring him from prison.[11]

With everyone else getting out of jail in the postwar period, it seemed a good time to win freedom for Yonnie. Columnist Drew Pearson, a man of influence, had adopted the newly formed J. Edgar Hoover Foundation as a pet project and was hammering away—along with Hoover—at the problem of juvenile delinquency. Certainly Yonnie Licavoli could appreciate the problem. His wife, mother, and daughter appeared in Washington to present Pearson with a five-thousand-dollar check on Yonnie's behalf. Other gangsters followed suit until Hoover became embarrassed. Twenty years later, when *Life* magazine referred to the episode,[12] C.D. DeLoach, formerly number two man in the FBI, wrote a letter explaining:

106

The "J. Edgar Hoover Foundation" to which you refer in your story was a proposal which was initiated in the late 1940s without Mr. Hoover's knowledge. Mr. Hoover protested this proposal and refused permission for the use of his name.[13]

So much for the battle against juvenile delinquency. Yonnie remained in prison. In 1969 Ohio Governor James Rhodes commuted his sentence, making him eligible for parole. The *Life* article created so much uproar, however, that parole was not granted until 1971, and Rhodes was defeated in his bid for re-election. Meanwhile, Yonnie wrote a novel, but his family felt it was too autobiographical to be published.

Yonnie Licavoli may have lacked the influence he needed in 1949, but Lewis S. Rosenstiel was able to get things done in 1950. In September of that year, the Internal Revenue Service was asked to approve an oral agreement between Rosenstiel and John L. Leban, then a vice-president of Schenley, which provided for Leban to buy Schenley stock at two-year intervals until 1970 at the price it was selling for in June 1950—twenty-six dollars and fifty cents a share. The IRS ruled on October 26, 1950, that the deal was improper.

The pressure started. Leban had raised up to forty-five thousand dollars for the Democrats in 1948, twenty-five thousand dollars in 1949, and eighteen thousand in 1950. Of course, Rosenstiel had contributed to the Republicans in 1948—the old game of playing both sides of the political street—but he had a good excuse: The Republican candidate, Thomas E. Dewey, was a personal friend.

Secretary of the Treasury John W. Snyder, got on the phone a few minutes after the unfavorable ruling was handed down. He told Charles Oliphant, chief counsel of the IRS and friend of Henry Grunewald, that he wanted the Schenley matter "expedited." It seems that "Rosenstiel sails on Sunday and this thing must be gotten out immediately." Five days later a reversal letter approving the Leban-Rosenstiel deal was written. Later, Oliphant resigned under fire when two congressional committees began probing the Rosenstiel affair along with sundry other matters of a similar nature.[14]

While all this, and much more, was going on, John Edgar Hoover was performing one of the greatest feats of public relations in history. Fred Cook wrote:

The persistent refrain of years that we had been absolutely secure because the FBI was guarding us was about to be changed to the shocking, the frightening, assertion that the Russians had stolen everything but our short pants. It is one of the most amazing paradoxes of history that the infallible policeman who had been taking all the bows for guarding us perfectly, was to take none of the blame for guarding us imperfectly. Houdini himself never wrought greater magic."[15]

To illustrate: Hoover, addressing a police convention in Miami on December 10, 1945, boasted that foreign powers had tried to steal the atomic bomb, but were foiled because "the counterespionage program which we developed did more than encircle spies and render them harmless. It enabled us to learn their weaknesses and their aims." Four years later, the FBI was taking bows for arresting Julius and Ethel Rosenberg, who were accused of stealing the secrets of the atomic bomb and passing them on to the Russians. The man who had left the barn door open, was given great praise for closing it *after* the horse had been stolen.

A new era of hysteria developed, comparable only to the period after World War I. An American public, unwilling to believe that the Reds could develop anything on their own, was still able to give them credit for devilish cunning in stealing another nation's secrets. Religion got mixed up in the picture so that no one could blame Hoover for being outsmarted by the devil himself. On the other hand, anyone who denounced the devil loud enough was automatically a hero. The refusal to admit that the Communists had any scientific knowledge, any technical ability, continued for years and ended only when the first Sputnik was fired into orbit in 1957 while America's rockets sputtered futilely on their launching pads. Only when Americans finally landed on the moon in 1969 was national pride assuaged.

It would serve no purpose here to describe in detail or even summarize the principal security cases of the period. Volumes would be required to do them justice, and many such volumes have already been written. It is obvious that during the long years of the New Deal, and especially during World War II, when Russia was our ally, persons of Communist persuasion achieved positions within the government. That some espionage was successfully achieved is also evident. But there was nothing to prove that this country's security was seriously impaired. Undoubtedly the atomic bomb would have been developed by Russian scientists and without the help of stolen secrets. No international conspiracy to overthrow the government existed, and the Russian drive in Europe was nothing more than a nationalistic impulse on the part of a country that had emerged—with plenty of aid from its allies—as the most powerful nation on the Continent.

It is equally apparent that, beginning with the *Amerasia* case in 1945, the Republicans seized upon the issue of "Communists-in-government" as a political weapon with which to drive the Democrats from power. John Edgar Hoover, who under a strong Roosevelt had played ball with the Democrats, now began to cooperate with his natural allies, the Republicans. Truman's unexpected victory over Dewey in 1948 surely shocked him, but the combination of local corruption scandals and the Communist issue made Republican victory in 1952 seem assured. To have fired Hoover after 1948 would only have confirmed Republican charges, and Hoover knew it. However, unlike that other hero of the right-wing, Douglas MacArthur, Hoover was smart enough to avoid a direct confrontation with the tough-minded Truman.

Opportunity for such a confrontation came in 1949 in the Judith Coplon case. Miss Coplon was employed in the Justice Department—an irony in view of the alleged efficiency of the FBI in checking out prospective employees. On March 6, 1949, she was arrested by the FBI in New York City and accused of passing confidential information to the Russians. The arrest was illegal—the FBI, for no apparent reason, neglected to secure a warrant. Nevertheless Miss Coplon was tried and convicted after prosecuting attorneys assured the court that there was no wiretapping in the case. While appealing the conviction, Miss Coplon was tried on a second charge. This time her attorneys won an admission that the FBI had indeed tapped her phones. When the judge ordered the records produced, he was told that most of the wiretap records had been destroyed.

This, it should be noted, became standard procedure. Years later, when the FBI was illegally tapping gangsters' phones, it promptly destroyed the tape recordings on the ground of economy—the tapes were needed for other taps. All that remained were so-called "logs," containing summaries of the conversations, and occasionally a full transcript of what the gangster was alleged to have said. There was, of course, no way to ascertain if the FBI agent had accurately recorded the conversation.

The judge in the Coplon case ordered the FBI to produce all its records that had survived. Hoover protested vigorously. Years before, Harry Daugherty had resigned as attorney general rather than produce Bureau of Investigation records, but Attorney General Tom Clark had no ambition to follow his example. Clark ordered Hoover to obey the court order and produce the records. When produced, the files not only won freedom for Miss Coplon in both cases, they made the FBI look silly. The files were merely a collection of gossip. Nothing, but nothing, had seemed too insignificant to escape the prying eyes of the FBI agents. Hoover, in a letter to his executive assistants, blamed it all on Clark.

I urged the Attorney General to seek a mistrial or a citation for contempt rather than produce these records with consequent devastating harm to the FBI's responsibility for internal security, as well as the disclosure of as yet incorroborated information in our files concerning individuals. . . .[16]

Of course the FBI still uses the "big ear technique." Proof came in 1971 when papers stolen from an FBI field office at Media, Pennsylvania, were leaked to newspapers. Any agency depending largely on paid informers cannot help but accumulate a lot of malicious nonsense, and the FBI files have far more chaff than wheat. Reckless, indeed, is the writer who relies on FBI files without double-checking them with independent sources. Unhappily, there have been more than a few such writers.

110

Hoover never forgave Tom Clark for the Coplon episode, and there is reason to believe he vented upon Clark's son the rage he was unable to direct against the father. Ramsey Clark, who was attorney general under President Johnson, became an object of Hoover's scorn. Not only did Hoover refuse to cooperate with Clark's "strike forces" against organized crime, but he called Ramsey a "jellyfish" because Clark didn't want the FBI to use wiretaps. Richard Nixon joined the chorus in 1968, promising loudly to replace Clark when elected.

One other espionage case deserves mention if only because it put Nixon on the long trail to the White House. Without help from Hoover, Nixon would have fallen flat on his face in the Alger Hiss case. Hiss was indicted for perjury after Whittaker Chambers produced the "Pumpkin Papers"—no one recalled the "Potato Papers" of the great Red scare—and suddenly Nixon was a national figure.

There were anxious moments. Nixon in his book, *Six Crises*, discussed the "complete shock" he felt upon being informed that the Eastman Kodak Company did not manufacture the type of film found in the pumpkin until years after the stolen documents had allegedly been put on the film. "We had been taken in by a diabolically clever maniac who had finally made a fatal mistake," Nixon wrote. A press conference was called to admit the error—an admission that would have ruined Nixon's political career. Five minutes before the reporters arrived new word was received—the film had been manufactured at the right time after all. The crusade could continue.[17]

Nevertheless, there is still much doubt today about the Hiss-Chambers case. The possibility cannot be dismissed that Hiss was framed by the FBI. Only one with complete faith in Hoover's integrity can ignore the suspicions, and no one who has studied Hoover's career in depth can cherish such faith. Hoover is no doubt sincere in his conviction that a Red menace threatens America—he decided that in 1919. To defeat that menace, he obviously believes that the ends justify the means. He is willing to do whatever is necessary. Except, of course, risking his job. Thanks to the secrecy of the FBI, the complete lack of review procedure, Hoover can do almost anything without risking his job. He is a law unto himself.

Ironically, the year that made Nixon a popular hero saw the formation of the American Jewish League Against Communism. Varied were the motives of the League's founders, but one of them was self-protection. How could anyone, in 1948, deny the vulnerability of people of Jewish background, many of them natives of Russia, where their parents had resisted the tyranny of the czar? Many of the intellectuals in America were Jewish. During the New Deal some had achieved high position. Moreover, Karl Marx himself was the son of a Jew who later became a Christian. To adopt the sane position, to resist unfair smears and the attempts of bigots to portray the Jew as pro-Red, might only make people mad. Better to go on the offensive against the Communist menace itself. Such was the attitude of some Jews—or at least the excuse they offered their friends—as national hysteria built up in 1948.

The possibility of the anti-Communism attack turning into a persecution of the Jews was very much on the minds of the government officials charged with prosecuting the alleged atom-bomb spies, Julius and Ethel Rosenberg. For that reason a Jewish judge was chosen, and the prosecuting staff selected to try the case was composed of Jews. One of their number was Roy Cohn.

More than concern for the Jews was involved in the formation of the League, however. Anti-Communism offered both political and business opportunities.

The League was formed at the home of Eugene Lyons, a right-wing author of note. Taking part in the first meeting were other right-wingers, including Louis Waldman, Lawrence Fertig, Issac Don Levine, and George Sokolsky. The prime mover was Alfred Kohlberg who, along with Lewis Rosenstiel, supplied most of the funds.

Sokolsky was a Hearst columnist. His stablemates were Westbrook Pegler and Fulton Lewis, Jr. The trio were hatemongers of the most vicious sort and, in fact, seemed engaged in friendly competition to out do each other in the purity of their vitriol. Sokolsky was especially close to Rosenstiel who, like other right-wing men, subsidized a stable of influential writers. Levine was the editor of *Plain Talk*, a far-right publication devoted to telling the American people the "facts" about their government and the Red menace. A close friend of Whittaker Chambers, Levine played a shadowy role in the Alger Hiss case. Kohlberg, the organizer, was well known as "the China Lobby man," who perhaps did more than any other individual to convince the public that the Democrats betrayed mainland China to the Communists. As a man who put money into the League, he deserves more than passing mention.

Born in 1887 in San Francisco, Alfred Kohlberg quit college in his sophomore year to enter business. All his ventures failed until in 1915 he visited China and went into the business of silks and laces. Soon he concentrated on handkerchiefs. The procedure became one of buying Irish linen in Belfast and shipping it to China, where what has been called "an army of Chinese women" did delicate embroidery as part of a cottage industry that spread over a large part of southeastern China. Kohlberg paid them sweatshop wages and shipped the finished product back to the United States, where it brought good prices—two hundred dollars a dozen. Despite the war, Kohlberg managed to keep the business going, but it shut down when the Reds drove Chiang Kai-shek to the offshore islands. Kohlberg kept his New York office open until 1957, using it for his campaigns to force the United States into war with Red China. Like Rosenstiel, he was a much-married man. His first wife died in 1919, and three more followed.

The "China Lobby," had no legal basis, although it was real enough. Naturally, it shared Kohlberg's interest in promoting war between the United States and China, and it was well financed by money from the Nationalist government on Formosa. Whether some of the money was supplied by American taxpayers who, in effect, subsidized Chiang Kai-shek is not on record. It remains a sinister possibility.[18] A group of five Chinese, from their headquarters in their embassy in Washington, manipulated the China Lobby. They reported directly to Chiang Kai-shek, using the code name "Kung" for the group. Being foreign nationals, they had to promote their aims through American citizens. Kohlberg was a natural choice. Rosenstiel kept out of sight, but if a third world war was going to break out, he wanted to know about it in advance. So, according to his fourth wife, he worked closely with the League and provided funds as needed.

Rabbi Benjamin Schultz was appointed executive director of the League. In testimony before the House Un-American Activities Committee in 1949, Schultz said he was a graduate of the University of Rochester, served as an assistant rabbi in Brooklyn from 1931 to 1935, and became rabbi of Temple Emanuel in Yonkers, New York, until he resigned in 1947 to fight "this evil of Communism." Others say his resignation was not entirely voluntary.

Not everyone approved the direction taken by the League. Issac Don Levine, one of the original founders, has put himself on record in the following statement:

We were exploring the ground, feeling our way, and Rabbi Schultz seemed to be the logical one to head such an organization. But I for one wanted this organization to function in the synagogues, among Jews. I was not in favor of an organization that would tell the country there is a handful of Jews fighting Communism, or which would use a public occasion to honor J. Edgar Hoover. I wanted one that would go from synagogue to synagogue, to carry the message. But before a decision was made I discovered that Mr. Kohlberg had taken the ball and had run with it. He installed Rabbi Schultz in a building he owned on 42nd Street, put a shingle up, and the organization was launched. I made it clear that I considered this action a little bit hasty, and I got out when I felt the committee had gotten off the track by neglecting the education of many Jewish people in the facts about Communism. But in setting up the AJLAC as he did, Kohlberg was being his impetuous self. He was given to impetuous actions. When an idea hit him he called in his secretary and started dictating.[19]

Despite Levine's defection, Schultz found plenty of others willing to play the game as he, and Kohlberg, wanted it played. The board of directors listed by Schultz in 1949 in-

114

cluded, in addition to Eugene Lyons and Kohlberg, such well known figures as Brigadier General Julius Klein and Abe J. Multer. Klein, of course, was to be even better known, thanks largely to his personal public relations campaign. In 1947 he formed Julius Klein Public Relations, Inc., and was elected national commander of the Jewish War Veterans, perhaps proving he was his own best client. The following year he wangled the post of "defense consultant" to the Republican National Convention. In short, Klein became a successor to Henry Grunewald, but a much more public one. He cultivated men of wealth and power, Presidents and liquor barons. Eventually, his associations with Senator Thomas Dodd caused that former FBI agent to be censured by the U.S. Senate. Before that happened, Klein had many profitable years as an influence peddler. For the record, Dodd was also a friend of Rosenstiel's.

Abe Multer, a Democratic congressman from New York, was closely associated with right-wing political and business activities. In 1960 he cooperated with Leonard Bursten of Miami Beach in a scheme to get ousted Cuban dictator Fulgencio Batista to this country. After all, Batista was anti-Communist, wasn't he? An FBI probe found no "predicate" for prosecution.[20] Others did object, and Batista was denied entry.

Rabbi Schultz was also anti-Communist. He told the House Un-American Activities Committee: "As a rabbi, a believer in God, a servant of mankind, I cry out against this black force of communism which is ushering a new dark age into much of our world."

And in words that sounded very much like the sentiments of John Edgar Hoover, he warned: "This country is in greater danger—because of the very subtlety of that danger—than it ever has been in all its history."

Years later, Hoover in his *Masters of Deceit* had a good word for the League. He wrote:

The American Jewish League Against Communism stated as early as 1948 that "Soviet Russia's million and a half Jews are the forgotten people of the world." The League lists among its proud achievements that "it was the first American organization to expose and document the communist anti-Jewish policies."

In 1948 the League's first goal was to become an effective force. It claimed "several thousand members in twenty-two states." Membership fees were "anything over $1," according to Schultz.

Right-wingers had no problem deciding which political figure to back in 1948. Thomas E. Dewey, the exgangbuster, had buried the hatchet with John Edgar Hoover and was considered certain to win the Republican nomination and the election. Some people, such as Klein, considered him too liberal and preferred Senator Robert Taft, but Rosenstiel put his influence, and his money, behind Dewey. As John Leban, then president of Schenley, told a House subcommittee in 1952:

> The chairman of my company [Rosenstiel] was a very good friend of Mr. Dewey's, and in 1948 I talked to a number of friends of mine throughout the country with whom we were doing business [liquor dealers], and I asked them if they were going to make any contributions to the Republican Party or if they thought they would like to do so, that I thought it would please the chairman very much. I wanted to do something to please him on it and that is why that came about.[21]

In simpler words, liquor dealers such as Joe Fusco in Chicago and Joe Linsey in Boston, were politely told to contribute to Dewey if they wanted to please Rosenstiel. In addition, Rosenstiel admitted contributing a total of five thousand dollars in personal funds to Dewey's cause.

As previously noted, Leban, on behalf of Rosenstiel, also gave money to the Democrats in 1948 to hedge his bet. That this paid off was indicated by another witness, Alfons B. Landa, an attorney working for Rosenstiel's chief rival, Seagram's. Landa, who said he raised money for the Democrats, planned to attend the inaugural ceremonies. He discovered, Landa said, that Rosenstiel was listed for a better seat than he could get. "I suggested to Mr. [Louis] Johnson that that place might be a more desirable place for a good Democrat."

Johnson replied, "He is a friend of ours too." Rosenstiel said he didn't bother to attend the inaugural.

The subcommittee that questioned Rosenstiel was investigating complaints that the Justice Department failed to make a thorough investigation into charges made in 1948 that major liquor distillers, including Schenley, had violated antitrust laws. The subcommittee wanted to know if political contributions to both parties had anything to do with that failure. Testimony disclosed that the Justice Department's probe was aborted when a "preliminary" investigation by the FBI failed to uncover evidence of collusion between the "Big Four" of the liquor industry. Other hearings brought similar complaints about the FBI, but investigating congressmen were given a ready explanation—the Bureau in each case has not been permitted to make a full probe. Being a well-disciplined agency, the FBI obeyed orders to the letter. If told to investigate on a limited basis it did exactly that—no more, no less.

When it came to buck passing, John Edgar Hoover was a professional civil servant.

The unexpected defeat of Dewey in 1948 upset a good many people, and made it necessary for the Jewish American League Against Communism to revise its program. It needed a new political figure behind whom it could rally. Coincidentally, the league had come into possession of a one hundred-page FBI report on Communist influence on government. The report was originally leaked to an intelligence officer in the Pentagon with instructions to pass it on to leaders of the league. There was nothing illegal in giving the FBI document to military intelligence, which is why it was done that way. Louis B. Nichols, Hoover's public relations expert, knew all the tricks. We have the word of none other than Roy Cohn that the secret FBI document was read, and conferences held, in New York and Washington. As Cohn put it, "a small group" took "upon itself the responsibility of getting the story across to America."[22]

The League decided it should approach a senator rather than a representative. At a meeting in Washington in November 1949, a special committee of the league "sifted carefully through the roster of United States senators for one

117

who might successfully undertake the task of educating his fellow Americans." They narrowed the list down to four possibilities, all Republicans. In turn, each senator was given a look at the FBI report. Each was urged to go on the warpath. Each was promised financial support. The first three men on the list refused. The fourth took the document home and read it carefully. Next morning he called a member of the League and told him he was "buying the package."

That fourth Senator was Joseph McCarthy.[23]

Joe McCarthy was largely a fraud. Born in 1908 in Outogamie County, Wisconsin, one of seven children, McCarthy made it the hard way. At age fourteen, he became a chicken farmer, went broke, and turned to managing a grocery store in a nearby town. When he was twenty, he decided to get an education. Thanks to cooperative teachers, he crammed four years of high school into one year, and entered Marquette University. He dated a reporter who gave him some favorable publicity, attempted to box but displayed no skill, and eventually decided that law rather than engineering offered the easiest course to a career.

Opening a law office in a little Wisconsin town, he made a living playing poker in the cheap gambling joints of the area. Old poker players remember him as "having the guts of a burglar," but the pickings were so small he moved to Shawano, a Republican town. Although Joe was a Democrat, he made some influential friends and ran for district attorney. He lost, but was not discouraged. By lying shamelessly about the incumbent circuit judge, he soon won a seat on the bench, and was on his way at last. Quickie divorces were his specialty.

With the outbreak of war, McCarthy decided his political career required him to serve. He applied for a commission on June 2, 1942, in the Marines. Later he was to brag that he enlisted as a buck private and won a commission on merit. He served thirty months, all the while hanging on to his judgeship in Wisconsin. Fellow circuit judges took over his case load and kept his seat warm. Meanwhile, McCarthy was shuffling papers as an intelligence officer in the South Pacific, and occasionally riding around in airplanes. He enjoyed firing the plane's machineguns, and won the distinction of firing forty-seven hundred rounds in a single day—at coconuts. Calling himself "Tailgunner Joe," McCarthy sent appropriate pictures to the newspapers back home.

A hero needs a medal, however, or at least a citation. Joe had broken his leg on June 22, 1943, during "shellback" ceremonies when his ship crossed the equator. He later used the injury to imply he had been wounded in action. Limping around, he would tell friends he had "ten pounds of shrapnel" in his leg. Somehow, he managed to get a citation which read in part: "Although suffering from a severe leg injury, he refused to be hospitalized." Vague as that was, it sounded good to the voters back home.

Voters were important even in the South Pacific. Ignoring a constitutional ban on incumbent judges running for another office, McCarthy managed to become a candidate for the U.S. Senate in 1944. The Marines let him come home on leave for the last few weeks of the campaign. Judge McCarthy held court in his uniform, and limped around impressively. In losing, he attracted more than ten thousand votes, and his political stock soared.

In February 1945 McCarthy decided that MacArthur could get along without him. He resigned his commission, came home, and resumed his activities on the bench. Soon he announced that he would oppose Senator Robert LaFollette. Campaigning as a war hero, he got help from the Communists. When asked about this, McCarthy commented: "Communists have the same right to vote as anyone else, don't they?"

McCarthy's Communist support didn't frighten the right wing. The *Chicago Tribune* endorsed McCarthy. General Robert E. Wood, former head of the America First Committee, backed him, as did other conservatives. McCarthy's alleged "good war record" was cited. In November, 1946, he won big—620,430 to 378,772.

Luck continued to follow McCarthy. *Life*, seeking a feature on a rookie senator's first day on the job, selected McCarthy as the man to feature. On his second day McCarthy called a press conference to advocate drafting labor leader John L. Lewis and his striking coal miners into the army. The announcement didn't solve the coal problem but it

119

served notice that McCarthy intended to live up to the expectations of his right-wing friends.

Soon he became known as the "Pepsi-Cola Kid." It came about in the following way. John Maragon, one of the "five percenters" of the Truman scandals, was working for Allied Molasses to get sugar rationing ended. Much of the company's molasses was sold to the Pepsi-Cola Company, which also—along with all the big liquor distillers—wanted rationing ended as quickly as possible. An ally was Russell M. Arundel, the self-styled "Prince of Outer Baldonia," an island off the coast of Nova Scotia. As a spokesman for sugar interests and the owner of two Pepsi-Cola plants, Arundel valued McCarthy's aid. Sugar rationing, one of the economic controls surviving the war, would have been lifted in any case, but it meant money in the pockets of Arundel and his associates if it could be ended sooner than scheduled. McCarthy led the fight that ended it sooner. Later, when McCarthy's bank back in Wisconsin, was about to call in some of the senator's personal notes, Arundel provided a "loan" to ease the financial crisis.[24]

By 1949, McCarthy was well established. He had done nothing distinguishing after his opening flurry, although he had proven his right-wing position by signing a letter calling for early hearings on a bill to aid Nationalist China. In a very real sense, he was looking for a new vehicle to ride, even as he had ridden his supposed war service into the Senate.

When McCarthy was offered the "package" on Communism, with its promise of financial support and ready data from FBI files, he didn't hesitate. As Roy Cohn put it:

Joe McCarthy bought Communism in much the same way as other people purchase a new automobile. The salesman showed him the model; he looked at it with interest, examined it more closely, kicked at the tires, sat at the wheel, squiggled in the seat, asked some questions, and bought. It was just as cold as that.[25]

On December 5, 1949, a cable signed "Kung" had gone directly to Chiang Kai-shek. One sentence spoke volumes: "Our hope of a world war so as to rehabilitate our country is unpalatable to the [American] people." Two months and four days later, on February 9, 1950, the climate began to

120

change. McCarthy, standing before the Ohio County Women's Republican Club in Wheeling, West Virginia, charged there were two hundred and five "security risks" in the State Department. The "nightmare decade," as Fred Cook calls it, had begun. John Edgar Hoover must have been delighted.

VII

HE United States in early 1950 was pictured as a great nation, weary of war, torn by internal dissension, disillusioned by graft and corruption. Harry S. Truman was seen as a weak President, betrayed by his friends and buffeted by a resurgent Republican Party determined to seize power in the next election. The American people, according to this view, were confused, frightened by bogeymen, at the mercy of conflicting forces, without a sense of national direction or purpose.

In contrast, the Communists were on the offensive in Asia. The mainland of China was under their control. Civil war raged in Indochina, and the colonial empires were crumbling. There was strife in Malaysia. In the Philippines, ancient tensions were alive. The Communists thought a strike into South Korea seemed not only logical but safe. Their evaluation of conditions within the United States convinced the Reds that America would not interfere in Asia.

No small factor in this misconception was the China lobby, representing as it did both the Nationalist Chinese and American businessmen who wanted a third world war. Building an anti-Communist climate in this country was party of their program. So was a campaign to encourage the

Communists into thinking the United States was a paper tiger.

On June 26, 1950, North Korean troops crossed the border and drove deep into South Korea. They advanced in confidence, contemptuous of the American will, or ability, to resist. President Truman reacted quickly, dramatically, effectively. Within twenty-four hours he announced plans to send air and naval forces to aid the South Koreans. On the same day, the United Nations in, perhaps, its finest hour, asked member nations to participate in repelling the invasion. Truman ordered American troops stationed in Korea in the midst of battle, a strange action for a man who had been, and would be, accused of being pro-Communist, of protecting traitors in government, of advancing the cause of the "International Communist conspiracy."

The big question mark was whether American intervention would bring in the Red Chinese and perhaps escalate the struggle into a third world war. On July 14, three weeks after hostilities began, the code name "Kung" was signed to a cable sent to Chiang Kai-shek by Alfred Kohlberg's Chinese allies in Washington:

> Whether the Chinese Communists send troops to Korea or not is of secondary importance, but the war in South Korea will be extended in any case. We must be patient at this time. Whether or not the war will extend to other places in Europe and Asia, we should make little comment and wait for development of the situation.[1]

Public comment, the Chinese members of the China lobby knew, should come from Americans—from right-wingers like Joe McCarthy and the American Jewish League Against Communism. That Kohlberg, founder of the League, used McCarthy as a spokesman is well illustrated. In the August 11, 1949, issue of *The China Monthly*, Kohlberg wrote: "Professor Jessup must therefore be honored by our State Department as the initiator of the smear campaign against Nationalist China and Chiang Kai-shek, and the originator of the myth of the democratic Chinese communists."

McCarthy in a Senate speech on March 30, 1950, used almost the same words: "Professor Jessup must therefore be credited by the American people with having pioneered the smear campaign against Nationalist China and Chiang Kai-shek and with being the originator of the myth of the democratic Chinese communists."

While McCarthy beat the drums, and mouthed the phrases of Kohlberg and others, Lewis S. Rosenstiel was hard at work. Convinced that World War III was at hand, he ordered Schenley to begin overproduction of bonded whiskey in what *Business Week* later called a "bad bet."[2] The huge stocks of liquor built up during Prohibition had given Schenley its start when Repeal came. Similarly, a huge supply of liquor had been manufactured on the eve of World War II, giving Schenley an advantage when wartime restrictions were imposed and giving such Schenley distributors as Robert Gould an edge in the black market that resulted. Louis B. Nichols put it this way in testimony many years later before the New York Joint Legislative Committee on Crime: "Everybody felt in 1950 that we were on the verge of World War III, and production would be shut off."

Not everybody. Just Schenley, which was unique in going out on a limb. Obviously, Rosenstiel gambled on inside information such friends as Kohlberg and the members of the American Jewish League Against Communism supplied. Kohlberg in a speech in 1951, was still confident: "I do not doubt the courage and patriotism of our young men who fight for us in Korea; and who *will fight in the months and years to come, in strange lands and seas, the names of which we scarcely know today."* (Emphasis added.) Kohlberg continued:

But for what do we ask them to fight? For moral principles, for liberty, for the right? Or for unworthy objectives that may be negotiated—or is it appeased?—next week or the week after in the UN or in some secret meeting with our enemies? Can we compromise our principles if only Joe Stalin or Mao Tse-tung would be willing to talk to us and not make the price too high?[3]

Implicit here is a fear that the third world war on which Kohlberg based his hopes for the restoration of his "cottage industry" in China, and on which Rosenstiel had gambled

124

many millions, might be averted by limiting the conflict to Korea. This fear grew steadily and became irrational in its intensity. Truman, who had instantly met the Communist challenge, was soon being accused of seeing peace without victory. One of those who was to shout the loudest was Douglas MacArthur.

Those pushing for a third world war hoped that the Chinese would be forced to intervene in Korea. This, they believed, would lead to full-scale war with China. Since the land mass was simply too large for an American expeditionary force to achieve decisive results without suffering the loss of hundreds of thousands of men, it seemed logical to believe the United States would employ the atomic bomb to bring China to her knees. Such use of the bomb would almost certainly bring Russia into action, not only in Asia but in Europe. A final showdown between America and the forces of godless communism would necessarily follow, and, of course, America would win.

That Truman hoped to avoid such a showdown marks him as a statesman in the eyes of reasonable men, but to the right wing his efforts to limit the conflict branded him a traitor.

When American armies led by MacArthur crossed the thirty-eighth parallel and invaded North Korea, the Chinese began to react as expected. Warnings were issued that if the advance did not stop, the Chinese would have to intervene. MacArthur ignored the warnings, plunged ahead, and at the same time, gave encouragement to Chiang Kai-shek, who was offering his veterans for combat from Formosa. On October 15, 1950, Truman conferred with MacArthur on Wake Island. MacArthur assured his President that the fighting would end by Thanksgiving. Asked if the Chinese might intervene, MacArthur said no.

Despite MacArthur's assessment, the Chinese did intervene. The general launched a new drive, which broke down as it encountered massive waves of Chinese pouring across the Yalu. Soon the Americans were in retreat. MacArthur estimated that "an aggregate strength of over two hundred thousand men is now arrayed against the United Nations forces in North Korea."

It was the moment the right-wingers had waited for. The

cry arose that the United States should throw in the reserves, bomb Manchuria, go all out to stop the Reds. MacArthur in a communiqué invited broad action.

MacArthur was not happy about limited successes. In a letter on March 20 to House Republican Leader Joseph W. Martin, he penned his famous phrase: "There is no substitute for victory." The letter, read on the floor of Congress, created a new uproar. Truman decided he had been patient long enough. On April 11, he announced that MacArthur had been removed from his command in the Pacific.

In a radio talk the next day Truman laid it on the line:

We do not want to see the conflict in Korea extended. We are trying to prevent a world war—not to start one. . . . A number of events have made it evident that General MacArthur did not agree with that policy. I have, therefore, considered it necessary to relieve General MacArthur so that there would be no doubt or confusion as to the real purpose and aim of our policy. . . . The cause of world peace is more important than any individual."

The Korean war slowly fizzled out. A military stalemate had developed by June 1951, and two years later a truce was signed. Nevertheless, the China lobby and its allies did not abandon their dream of a third world war. In 1971 a witness before Senator William Proxmire's Joint Economic Committee told of secret activities that:

1. Created crises in the Taiwan Strait (that body of water between mainland China and the off-shore islands protected by the United States) in 1954 and 1958.

2. Added to the flames of a revolt in Tibet against Red China in 1959.

3. Contributed to the development of a "war" between China and India in 1962.

The witness, Allen S. Whiting, a former Chinese expert for the State Department, said the crises "triggered Chinese Communist military reactions which, in turn, have been used to justify a vast expansion of U.S. military programs throughout Asia, ostensibly to contain the threat of Chinese-Communist aggression."[4]

Meanwhile, John Edgar Hoover faced a crisis of his own. Word circulated that attorney-scholar Max Lowenthal had penned an unflattering book about the FBI. This was a shock to Hoover who, over the years, had enjoyed a good press. With the exception of a few leftish-liberal journals, most publications accepted and elaborated upon the developing Hoover myth as fed them by Nichols. A steady stream of books and magazine articles had praised Hoover as a noble knight on a white horse. Many of course, had been ghost written under Hoover's name. In 1938 he had published *Persons in Hiding*, three hundred and eighteen pages dealing with the FBI's exploits against criminals. The *New York Times* had not been complimentary. Robert Van Gelder in a review noted:

It is time that Mr. Hoover gave his ghost some fresh material. This book is washed over and dimmed by banalities. Those who take it up after reading Courtney Ryley Cooper's earlier books will hardly escape the conviction that they have read it before. Mr. Hoover continues to come out against Robin Hood, the sentimental "moo cows" who can't be quite persuaded that all criminals are rats and nothing more. Pages are devoted to proving that criminals are selfish. . . .[5]

Hoover took the hint. In 1943 Frederick L. Collins published *The FBI in Peace and War*, with an introduction by Hoover. This book added some spy stories to the by now old-hat tales of Karpis and Ma Barker, and countless magazine articles picked up the theme. Hardly a day passed without some columnist—Walter Winchell, George Sokolsky, Eugene Lyons—devoting newspaper space to polishing the halo around Hoover's dyed hair.

Now suddenly word was out that Lowenthal, an attorney whose government associations began as secretary to the Wickersham Commission on Law Enforcement set up by Herbert Hoover, had exposed John Edgar Hoover as a fraud. Immediately an attempt began to blunt the impact of the book even before its publication. The obvious method was to smear the author. *The Nation* described the preliminary campaign: "During August [1950] several eminent radio gossipers gave advance 'reviews' of the book which they hadn't read—describing the author's character ('sinister') and his personal associations ('communists')."[6]

Then on September 1, 1950, Michigan Congressman George Dondero arose to address his colleagues. Representative Dondero had long proved his devotion to right-wing Americanism. In 1949, for example, he had bitterly attacked art critics and modern art as tools of the Communist conspiracy. Dondero was no less blunt about Lowenthal. He began: "Mr. Speaker, I want to discuss a man of mystery this afternoon and for the first time take off the mask behind which he has been hiding for years and even avoiding service from the Committee on Un-American Activities."

Dondero confessed "I still do not know the full story because he is a man of mystery. He has reached pinnacles of great power. A recommendation from him was tantamount to success. There are few men in Washington who have dared to stand up against him."

The full flavor of the attack is seen in one sentence describing Lowenthal's education. "Then like many other parlor pinks, fellow travelers, Communists and convicted perjurers, he attended Harvard Law School, graduating in 1912." While at Harvard, Dondero added, Lowenthal came "under the influence of another man who through the years has manipulated the Charlie McCarthys in Government office." Who was this other man? Justice Felix Frankfurter.[7] The congressman continued a long recital of Lowenthal's career, his alleged Communist associations, his power for evil. Not once was Lowenthal's book mentioned. Nor was there any reference to Hoover. Exactly why Dondero suddenly found it necessary to expose this dangerous menace was not made clear.

The House Un-American Activities Committee picked up its cue, however, and called Lowenthal to Washington to testify in executive session on September 15. A literate, intelligent man, Lowenthal fielded all questions with ease, but the implication that he was a conscious agent of the international Red conspiracy was firmly established. One day before the book was published, the committee made his testimony public.

The Federal Bureau of Investigation is referred to several times in this volume. It is an excellent source book, scholarly, nonsensational, well documented. There is nothing in it to which Hoover or anyone else could take just exception. Nevertheless, as William V. Shannon wrote in the *New York Post*:

> One American is learning that there is a high price tag attached to his right to criticize a powerful government agency. The man is Max Lowenthal, a New York attorney whose book is highly critical of the methods and operations of the FBI and its director, J. Edgar Hoover. The news that Lowenthal was planning to publish such a book plunged him into a half-lit shadow world of vicious attack, false innuendo and deliberately contrived mystery.[8]

Shannon pointed out that the detailed information used by Dondero "could have come from only one source—the FBI files."

The Nation, in discussing the episode, commented: "Apparently our thought police are running out of communists. Who's next?"

The attack on Lowenthal's FBI book was only partially successful. In part, it diverted attention to the book and perhaps guaranteed it would be read by thoughtful people. Unfortunately, perhaps, its scholarly approach possessed none of the "bing-bang" thrills to be found in the pro-Hoover books, so the study never achieved a popular success. In a very short time, the book became almost impossible to find. Even today, libraries well stocked with Whitehead, Collins, and Hoover, do not have Lowenthal on their shelves.

To his credit, Lowenthal became Hoover's pet hate, to be supplanted in time by Fred Cook whose *The FBI Nobody Knows* drew heavily on Lowenthal's original research and became a best-seller in 1964. Cook had his problems as well, and so have other writers who have dared to be critical of John Edgar Hoover. None of the criticisms, it should be added, did any serious damage to Hoover's image. He had become a legend in his own lifetime.

Hoover was so powerful that the Kefauver Committee's probe of organized crime in interstate commerce did not hurt his prestige, despite the fact Kefauver proved beyond a shadow of doubt that Hoover had been criminally negligent in fighting the crime syndicate. Once again the public simply refused to blame him for his failures.

Carey Estes Kefauver was born in 1903 in Tennessee. Tall and lanky, he pursued gangsters with the zeal of a Davy Crockett on the trail of redskins. To win his Senate seat he had to defeat the well-established political machine of Edward "Boss" Crump, an exploit that gave him considerable insight into the alliance of crime, business, and politics. The Kefauver probe began in Miami on May 26, 1950. In the months to come, it at times drove Joe McCarthy and his allegations about Communists-in-government off the front page. The first people to testify in the series of public hearings were Ben and Seymour Eisen, accountants for Meyer Lansky.[9] Much later, Lansky himself testified. Among other things, he told his version of "Operation Underworld," that mysterious conspiracy to parole Lucky Luciano as a reward for his aid to the war effort. The Kefauver Committee stated bluntly: "It now appears that the parole must be justified on some basis other than that of Luciano's contribution to the war effort."

Almost every major gangster in the nation appeared before Kefauver. Many refused to talk and were cited for contempt. Others testified more or less frankly. Their stories revealed the interlocking relationship of criminal activity in almost every city in the country. In the vast majority of cases, the men got their start during Prohibition, went on into organized gambling, loan sharking, labor racketeering, and legitimate businesses.

The Kefauver Committee found that "one of the most perplexing problems in the field of organized crime" was gangster infiltration of legitimate business. It listed fifty areas of gangster activity ranging from advertising to transportation. Banking, newspapers, hotels, insurance, racing, restaurants, amusements, steel, and television were a few of those listed. In the liquor industry the committee found that

. . . leading hoodlums have penetrated the liquor industry, principally the distribution end of the business, due to the failure of the industry to assume its proper share of responsibility. . . .

130

Many of the Nation's leading hoodlums got their start as boot-leggers during prohibition. Many have a history of prohibition arrests. The transition from bootlegging to the legitimate liquor business was a natural one. Unfortunately, however, many rack-eteers found it hard to drop the methods of operation which characterized their rum-running days and consequently, the committee was not surprised to find hoodlums involved in huge liquor black-market deals during World War II. . . .

Turning to another basic aspect of the problem, the committee noted:

The most shocking revelations of the testimony before the committee is the extent of official corruption and connivance in facilitating and promoting organized crime. . . . The committee found evidence of corruption and connivance at all levels of government—Federal, State, and local. . . .

As to organized crime itself, the committee reported:

The structure of organized crime today is far different from what it was many years ago. Its power for evil is infinitely greater. The unit of organized crime used to be an individual gang consisting of a number of hoodlums, whose activities were obviously predatory in character. Individual gangs tended to specialize in specific types of criminal activity such as a payroll, or bank robbery, loft or safe burglary, pocket picking, and so on. These gangs normally confined their activities to particular areas of the country or particular communities. . . .

This description was obviously a bow to John Edgar Hoover who had specialized in the nineteen thirties in extermi-nating the major bank robbers. That in doing so Hoover ignored the more dangerous criminal syndicate was implicit in the committee's next words:

New types of criminal gangs have emerged during prohibition. The huge profits earned in that era together with the develop-ment of twentieth century transportation and communication, made possible larger and more powerful gangs, covering much greater territory. Organized crime in the last 30 years has taken on new characteristics. The most dangerous criminal gangs today are not specialists in one type of predatory crime, but engage in many and varied forms of criminality. Criminal groups today are

131

multipurpose in character, engaging in any racket where ever there is money to be made. . . . The more dangerous criminal elements draw most of their revenues from various forms of gambling, the sale and distribution of narcotics, prostitution, various forms of business and labor racketeering, black-market practices, bootlegging in dry areas, etc.

Noting that "modern crime syndicates" have "copied some of the organizational methods found in modern business," the committee listed two major syndicates in New York and Chicago, and said that there "are many other criminal gangs throughout the country that have more than a local importance." As to the Mafia, the committee commented:

The Mafia, the committee is convinced, has an important part in binding together into a loose association the two major criminal syndicates as well as many minor gangs and individual hoodlums throughout the country. Wherever the committee has gone it has run into the trail of this elusive, shadowy, and sinister organization.

While today, given much new information and additional insight, one might quarrel with some of the committee's conclusions about the structure of organized crime, no one can quibble over the importance of its basic achievement. Kefauver for the first time bared the intimate relationship between crime, politics, and business, and documented that relationship in every major city in the country. In comparison, the work of John Edgar Hoover shrivels to the level of that of a Keystone cop.

What did Hoover think of the Kefauver committee and its findings? Largely, he ignored it. McCarthy's crusade against Communism occupied much of his time during the period the committee was holding hearings. Nevertheless, Hoover was too much the civil servant to allow such important work to be done without in some way—however minor—associating himself with it. Joseph Nellis, a Kefauver aide, now a prominent attorney in Washington, told the author that Senator Kefauver considered it a "great coup" when Hoover accepted an invitation to testify before the committee. Appar-

132

ently Hoover, even then, had become so powerful he could and did ignore such requests from congressional committees if he desired.

On March 26, 1951, Hoover testified in Washington. He was accompanied by Attorney J. Howard McGrath who noted that both he and Hoover opposed the formation of a national crime commission on the grounds "such a body might tend to derogate from the basic State and local responsibility for criminal law enforcement and lead to the creation of a national police force."

Hoover began by praising the committee in a prepared statement. "You have developed facts which brought out into the open," he said, "entanglements between the underworld and the upperworld, and unholy alliances between the criminal element and officialdom which established a shocking disregard for law and order."

Despite these unholy alliances, Hoover continued,

this nation has no need for a national police force. . . . My experience has demonstrated that the present system of law enforcement, national, State and local, is the best system. The peace officer must be the servant of the people, protecting their interests and responding to their will. The law-enforcement agency must be an integral part of the community.

Perhaps recognizing that it was inconsistent to admit that shocking conditions existed, while maintaining that the system which permitted those conditions to develop was the best, Hoover made this point:

The mere fact that conditions have been exposed which are shocking, to say the least, is no reason to depart from our traditional concepts of constitutional government. In the deplorable conditions which have been exposed by the committee, it was not the system that was at fault but the men who were responsible for its proper functioning and, more important, the citizens who failed to raise their voices or to exercise their responsibility at the ballot box.

This statement sounds lofty but ignores realities. The "system," any system, depends upon men to operate it. The operators are thus part of the system. To vindicate the vehicle and blame the driver is to ignore the necessary relationship between the two. And when Hoover makes the additional comment that the solution to crime is simply to "enforce existing laws fairly and impartially," he is again ignoring the true nature of organized crime. Unperturbed, Hoover continued in the same vein, concluding with an appeal for "a return to the fundamentals upon which this Nation was founded—a moral reawakening—a revitalized spirit and a rededication of services to our fellow man."

In other words, if everyone would be good and not break the laws, there would be no crime problem. And if they won't be good—well, it's still a local problem. The FBI, he made clear, would "always be willing to lend all possible assistance to local agencies without usurping local functions, prerogatives or jurisdiction." Just no responsibility, please.

The questioning of Hoover was mild enough. He was asked if the men who began in Prohibition did not turn next to gambling. He replied:

I think a great many of the present underworld leaders and the underworld scum are descendants from the prohibition era. They started in at that era with easy money and, of course, they had to buy local officials in order to be able to carry on their nefarious activity. As that passed out of the picture, a few turned to the era of kidnaping and bank robbers which we had in the thirties and late thirties. That was pretty effectively broken, and then the great bulk of them gravitated into the gambling racket that you have today.

By making this statement, Hoover was revising history to suit his purposes. By inserting the "era of kidnaping and bank robbers" between Prohibition and gambling, he distorted the facts to justify his own activity in the thirties. In passing Hoover took a dig at Miami Beach, one of his favorite vacation spots. "In the winter season," he said, "Miami is the winter capital of the criminal underworld, and the scum go with it."

When asked if he believed "it would help some in this country if your jurisdiction were extended," Hoover replied firmly:

"I do not. I am very much opposed to any expansion of the

134

Federal Bureau of Investigation. I think it is too big today."

In other words, despite the fact that shocking conditions existed, that the "system" didn't work too well because of human nature, that corruption was widespread on every level—despite all this, Hoover wanted no additional duties, no responsibility to do anything about it. The professional civil servant was happy with his empire—he wanted nothing changed that would bring his agency into conflict with powerful political or economic interests.

Hoover's appearance, the respect shown him by the committee, the prestige he enjoyed even then, make one fact clear: had Hoover suggested that organized crime was a matter worthy of his attention, he would have quickly been given all the necessary authority, all the necessary funds, to lead a fight against it. Instead, he insisted crime should be left to local officials, corrupt as they might be, and specifically declined a suggestion that his jurisdiction be extended. His testimony did not name a single gangster convicted as a result of the FBI's investigations.

Hoover must take responsibility for the failure of law enforcement to deal effectively with the greatest crime problem a democratic society has had to confront. In the next decade, organized crime would become even more powerful—thanks to Hoover's apparent refusal to step on the toes of the men who supported him. The power that could have been mobilized against the crime syndicate was used to protect Hoover from criticism. As he put it in 1951, "Law enforcement is only as effective as the citizens demand."

This author was the last writer to interview Kefauver. He looked tired and ill on that day, August 8, 1963, but he plucked at his old-fashioned suspenders and talked about the need for a national crime commission. The committee in 1951 had recommended the creation of such a body, but in the face of Hoover's continuing disapproval, the proposal never got off the ground. Hoover wanted no commission of any sort looking over his shoulder.

Kefauver died two days later. The work of his committee remains as his monument. No investigation before or since has come close to it. Unfortunately, in the turmoil of the McCarthy era and the arid desert of the Eisenhower-Nixon years that followed, its value was never fully appreciated and its recommendations never fully implemented. It was one thing to watch Frank Costello's hands on television—the New York hearings were the sensation of the day—but it was easier to accept McCarthy's allegations about Reds in government. To do something about organized crime would have required overhauling the socioeconomic system, whereas, with the Reds, one could leave everything to Joe and John Edgar Hoover.

By 1952 it was apparent that a third world war was not going to start so long as Truman was President. It was also obvious that McCarthy, despite the headlines he had secured, needed some help. McCarthy was too shallow, too impulsive, too lazy to use the material given him in an effective manner. His attacks on the Democrats for "twenty years of treason" had helped prepare the way for a Republican to assume office, but the hard-headed leaders of the GOP were looking beyond McCarthy for a suitable candidate. Hopes that Mac-Arthur might fill the bill quickly vanished, and the right-wingers were forced to settle on Senator Robert Taft. This prospect was enough to worry many people—including Harry Truman.

Dwight Eisenhower revealed that on December 18, 1951, Truman wrote him a longhand letter disclosing his desire to retire to Missouri. He expressed a further wish "to keep isolationists out of the White House." The implication was clear—if Eisenhower would agree to run, Truman could safely call it quits.[10]

Republicans collected under Eisenhower's banner not because they appreciated his political philosophy—few knew what that was—but on the logical grounds that he alone could beat the Democrats. Even McCarthy got in line. Eisenhower won the nomination easily after making a concession to the right wing by accepting that young Red hunter, Richard Nixon, as his running mate.

One result of the Eisenhower-Nixon victory was to sweep into Congress enough—barely enough—Republicans to provide a GOP majority. This meant that McCarthy, as ranking Republican, would be the new chairman of the Senate Permanent Subcommittee on Investigations. It would enhance his investigatory powers and also give him an almost free hand in the selection of a staff. The right wing decided to assign to the committee a trained legal mind to keep the erratic senator on the track and perhaps actually find some Reds in government. The men who had originally selected McCarthy knew exactly whom they wanted for the job—Roy Cohn. Various individuals have been given credit over the years for directing Cohn to McCarthy—Winchell, Sokolsky, Rosenstiel. Cohn insists that McCarthy approached him in person, but even Cohn's account makes it plain that someone had been giving the young lawyer quite a build-up. He quotes McCarthy as saying, "You can't possibly be one-tenth as good as everyone says you are."[11]

Cohn was not the choice of one man, but the nominee of a group—the American Jewish League Against Communism. How better to achieve the aims, or at least the avowed aims of the League, to prove Jews were anti-Communists, than to present McCarthy with a Jewish chief counsel?

Young as he was, Cohn at the age of twenty-five had quite a record of anti-Communist activity. The son of a Bronx County judge, well educated, he had had some small part in the trial of eleven Communists charged under the ancient Smith Act with conspiring to overthrow the government. As an assistant United States attorney, he was one of the Jewish staff that convicted the Rosenbergs. More recently he had led a grand jury in New York into a probe of alleged Communists in the United Nations. That investigation eventually bogged down—or so it was charged—when someone in the Justice Department ordered the FBI to quit supplying Cohn with the names and background data of potential witnesses. The Chelf subcommittee of the House—the same group that had investigated Rosenstiel's political contributions—looked into the matter and expressed shock to learn that some of the witnesses called by Cohn had refused to say whether or not they believed in God. Exactly why that was any business of a Federal grand jury, no one bothered to inquire. The committee commended Cohn highly for his efforts to root out the godless Americans working for the United Nations.[12]

Transferred to Washington, Cohn helped convict William Remington on perjury charges. The first conviction was thrown out on appeal. Rather than try that case again, the government secured a new indictment and this time made it stick despite a dissent from Judge Learned Hand, who vainly argued the conviction should be reversed and the indictment quashed.[13] A few months later Remington was murdered in his prison cell.

With Remington's scalp on his belt, Cohn moved to take over as McCarthy's chief counsel. To celebrate the event, a party was given in his honor. Attending were Vice-President Nixon, John Edgar Hoover, a number of right-wing senators, various right-wing columnists and business leaders. "It was heady wine," Cohn has since admitted, and his subsequent behavior proved it.

In time, Cohn would become an attorney for—he was already a personal friend of—Rosenstiel, and, with Louis B. Nichols, achieve a weird influence over that stubborn multimillionaire. He would become involved with Las Vegas gamblers—exbootleggers, such as Moe Dalitz and Sam Tucker—and with other wheeler-dealers of right-wing persuasion. He was to be indicted, acquitted, indicted, and acquitted again. In short, after his services to McCarthy, he found a place in that gray world where conventional lines of honesty are blurred and indistinct.

Cohn's friend, traveling companion, and fellow comedian in the McCarthy circus, G. David Schine, was born to that world. As the son of wealthy Meyer Schine, he was rich and sophisticated by the standards of Miami Beach. His father had been a witness before the Kefauver Committee, admitting reluctantly that he had lease arrangements with bookmakers at his Miami Beach hotels. Frank Erickson, the syndicate's official betting commissioner, paid forty thousand dollars for the privilege of operating a handbook for three months—the winter season—at the Roney Plaza. Schine received another twenty thousand a year for bookmaking at the Boca Raton Club in Boca Raton, Florida.[14]

The Schine hotel chain included the McAllister Hotel in Miami and the Gulfstream on Miami Beach. The Kefauver Committee did not explore the subject, but, had they bothered, they would have learned that the Gulfstream—a combination hotel and apartment house—was the favorite stopping place for John Edgar Hoover when he came to the Miami area to play the horses. Here is the way one FBI agent in Miami put it: "The Director always stayed at the Gulfstream Hotel on Miami Beach, where they always picked up his tab." A Negro special agent—one of the very few in the FBI at the time—served as his chauffeur. The agent would "drive over to the Gulfstream every morning, then drive the Director to the racetrack." He used, of course, the armor-plated Cadillac kept the year round in Miami for Hoover's convenience.[15] Later, Hoover moved to the Key Biscayne Hotel, owned by the Mackle brothers. Other frequent guests there were Richard Nixon and Joe McCarthy. The Mackles were land developers, building among other things a city on Marco Island off the west coast of Florida. When Louis B. Nichols decided he needed a winter home, he found one on Marco Island.

In his testimony before Kefauver, the elder Schine insisted that he tried to keep the Roney Plaza clean. He said:

> For three years we were accosted by various people to let them make book, and we wouldn't. And because we tried to keep it what you might call ultra clean we refused to take on anybody, but it got so bad that the help and the guests and the sneak bookings were bad, and finally he came to me and talked to me about it. Erickson—and to me Erickson is no different than any other bookmaker. They all seem to be alike. And I talked it over with the manager, and they all agreed it would be better to give it to a man who was responsible rather than to one who was fly-by-night, as you might say.

How did they arrive at the figure of forty thousand dollars? "Well," said Schine, "we just asked him fifty. Then he offered twenty-five, and it was gotten together that way." Why the figure of twenty thousand at Boca Raton? "Well, we figured we couldn't get any more."[16]

According to several authorities, David Schine's career as a Communist-fighter began in the Schine hotels at Miami Beach. For reasons not clear, he had written a six-page monograph called "A Definition of Communism," which was placed beside the Gideon bible in every hotel room. According to Richard Rovere, the paper was "a bedside treasury of

139

wrong dates and mistaken identities and misunderstood principles." Nevertheless, Rabbi Schultz read the paper, which bore the symbol of the Schine hotels, and decided that it was a masterpiece. He called Schine to the attention of George Sokolsky, one of his colleagues in the American Jewish League Against Communism, and Sokolsky persuaded McCarthy to hire the young expert as a "consultant." Schine served at a dollar a year and was well worth the money. After all, he made his suite in the Waldorf Towers available to the committee, and Cohn opened an office there at no cost to the taxpayers.

David Schine was taller than Cohn, good-looking in the sleek, sleepy-eyed style of the stars of the silent films. He had attended Harvard—although no one accused him of picking up any left-wing ideas there. Next to his paper on Communism, he was perhaps proudest of his cigar collection.

Exactly why Cohn became so fond of Schine remains something of a mystery. The two young bachelors were inseparable—and later, when Schine was drafted, Cohn seemed willing to destroy the army to make sure his friend continued to live in the style to which he had become accustomed. The Cohn-Schine expedition to Europe made McCarthy a laughingstock and brought on the McCarthy army hearings. Cohn, in retrospect, admitted the trip was a "colossal mistake." He wrote:

> David Schine and I unwittingly handed Joe McCarthy's enemies a perfect opportunity to spread the tale that a couple of young, inexperienced clowns were bustling about Europe, ordering State Department officials around, burning books, creating chaos wherever they went, and disrupting foreign relations.[17]

Nothing needs to added to that summary—it sums up beautifully the Cohn-Schine effort to cleanse State Department libraries.

While the Cohn-Schine roadshow was going on, Hoover's boss, Attorney General Herbert Brownell, was engaged in an equally bizarre project—smearing a dead man. In a Chicago speech on November 6, 1953, Brownell charged that Harry Dexter White was a Communist underground agent. White

140

had been accused in 1948, had denied the charges in a polished performance before the House Un-American Activities Committee, and won applause from the audience. Before testifying, he had told the committee that he suffered from a heart condition; nevertheless, he had been grilled mercilessly. A few days later he died of a heart attack. Now, five years after his death, the charges were renewed.

Brownell, however, was shooting at bigger game than White. He insisted that the FBI told President Truman about White's work for the Reds before Truman appointed White to a high government post. Brownell's implication was plain—Truman had knowingly promoted a Russian spy.

From Independence, the ex-President made characteristic reply. Noting that the Republicans had lost heavily in the 1953 elections, he accused Brownell of reviving an old scandal for smear purposes. Then, apparently confused, he insisted he had promoted White so the FBI could keep an eye on his activities with less difficulty.

The fat was in the fire. Hoover, who had always fought to keep FBI records secret, appeared before a Senate subcommittee and confirmed Brownell's charges. Copies of FBI documents were submitted. They proved only that accusations against White had been made by professional informers such as Elizabeth Bentley, and that Truman had disregarded the information. Allegedly there was "corroborative evidence," which, according to Brownell, could not be divulged without impairing the efficiency of the FBI.

Hoover was in good form. "Our American way of life," he said, "has been brought into conflict with the godless forces of Communism. These Red Fascists distort, conceal, misrepresent and lie to gain their ends. Deceit is their very essence."[18] By implying that Truman was a traitor, Hoover cast aside all pretense of objectivity. Publicly he joined with McCarthy, who had been shouting that the Democratic years from Roosevelt through Truman were "years of treason."

The controversy got big play in the press at home and abroad. Few writers bothered to note that all the evidence against White had been submitted to a grand jury in 1948— the same grand jury that indicted scores of the top leaders of the Communist Party. After thoroughly studying the case against White, the grand jury refused to indict him.

Eisenhower defended Truman's loyalty, and eventually the uproar subsided. Hoover, however, had flexed his muscles in daring to contradict a former President, and had acted in plain view of all who cared to notice as if he were the most powerful man in the United States.

In comparison, McCarthy seemed an awkward clown.

VIII

VERY little is known about John Edgar Hoover's private life. It has been customary to say he is "wedded to his work." Certainly he is not married to a woman. Even in his nightclub period his name was not linked to anyone, with the single exception of Mrs. Leila Rogers, mother of movie star Ginger Rogers. But Mrs. Rogers's comment to *The National Observer* in 1971 was not that of an old flame. "That poor little boy," she was quoted as saying. "I sometimes wish I could just take him and comfort him."[1] The "closest thing to a love affair" he ever had, she added, was his affection for Shirley Temple, back when Miss Temple was a child star and not a right-wing politician. Hoover's chief companion for years has been Clyde Tolson, an aging assistant. They go everywhere together—even, as we shall see, on Hoover's "working vacations." Tolson is also a bachelor. Often their vacations involve horseracing.

Hoover's love of the so-called "sport of kings" has received very little attention over the decades. His press agents have referred to it occasionally to prove that Hoover does have some human qualities in common with other mortals, and his critics have poked mild fun at Hoover as the following

143

excerpt from the *New York Times* of May 15, 1937, illustrates:

On the same day that George VI received his crown in London, England, it was revealed, though not so conspicuously reported, that J. Edgar Hoover, Chief of the U.S. Bureau of Investigation, lost his hat at Churchill Downs, Kentucky.

It is fair to assume that the hat was, so to speak, a Derby hat, because it vanished during the running of the race of that name. A hurried inquiry by a conclave of the U.S. Bureau of Investigation, represented in the person of Mr. Hoover, decided that the hat was stolen, or, possibly, kidnapped. No ransom notes have been received, but it is hoped that the hat may be traced through the federal system of fingerprints. If it is not, Mr. Hoover may be comforted by the thought that many other visitors to Churchill Downs lost their shirts.

Hoover's press agents could turn off the flow of publicity as easily as they could turn it on when needed. Typical coverage was this item in the *New York Times* of August 24, 1954, datelined La Jolla:

Senator McCarthy relaxed on a vacation here today, which, he said, merely coincided for the second year with the annual visit of J. Edgar Hoover, Director of the FBI, at the ocean resort hotel of Clint W. Murthinson and Sid Richardson, wealthy Texans.

La Jolla is located on the coast of the Pacific near San Diego. It began as an art colony shortly after the turn of the century, and developed into an exclusive retreat for the very wealthy. Its beach, a long, lonely stretch of golden sand, is called Windansea, and its surf is considered the best east of Hawaii. But natural beauty is not the principal lure for Hoover. It is the nearby Del Mar Racetrack, "where the turf meets the surf." The Del Mar racing season comes in June, neatly counterbalancing the winter season in Miami, and permitting Hoover to enjoy his favorite sport under the most ideal conditions.

The Hotel Del Charro opened its doors in June 1953, just in time for the racing season. Richardson and Murchison, the owners, called it the "KKK West," a reference to their exclusive "Koon Kreek Klub" back in the Lone Star State. Murchison and Richardson grew up together in the little Texas town of Athens. Clint actually went to college, got into trouble shooting craps, and decided he could get rich without a formal education. While still boys they began to trade, dealing in cattle, land, horses—anything that was handy. As one of their friends put it: "They have only the simplest, most innocent desire in the world—to make money. All they want is more."[2]

Oil provided the opportunity. Both men began as wildcatters, and struck it rich quickly. As the millions poured in, they invested it—in more oil wells, in ranches, in big-city real estate, in banks, in insurance companies, in motels, in steamship lines, in restaurants, in book-publishing companies, in race horses, in racetracks, in cab companies, in candy companies, in railroads. With wealth came the fears of wealthy men everywhere and especially of the nouveau riche. They had made the money the hard way—aided, of course, by a lot of luck—and they resented any suggestion of change in the status quo. Recognizing, like Mark Hanna decades before, that politics if properly controlled can be good for business, they set out to fill all key elective offices with right-thinking men. Locally, on the state level, there was little to worry about. The big danger was Congress, where, year after year, left-wing liberals tried to tinker with that most valuable possession—the oil depletion allowance. That such liberals were really Reds in disguise, no true-thinking Texan doubted.

A Murchison lieutenant, Robert Thompson, brought McCarthy to Murchison. Later, when the political climate in Washington changed, he introduced him to Bobby Baker,[3] thus proving once again that business is basically unconcerned with party labels. It is the character of the individual, not his professed political faith, that is important. Much impressed with McCarthy, Murchison and Richardson contributed generously to the war on godless communism and to the defeat of McCarthy's enemies—Millard Tydings of Maryland and William Benton of Connecticut.

The Hotel Del Charro, where the minimum rate was a hundred dollars a day, European plan, accommodated a fantastic group of big name freeloaders. In addition to Hoover and McCarthy, other "special guests" during the 1950s included Vice-President Nixon, Senator John Connally, Senator Clinton Anderson, Senator George Smathers, Lewis S. Rosenstiel, Arthur Samish, and a wide assortment of top gangsters from Las Vegas.

During the winter Murchison maintained a watering spot for his friends on tiny Spanish Cay in the Bahamas. Politicians from around the country were flown there in Murchison's private plane. It was a standing joke in Frankfort, Kentucky, for example, that when the governor—be he Democrat or Republican—announced he was flying to New York on business, he headed instead for Spanish Cay. Tecon, a Murchison engineering firm, had many highway contracts in Kentucky, so it was only good business to keep the governor happy. Murchison also owned a thousand-acre island in the Gulf of Mexico, a seventy-five-thousand-acre ranch in Mexico, and a twenty-five-room house in Dallas. The house had nine bedrooms, one with eight beds so "the boys" could talk all night if business was urgent.

It was at La Jolla that Murchison persuaded Hoover to write—or have his ghost write—*Masters of Deceit*. Clint had purchased the old and honorable Henry Holt Publishing Company, and he believed that a book by Hoover would give the troubled firm a shot in the arm while, of course, simultaneously alerting the nation to the Communist menace. He was right—the book sold two hundred and fifteen thousand copies in its first two years and made Hoover a pile of money. *Masters of Deceit* was a fitting stablemate to *Folk Medicine*, by Dr. DeForest Clinton Jarvis, another Holt best-seller, of the same period, which extolled the virtues of honey and cider vinegar.[4]

In 1954 Richardson and Murchison got control of the Del Mar racetrack and set up a foundation, "Boys, Incorporated," to operate it. Profits were to go to the foundation, which was supposed to benefit underprivileged boys. General Howland "Howling Mad" Smith, the hero of Guadalcanal and a resident of La Jolla, was retained to serve as front man for the foundation. Soon Smith was disenchanted. He sounded off in an interview with the *San Diego Evening Tribune*. The story, which criticized Murchison, ran in only

146

one edition before being killed, but Murchison decided it must be countered. He wheeled forth his big gun, John Edgar Hoover, who paid tribute in the same paper to Murchison as "the type of rugged individualist that made this country great." For good measure, Hoover granted an exclusive interview to Oscar Otis of *The Morning Telegram*, the racing publication once owned by Moses Annenberg. Asked specifically about the "charity aspect" of Del Mar racing, Hoover replied:

I know Clint Murchison quite well and I think he would be the last person in the country to use such a plan as a clever tax or business subterfuge. In fact, I spoke to Murchison about ten years ago about devoting some time and help to youth work and the charitable corporation of Del Mar is one of his answers. This work helps directly in making the nation sturdy, for communist penetration is currently directed mainly at labor organizations and youth organizations.

Hoover went on to declare that he found racing a "wholesome diversion" from "a gruelling week of work at the FBI." He saw no moral issue in betting—unless one overdid it, and he added:

Actually, from a law-enforcement standpoint, a well-conducted racetrack is a help to a community, if only for the reason that the people at the track are finding an outlet for their emotions, are enjoying a diversion, if you will, which time, if they weren't at the track, they might use for less laudable escapes.

Hoover's pronouncement flatly contradicts the opinion and experience of most police chiefs in cities having horse or dog tracks. From Louisville to Miami Beach, police chiefs customarily warn citizens to expect an influx of pimps, touts, pickpockets, gangsters, and burglars during the racing season. The crime rate goes up while the horses are running, as Hoover would know if he only studied the FBI's famous figures.

Lest the public worry about Hoover being at the track every afternoon, the FBI chief hastened to reassure them that "I always arrange it so that I can be reached instantly in case I'm needed." During the interview he also had time for some

147

philosophy: "At the FBI we often judge a man by who is damning him as well as by who is praising him. An example, the more the communists damn the FBI, the better the job we must be doing in fighting them, America's number one menace." Hoover also commented that while "there have been some bad people in racing," he thought that "they have been pretty well eliminated. . . . You can take it direct from the FBI that no human activity of consequence that is organized has been free of scandal. We've had crooked lawyers, doctors, and bankers."

The country has come to accept journalistic prostitutes who will give a good word, or column, to anyone in return for freeloading plums; it is still shocking, nevertheless, to see the FBI chief allow himself to seem to be sinking to the same level. And, one might add, for the same apparent reason. In passing, Hoover also put in a plug for his fellow sponger on Murchison's hospitality. "I never knew Senator McCarthy until he came to the Senate," Hoover told the San Diego newspaper. "I've come to know him well, officially and personally. I view him as a friend and believe he so views me."

And so, year after year, the nation's top Red hunters—Hoover, McCarthy, Nixon—gathered each June at the Hotel Del Charro to plan their campaigns while enjoying every luxury that money—Murchison's money—could buy. That it was sometimes necessary to brush elbows with top gangsters bothered no one—the gangsters, after all, were loyal Americans who opposed any effort to change the status quo that had given them their big opportunity to become rich.

A sidelight to the La Jolla interlude is provided by the story of Allan Witwer. If nothing else, it supplies new insight into the interrelationships of which our amoral society is comprised.

Witwer was a native of New Jersey, growing up with Jim Bishop, his closest friend. Witwer's father had been a writer of some distinction, and the youth shared literary ambitions with Bishop. Getting started was difficult, but the two men helped each other along.

The Kefauver Committee in 1951 got Bishop to admit that three years earlier he had carried a three-hundred-thousand-dollar bribe offer from Zwillman, who was known as the "Al Capone of New Jersey" to a candidate for governor. The candidate turned it down, and Bishop chalked up the episode to his political education.[5] Witwer meanwhile was learning the ropes in Hollywood. Bishop helped him get a job with *Liberty* magazine. When it folded, he banged around Los Angeles awhile, became friendly with a Murchison lieutenant, and ended up as vice-president and general manager of the Hotel Del Charro Corporation. To get the job he had to get security clearance from the FBI.

Being a thrifty soul, Witwer kept a close eye on the big-name freeloaders he was required to entertain. What's more, he kept copies of their hotel bills, showing how the bills were charged off as business expenses to one of Murchison's many corporations. In time, he accumulated two large suitcases full of records. Something happened, and Witwer was fired. He turned as usual to Bishop, who by now was a syndicated columnist. In the good old days at La Jolla, Bishop had been a frequent freeloader, paying for room and board with plugs in his columns. Witwer was the subject of several flattering columns.

As usual, Bishop had an angle. He helped his boyhood friend find a job on Grand Bahama Island, where Meyer Lansky was in the process of developing the first major casino in the Caribbean. Security was slack in those early days, and Witwer—ever tidy—collected a vast amount of documentation, showing, among other things, the huge pay-offs made to Bahamian officials. When he had enough data, he resigned his job as public relations expert, and announced loudly that he was going to Miami to write a book—*The Ugly Bahamians*. He actually did write a few chapters, but most of his efforts went into preparing a detailed outline of the proposed book. In a complicated deal, Witwer soon sold the outline and, allegedly, all documentation, to Exposition Press for fifty thousand dollars, plus some three thousand dollars in expenses. The publisher then sold the material back to the public relations firm for which Witwer had worked, making a neat profit for doing nothing. Needless to say, *The Ugly Bahamians* was never published.

The story, however, was not ended. Witwer, it developed,

had kept copies of all the documentation. Several copies. Robert Morgenthau, the U.S. attorney in New York, was able to subpoena them. Leaked to the *Wall Street Journal,* they won that newspaper a Pulitzer Prize. The publicity led directly to the overthrow of the white government of the Bahamas headed by Sir Stafford Sands.[6]

Afterward, Witwer and Bishop became bitter enemies. Bishop no longer wrote columns in praise of his former friend. In 1971 he gave his version of Witwer's Bahamian coup. Referring to his schoolboy chum as "Willy," Bishop wrote:

> So I got him a job as a publicity agent. He worked a couple of years, smiling his way from one typewriter to another. Then he showed me a jumble of the most incoherent writing I've ever seen. It was an exposé of his boss. I'm a slow thinker. He didn't want to publish the junk; he wanted the boss to buy it from him. The boss did: for $60,000. So I lost two friends in one shot.[7]

Witwer replied: "Jim Bishop would have written a column telling the world what a grand guy Judas of Iscariot was if he and his family had been invited to the Last Supper."[8]

Apparently what provoked Bishop's 1971 outburst was Witwer's reappearance in Miami with two suitcases full of documents detailing Murchison's hospitality to Hoover, McCarthy, and Nixon back in the days when Witwer was managing the Hotel Del Charro. The documentation was allegedly being peddled to any writer who would shape it into a book—but, strangely enough, Witwer backed away when anyone displayed interest. Nor would he allow a prospective author to examine the contents of the locked suitcases. Occasionally, as if to whet the writers' appetites, he would whip out a document. One such, on FBI stationery, was dated August 23, 1958. Addressed to Witwer at the Hotel Del Charro, it began:

> Dear Allan:
> It is always hard to leave one's friends after such an enjoyable stay as Clyde and I have had these past few weeks. However, we certainly could not leave without expressing

our thanks to you for making our visit to Del Charro and to La Jolla so very pleasant. We appreciated the superb accommodations and your many contributions toward our comfort and enjoyment of this trip. We truly had a grand time.

With best wishes to you and the family, in which Clyde joins me,

Sincerely,
Edgar [in longhand][9]

To supplement the documentation—which he was always going to show in full at the next meeting—Witwer told many tales of life at La Jolla. He told of the night Mrs. Murchison became alarmed after a burglary in the area and of Hoover assigning an FBI agent to stand guard outside her cottage. And he told the weird story of a woman partner of Murchison's who mysteriously died at sea. If Witwer is to be believed, she died calling for someone to contact John Edgar Hoover by ship-to-shore telephone.

The Miami office of the FBI, hearing of Witwer and his suitcases, called him in and questioned him. When, however, no one offered to buy his unwritten book a second time, he took his suitcases and melted away. Later he was heard from in Las Vegas, where Hank Greenspun, former press agent to Moe Dalitz at the Desert Inn and owner of the *Las Vegas Sun*, was dickering with him.

If, indeed, Witwer was attempting to pressure Hoover, he had a basic problem: the FBI director's freeloading at La Jolla was not news. It had been reported many times. Moreover, John Edgar Hoover's image was virtually scandal-proof. Any attack upon the man could be written off as a Communist-inspired effort to degrade the nation's most valiant Commie-fighter.

Bishop, meantime, had become the chief booster, through his syndicated column, of Louis E. Wolfson, the multimillionaire whose friendship with Associate Justice Abe Fortas caused Fortas to step down from the Supreme Court. In his 1971 column about "Willy," Bishop related how he told Wolfson about his former friend. He quoted Wolfson as saying in reply, "He wrote a note to me awhile back. Said he wanted to see me about something important. I turned him off because, in his letter, he said he knew you and that you're a phony."[10]

In short, Bishop was happy in the knowledge that Wolfson, just out of Federal prison, was his good friend.

Bishop's column continues to be carried daily in hundreds of newspapers. In it he continues to say nice things about the Wolfsons, the Murchisons, and the Hoovers of our society. Bishop, of course, is not unique. The Winchells, the Sokolskys, and others of their ilk did their bit to make Hoover a legend and McCarthy a power. Such is the influence of the right wing on American journalism today that in many cases the accuser becomes the accused and is smeared like Max Lowenthal was.

It is worth noting that organized crime also makes good use of the prostitutes of the press. When, in 1952, Batista—with help from Lansky—regained power in Cuba, he was hailed as a bulwark against Communism. The plush casinos Lansky developed there in the next few years became favorite vacation spots for the wealthy businessman and the politicians. This is how the fourth Mrs. Rosenstiel in 1970 described to the New York Joint Legislative Committee on Crime her first visit to Havana:

Q. Did there come a time during this period when you went to Havana?
A. . . . We went in February of 1957 with Mr. Jack Amiel.
. . . .
Q. Who was Mr. Amiel?
A. He owned Jack Dempsey's restaurant and also real estate in Brooklyn.
. . . .
Q. Had you ever been in Havana before this?
A. Never.
Q. When you got to Havana, would you tell the Committee what happened?
A. We arrived in Havana and then we went to the Nacional Hotel and we were escorted up to our suite, and we had a very big suite, and it was filled with flowers. I thought it was more of a funeral, so I looked at the card, and the card said, "Welcome, Supreme Commander, to Havana. Meyer and Jake.

152

So, I asked my husband who Meyer and Jake were, and he said that is Meyer and Jake Lansky, very good friends of his.

Then he called Jack Amiel on the telephone and he said, "Let's meet down in the lobby, and we will go right into the gambling room."

So, in about five or ten minutes, we went right down to the lobby, and the gambling room was off the lobby, and Meyer Lansky was there waiting our arrival. And he was very happy to see the Supreme Commander, and Jack Amiel and I were introduced.

Then he [Meyer Lansky] told whoever it was—I think his brother ran the gambling—he said, "Unlimited credit."

So, then Mr. Rosenstiel got thousands of dollars worth of chips and started to gamble at the roulette wheel, and Mr. Amiel went over to the crap table, and I set next to Mr. Rosenstiel, and he said that I could have $100. Then he was gambling and gambling, and Meyer Lansky came back and said, "Supreme Commander, where would you like to have dinner tonight?"

And the Supreme Commander said that wherever Meyer thought was the best restaurant. So he suggested a restaurant down the street.

This was about 6:30. So, we went upstairs to change, and then we went to the restaurant, and the restaurant reservation was under the name of Meyer Lansky, and the three of us had dinner there. And there was no check.

After dinner we went to the Tropicana to see a show, and then the Supreme Commander wanted to gamble some more; so we went into the gambling room and he and a friend of his he introduced me to by the name of Lefty Clark, told him he should not gamble there. He did not give any reason why.

So, he said, "Let's go back to the Nacional," and we went back and he gambled, I would say, until about one or two in the morning. And then we went upstairs to bed.

The following day we had lunch with Meyer around the pool with Jack Amiel, and they introduced me to someone by the name of Ray Ryan that had the cabana next to us. In the evening we went to the same restaurant and instead of going to see another show, we came right back to the Nacional. Then Sunday night we had dinner with Meyer Lansky, and Monday we left for Florida.[11]

Lewis S. Rosenstiel, asked by the press to comment on the charges his fourth wife had made under oath, denied he had ever met Meyer Lansky or had dealings with him. New York State Senator John H. Hughes, who headed the Joint Legislative Committee on Crime, offered Rosenstiel an opportunity to rebut his wife's testimony under oath, but Rosenstiel declined on the basis of health. Sometimes later, Hughes told newsmen, "Her [Mrs. Rosenstiel's] testimony in Executive session last year has been checked and the committee has every reason to believe she is telling the truth." Some months later, Louis B. Nichols testified before the same committee and volunteered the information that "If Rosenstiel had visited Havana he would have met Jake Lansky." Presumably by chance, since, said the exassistant to Hoover, "Rosenstiel avoided organized crime like the plague."[12]

Senator George Smathers, known to his Florida constituents as "Gorgeous George," was a strong supporter of Batista, and thus, indirectly, of Lansky. Smathers won his Senate seat by defeating Claude Pepper in a campaign that was copied by Nixon in his California race against Helen Gahagan Douglas. Smathers labeled his opponent "Red Pepper"; Nixon called Mrs. Douglas "the Pink Lady." The voters of California were a little too sophisticated, however, for another technique Smathers found effective in the piney woods of North Florida.

"Are you aware," asked Smathers, "that Claude Pepper is known all over Washington as a shameless extrovert? Not only that, but this man is reliably reported to practice nepotism with his sister-in-law, and he has a sister who was once a thespian in wicked New York. Worst of all, it is an established fact that Mr. Pepper, before his marriage, practiced celibacy."[13]

After his election, Nixon went to Florida for a vacation. Smathers asked his good friend, Charles G. "Bebe" Rebozo, to see that he had a good time. Accompanying Nixon on the 1952 trip was Dana C. Smith, an old supporter who would shortly be identified as the administrator of the "Nixon Fund"—that secret, self-renewing supply of cash provided by the right wing to help build Nixon into a national figure. Disclosure of the fund's existence during the election campaign that fall caused a scandal, but Nixon retrieved his position as candidate for Vice-President with his famous "Checkers" speech.

After a few days in Miami, Nixon and Smith decided they wanted some action. Accompanied by former FBI agent, Richard Danner, they hopped over to Havana. Danner had been former city manager of Miami and, in that capacity, had become acquainted with many of the gangsters operating in Cuba. One such Miami-based hood was Norman "Roughhouse" Rothman, current boss of the Sans Souci. Smith promptly lost all his cash at the Sans Souci and was permitted to play on credit. He wrote a check to cover his losses, but when he returned to the States, he stopped payment. An angry Rothman threatened legal action, or worse. Nixon asked the State Department to intervene on behalf of Smith, and eventually the gangster was soothed.[14]

Smathers, who became known as "the Cuban senator," was not alone in supporting Batista as an anti-Communist hero. And, since men often see only what they want to see, practically no one took Castro seriously. Almost to the last day of 1958, Havana was a gay place for tourists and for junketing politicians. The skyline of Havana changed as, under Lansky's strict control, huge new hotel-casinos were erected. The spectacular growth of Las Vegas was duplicated in Cuba. At the same time, the crime syndicate had regional gambling centers serving the East and West coasts, with smaller operations still functioning in Newport, Kentucky; Hot Springs, Arkansas; and a dozen other cities such as Biloxi, Gretna, Revere, and Cicero. The skim from all these operations totaled hundreds of millions. The take flowed through syndicate banks to Switzerland, and returned dry cleaned for investment in hotels, food chains, television stations, book publishers, and anything else that offered a respectable haven.

Against this background the Eisenhower administration dealt gingerly with the problem of McCarthy. The senator from Wisconsin was no longer content to blame Democrats. He turned his guns on the Republicans. As usual, the guns were loaded with blanks, but made a loud noise and much smoke. Also, as usual, there were those ready to assume that where there was smoke there must be fire.

The story of the McCarthy army hearings is fascinating and sordid. It all began when G. David Schine, "consultant" to McCarthy's committee, was drafted. Roy Cohn lost his head trying to keep Schine out of the service, arguing that his expert knowledge of communism was essential to the work of the committee. Cohn desperately commuted to New York almost every weekend, seeking advice from George Sokolsky and other members of the American Jewish League Against Communism on how to save Schine from the army.

The televised hearings brought McCarthy into the living rooms of America, giving many citizens their first real understanding of the man and his methods. They were not aware, of course, that behind the scenes men like Nixon and Senator Everett Dirksen were trying desperately to work out a compromise that would save the army's face and still preserve McCarthy's image. Eisenhower, however, had made up his mind that McCarthy would have to go, and he refused all proposed "deals."

Left to fight it out, McCarthy resorted to his usual tricks. On May 4, 1954, he produced what he obviously thought would be a bombshell. He said he had a letter from FBI Director Hoover to army intelligence, alleging espionage at Fort Monmouth, New Jersey, where, after months of effort, McCarthy had indeed turned up a "pink dentist." The two-page letter bore the typewritten closing, "Sincerely yours, J. Edgar Hoover, Director." Hoover, when challenged, denied the authenticity of the letter, though he did admit it contained seven paragraphs of a report he had sent to the Army in 1951. How did McCarthy get the document? According to Cohn, it was given to the senator by an officer in G-2 who was "disgusted" over the army's failure to do anything about the alleged information it contained.[15]

The Monmouth letter does bear a striking resemblance to the one-hundred-page FBI report that was leaked in 1948 to members of the American Jewish League Against Communism, and shown to McCarthy by league members as part of their attempt to recruit him. Other FBI documents had provided ammunition to McCarthy during his four-year campaign. There is thus little reason not to assume that the document introduced at the McCarthy army hearings was but one in the series. Cohn noted that while Hoover did say the letter was not an exact copy of his original report, he did not say "that the information it contained was unfaithful to the text of his memorandum." On his own responsibility, Cohn added: "It was not." Cohn's remark can only mean that Cohn was familiar with the text of the original FBI report.[16]

Hoover, like McCarthy, was skating on thin ice, but such was the prestige of the FBI director—and the growing disgust with McCarthy—that the episode became known as "the case of the purloined letter." It was easier to believe that McCarthy had stolen the document, or manufactured it, than it was to assume that Hoover cooperated in making it available.

Hoover's letter, purloined or not, was to receive considerable attention from the "Select Committee to Study Censure Charges Against the Senator from Wisconsin, Mr. McCarthy." Following the inconclusive, from an official point of view, McCarthy army hearings, Senator Ralph Flanders of Vermont on July 30, 1954, introduced a resolution to censure McCarthy. Flanders had been restless for some time. In an earlier speech he had commented:

He [McCarthy] dons his war paint. He goes into his war dance. He emits his war whoops. He goes forth to battle and proudly returns with the scalp of a pink Army dentist. We may assume that this represents the depth of the seriousness of Communist penetration at this time.

Nixon was given the—for him—unpleasant task of selecting the members of the lynching party. Ever the expedient man, the Vice-President recognized that the tide was turning against his fellow freeloader. Having cooperated with McCarthy in his rise to power, he was now ready to destroy him as the changing political picture dictated. Nixon named Republican Senator Arthur Watkins, a former judge, as chairman of the select committee. Columnist Stewart Alsop commented that the "man-eating tiger" was about to face an "elderly mouse," but, as sometimes happens, Alsop was mistaken.

157

The matter of the "purloined letter" came up immediately. As Senator Watkins put it, "the question had immediately arisen as to how McCarthy could have obtained such a document and whether his possession of it was a breach of Federal espionage laws."[17] One witness was Winchell, the columnist who had worked with the syndicate in arranging the surrender of Lepke to Hoover. In a column published in May, Winchell had claimed to have a copy of the famous letter. When asked, he could not remember who had given it to him. But he did assure the committee that John Edgar Hoover was still the tough law-and-order man he professed to be. He asked John, he said: "Would you arrest me if I published it?" To which he testified John replied, "Yes."[18] While this sounded good, it didn't explain why Hoover made no move against McCarthy for publicizing the document. As usual, Hoover was not asked to testify. Apparently even Watkins had no desire to probe too deeply into the matter. In the end, "the Select Committee went on to conclude that it preferred to give Senator McCarthy the benefit of whatever doubts and uncertainties may have confused the issues in the past," as Watkins put it. It did accuse him, however, of a "lack of regard for responsibility" in the matter. The Eisenhower administration, Nixon in particular, while ready to censure McCarthy, had no desire to bring Hoover into disrepute. He had served the Republicans too well in the past—as the recent Harry Dexter White case illustrated.

As the hearings continued it became apparent that McCarthy had given up hope of winning his battle before the committee. He turned, instead, to the court of public opinion. On the whole his conduct within the hearing room was —for him—discreet enough. He had promised his unofficial attorney, Edward Bennett Williams, to behave, but Williams had neglected to make him promise to behave outside the chamber. Williams, of course, was accustomed to serving as an attorney for top gangsters, who were happy enough for him to do their talking. That McCarthy should turn to a criminal lawyer for advice was not without precedent. In the 1920s, Attorney General Daugherty had retained Max Steuer, the Edward Bennett Williams of his day, to represent him. Steuer later defended such gangsters as John Torrio in the Prendergast-Davies case.

Day after day, McCarthy gave statements before the television cameras waiting in the hall outside the hearing room. He attacked the individual members of the committee. The attacks were effective. Soon thousands of letters, many almost identical in language, poured in. The American Legion rallied to McCarthy's support. On August 7, as the hearings ground on, McCarthy appeared before two thousand legionnaires in Washington, and assailed the committee. On November 7, at a communion breakfast of Catholic War Veterans, Msgr. Edward R. Martin, appearing as the personal representative of Cardinal Spellman, charged that the attack on McCarthy was an attack on "Catholic ideals." McCarthy, of course, professed to be a Catholic. Despite the efforts of the American Jewish League Against Communism to rally Jews to McCarthy's defense, the bulk of his supporters were Catholics. It is perhaps significant that Rosenstiel, one of McCarthy's admirers, was converted to Catholicism. Louis B. Nichols, defending Rosenstiel in 1971, said the liquor baron "enjoyed the friendship of the late Cardinal Spellman" and, even then, was "serving with His Eminence Cardinal Cooke as one of the three trustees of the Cardinal Spellman Foundation."[19]

Nevertheless, the American Jewish League Against Communism got its two cents in. On Veterans Day, a crowd of three thousand gathered at Constitution Hall in Washington, D.C. The rally was organized by Rabbi Benjamin Schultz, national director of the League, and Schultz brought a special train full of supporters from New York. Prominently displayed on the stage were relatives of men believed to be Communist prisoners in Korea. McCarthy reduced some of the prisoners' relatives to tears when in an emotional speech he told them, "You are the victims of a massive appeasement that has been going on for years. It knows no political bounds."

Other speakers included Senator Barry Goldwater, Senator Herman Welker, Senator Karl Mundt, former Senator Burton K. Wheeler—now a strict isolationist—former Representative Hamilton Fish, and, ironically enough, the most

159

antidemocratic columnist of them all, Westbrook Pegler—in short, almost all leaders of the right wing. "Regardless of what the Senate may do," shouted McCarthy, "the fight to expose those who would destroy this Nation will go on and on and on."[20]

On November 14 the formation of what was inaccurately called "Ten Million Americans Mobilizing for Justice" was announced. The organization proposed to combine all "pro-America" groups, all veterans organizations, and so on, to distribute petitions on behalf of McCarthy. A disturbing feature of the group was the fact that so many high-ranking military men allowed their names to be used. Included were retired Lieutenant General George F. Stratemeyer, retired Admiral John G. Crommelin, retired Admiral William H. Standley, and retired General James A. Van Fleet. Douglas MacArthur was, of course, too egotistical to be but one of such a group, although his name was freely mentioned as a supporter. The fact that military men were willing to be used in the defense of a rabble-rouser like McCarthy offers food for sober thought. The industrial-military complex against which Eisenhower warned is basically as right wing as the leaders of the crime syndicate. As a potential threat to the Republic, the military-industrial complex is far more dangerous than the disorganized radicals of the left.

Despite its promises, the committee was able to secure only one million, eight hundred and sixteen signatures to its petitions. They were delivered by armored truck to the Capitol and presented to Vice-President Nixon, who accepted them "on behalf of the Senate." After pictures were taken, the petitions were carried out to the armored trucks and returned to New York.

The flood of mail continued. As Senator Watkins noted, the letters ranged from reprints of articles by the prince of anti-Semites, Gerald K. Smith, to copies of *American Legion Magazine* articles by "the respected head of the FBI, J. Edgar Hoover." The Hearst press, the *Chicago Tribune*, and other right-wing newspapers—especially in Texas, where Murchison and his fellow oil barons owned many—kept up the attack against McCarthy's critics. Pro-McCarthy senators did their bit on the floor of the Senate. Typical is a comment from Senator John Bricker: "Today the hue and cry is on throughout the land. The pack which hunts the hunters of communism has caught the smell of blood."

Senator Goldwater got into the act with this statement:

We know that this censure move is not a disconnected happening either in the career of Senator McCarthy or in America's fight against communism. It is a part of a sequence of events. Actually, those unknown engineers of censure hope that this will be the culminating act in the merciless fight to destroy a United States Senator and the fight against communism . . . The masterminds of this fight have said one thing and meant another. Their propaganda has dripped with idealism, high-mindedness, and lofty sentiments. Their deeds have come from darkness . . .[21]

On September 27 the Watkins committee made its report. President Eisenhower described it in this fashion:

While bending over backward and giving Senator McCarthy the benefit of the doubt on some points, the committee recommended censure on two charges: contempt of the Senate, and the senator's treatment of General Zwicker. In view of the senatorial restraint toward colleagues, this was a victory indeed for the anti-McCarthy forces. There the matter sat until after the congressional elections.[22]

Exactly what role the McCarthy battle played in the Republican defeat in 1954 is a matter of conjecture. The affair was fought out at the height of the campaign. Certainly, McCarthy's appeal to the public was designed to make him the big issue, but whether citizens voted for the Democrats because McCarthy was a Republican, or because the Republican leadership, on the executive level, at least, was attempting to censure McCarthy, is impossible to determine. The results, however, were disastrous for McCarthy. The Democrats captured control of both houses of Congress, and this action stripped McCarthy of his cherished chairmanship of the Senate permanent investigating subcommittee. Thus, in a very real sense, it was the voters of America who forced McCarthy from the reins of power. McCarthy's loss of the chairmanship was also a factor in the Senate debate on the censure resolution that followed the elections. Suddenly,

161

the senator was no longer so formidable, and hesitant senators were able to find the courage to vote against him. Of course, there were last-minute compromises. The censure charge involving one Army General was dropped. The word "censure" was changed to "condemned," allegedly by Richard Nixon's facile pen. Watkins later maintained that "condemn" was the stronger word, but at the time pro-McCarthy forces found a sad satisfaction in the word change.

The roll call of the Senate brought sixty-seven votes to condemn McCarthy and twenty-two to reject the resolution. Six senators abstained, including Bricker, Smathers, and John Kennedy, who was ill. All the Republican Senate leaders with the exception of Leverett Saltonstall, voted for McCarthy. Goldwater, Hickenlooper, Bridges, Knowland, Mundt, Welker, Milliken, and Dirksen were among them. President Eisenhower, who earlier had called McCarthy a political problem for the Democrats, left no doubt of his new position. Two days after the vote he called Senator Watkins to his office to commend him for "his superb handling of a most difficult job." Hearing of the meeting, McCarthy apologized to the American people for supporting the President in 1952. Eisenhower was later to write:

By a combination of the Senate's vote and the loss of his committee chairmanship, the senator's power was ended. Senator McCarthy died an untimely and sad—even pathetic—death in 1957, but as a political force he was finished at the end of 1954.

The President added a final thought that has meaning even today when law-and-order advocates suggest waiving the Bill of Rights in pursuit of radicals:

Un-American activity cannot be prevented or routed out by employing un-American methods; to preserve freedom we must use the tools that freedom provides.[23]

The end of McCarthy may have been apparent to Eisenhower, but not to others. Even a dying snake can bite. Friends of McCarthy took great pleasure in defeating Senator Watkins when he came up for reelection in 1958. The man who succeeded him was the former Governor J. Bracken Lee of Utah, staunch defender of McCarthy, president of a "pro-America" group made up of wealthy Texas and California conservatives.

Before leaving McCarthy to drink himself to death, however, one subject raised by Roy Cohn deserves attention. In his book on McCarthy, Cohn noted: "It had been widely whispered about that McCarthy was a homosexual, a charge widely accepted by many of his enemies who were undeterred by its patent falsity." According to Cohn, Senator Flanders referred to this "rumor" when in the middle of the McCarthy army hearings, he arose on the floor of the Senate to complain: "The committee has not yet dug into the real heart of the mystery. That mystery concerns the personal relationships of the army private [Schine], the staff assistant [Cohn], and the Senator." Again according to Cohn, army counsel Joseph Welch had the homosexual charge in mind when in the course of the McCarthy army hearings, he mentioned the word "pixie." McCarthy interrupted to ask for a definition of the word. Welch replied, "Yes, I should say, Mr. Senator, that a pixie is a close relative of a fairy. Shall I proceed, sir? Have I enlightened you?" He had definitely enlightened his audience for, as Cohn observed, it "roared" with laughter.[24]

McCarthy was, of course, for many years, a bachelor. Eventually he married his secretary, and in January, 1957, the couple adopted a baby. Schine was also a bachelor. Years later, after his role in the army was forgotten, he married a former Miss Universe, and moved to Hollywood where "he lives elegantly like an old time movie mogul" in a mansion. Cohn was also a bachelor, and at the time of this writing has not yet married. Furthermore, the gossip columnists have never identified him with a woman. When one remembers how Senator Goldwater attempted to characterize the Johnson administration as "this curious crew," after a Johnson aide was arrested on a morals charge, one can only conclude that —despite Cohn's indignation—the critics of McCarthy were not as unkind as they might have been.

McCarthy died on May 2, 1957. At Mrs. McCarthy's request he was given a state funeral in the same chamber where less than three years before he had been condemned. An era had ended.

The American Jewish League Against Communism survived. When Rabbi Schultz despaired, the leadership was taken over by Sokolsky. When he died, Roy Cohn assumed the mantle. Opposed by several leading Jewish organizations, the League today exists only as a vehicle for Cohn's ambitions.

IX

THE relationship between organized crime and politics is well illustrated by an event that followed the McCarthy army hearings. After the hearings, Roy Cohn, a lieutenant in the National Guard, was assigned to Kessler Air Force Base at Biloxi, Mississippi, for two weeks of summer training. Biloxi was at that time a junior-league syndicate town, offering small casinos on the beach to tourists and bust-out joints downtown to servicemen. Apparently Cohn couldn't have cared less. Not too far away was New Orleans, where major casinos founded by Lansky and Costello still operated in Jefferson Parish. Cohn went to New Orleans on weekend passes. In his book he makes no mention of the city's attractions, but he does tell about getting a room at the Roosevelt Hotel. Upon phoning for a reservation, he was told none were available. Cohn was not accustomed to taking no for an answer. As he told it:

I got through to Seymour Weiss, the owner of the hotel, whom I knew and who has a "soft spot" for any Communist fighter, and asked if he had some "house" rooms available such as are generally set aside by the management. Weiss told us to come on over at once—he had a fine suite for us.

165

The suite, as Cohn discovered, had been assigned to General Matthew B. Ridgeway, hero of Korea and army chief of staff. Ridgeway was placed in "less desirable quarters."[1]

Who was Seymour Weiss, this man with a "soft spot" for Communist-fighters, who would move the army chief of staff to make room for Roy Cohn and his buddies? Weiss was a former lieutenant of Huey Long, an ex-convict, who had been very active in the syndicate's gambling operations in and around New Orleans. Beginning as the manager of the barber shop in the Roosevelt Hotel in 1923, Weiss moved up to assistant manager of the hotel by 1925, and became Long's right-hand man. When the intelligence unit of the Internal Revenue Service went to New Orleans on Roosevelt's orders, Weiss was a prime target. The murder of Long prevented his indictment on tax charges, but the pressure on his lieutenants continued. Weiss, along with Long's successor as governor, Richard W. Leche, and Robert S. Maestri, Mayor of New Orleans, attempted to run the Long machine after the Kingfish's death. In 1939 Weiss was indicted on income-tax and mail-fraud charges, growing out of the graft of the period, and was sentenced to four years in prison. He served sixteen months before being paroled.[2]

Two months before the indictments were returned, Governor Leche—who was also indicted—entertained Attorney General Frank Murphy and John Edgar Hoover at a reception at the Governor's Mansion.[3] A week before the indictment, Hoover's assistant, Louis B. Nichols, gave Leche and Weiss a personally guided tour of the FBI offices in Washington.[4] Apparently Murphy, Hoover, and Nichols were completely oblivious to conditions existing in New Orleans, including the alliance of organized crime and politics. And Roy Cohn, eighteen years later, knew Weiss well enough to ask for, and receive, special favors. Truly, the life of a "Communist-fighter" has its compensations.

The New York Joint Legislative Committee on Crime in 1970 heard sworn testimony linking Lewis S. Rosenstiel to business deals in New Orleans involving Costello, Weiss, and other Long lieutenants. Completing the pattern, is the fact that both Cohn and Nichols found employment with Rosenstiel after quitting their official duties in the battle against

166

the international Communist conspiracy. Prior to their employment, Rosenstiel retained Thomas E. Dewey, excrimebuster, exgovernor of New York. He served as Schenley counsel from, as Nichols noted, "the early 50's until the 60's."[5]

Rosenstiel's big problem in the 1950s was what to do with the vast quantity of surplus liquor he had ordered manufactured at the time of the Korean war. The deadline for action was 1958, when one and a quarter billion dollars in taxes would come due on the stored liquor. That Dewey with his vast political influence could help was obvious, but Rosenstiel wanted to leave no stone unturned. For this reason he asked Nichols to quit his job with the FBI in December 1957. Nichols has since boasted, "I could have had anything I wanted in the FBI,"[6] but he accepted Rosenstiel's offer to become executive vice-president of Schenley at one hundred thousand dollars a year, and fringe benefits. Before accepting the job, Nichols said, he checked out Rosenstiel completely. The check, he admitted, included the FBI files. He found nothing adverse. Later he admitted to the New York Joint Legislative Committee on Crime that he knew nothing of the Prendergast-Davies case involving the brothers-in-law of Rosenstiel and Torrio, until he "read about it" in 1970. Interestingly enough, he was first introduced to Rosenstiel by George Sokolsky, one of the founders of the American Jewish League Against Communism. He also knew exbootlegger, Joe Linsey, he said, but didn't know that Linsey had solicited Meyer Lansky for contributions to Brandeis University "until I read it in the papers."

Presumably, Nichols was more convincing in his efforts on behalf of the Forand Bill in 1958 than he was in selling Rosenstiel's virtues in 1971. The bill provided that the taxpaying period for stored liquor be extended from eight to twenty years. Nichols, who had represented the FBI on Capitol Hill, admitted he lobbied for the Forand Bill even after being confined to bed. As he described it:

While I was recovering from a heart attack at the time, I did exercise my right of petition in discussing the merits of the bill. The great job of advocacy before the Committee was performed by a colleague, Ralph Heymsfeld, now deceased. The Company

167

[Schenley] did have a service office in Washington. But any charge or suggestion that money was passed to obtain favorable votes is a lie.[7]

Not only did Schenley get the relief it wanted—thus saving the company from bankruptcy—but Schenley proved it could make money as well as save it. Senator Thruston Morton of Kentucky, in a speech opposing some provisions of the bill, noted that on July 25, 1958, when the Senate Finance Committee approved the bill, Schenley's stock suddenly soared. Morton commented:

Mr. President, I think the committee adjourned about 10 minutes of 1, having taken this action. I think the stock exchange closes at 3 o'clock. In those two hours and ten minutes, Schenley stock sold in the amount of 103,000 shares. It was the second most active stock, and it increased ten percent in value.

On Friday, August 1, the bill was actually reported—on the previous Friday it had been ordered reported—and Schenley stock took another spectacular leap and was the most active stock on the board. On Monday, August 4, yesterday, it was again the most active stock on the board and closed at $30.50 per share. Earlier this year the stock sold at $18. This spectacular rise of 67 percent can be attributed only to the fact that the investor and speculator believe this bill gives a windfall to Schenley. I do not believe the American investor and the American speculator can be so far off.[8]

Morton's efforts—and that he was sympathetic to Schenley rivals cannot be doubted—were futile. The bill passed, and Schenley had been bailed out in de luxe style. Rosenstiel's "bad bet" of 1950 had turned out very profitably even if there had been no third world war as he had anticipated.

While Nichols was checking out Rosenstiel prior to quitting the FBI, the nation was shocked by a gathering of Mafia hoods near Apalachin, New York. The meeting represented a desperate effort by leaders of the Mafia to organize opposition to Meyer Lansky who, gradually over the decades, had become unofficial chairman of the board of the national crime syndicate. The Mafia convention was originally called by Albert Anastasia who was attempting to depose Lansky as boss of Cuban gambling. Anastasia was murdered on October 25, 1957, so his allies held the scheduled meeting without him. State police broke it up, and the heat kept the Mafia immobilized for months, much to Lansky's amusement.[9]

While not fully understood, the meeting at Apalachin was clear-cut evidence of the power of organized crime, and as such it couldn't be ignored by the Eisenhower-Nixon administration. Hoover wanted no part of an attack on the syndicate—at this late date he still refused to admit that there was a Mafia—so on April 10, 1958, Attorney General William P. Rogers announced the formation of a "special group" in the Justice Department to investigate the syndicate. Milton R. Wessel, a Harvard Law School graduate and former assistant United States attorney was appointed head of it. Exactly a year after the group was formed, the news broke that the group was being disbanded—although Mafia figures who had attended the Apalachin meeting were being prosecuted. Wessel commented later that "according to the stories, our unit was dissolved because we had aroused the jealousy of older agencies that resented our authority over crimes in their jurisdiction."[10]

Other sources close to the situation put the blame entirely on John Edgar Hoover. Wessel and his men had apparently received too much publicity to suit Hoover. Their activity had made the FBI suffer in comparison. Before calling it quits, the special group prepared a final report that began as follows:

This report recommends a streamlining of federal criminal prosecution to equip it to deal effectively with modern syndicated crime.

Syndicated crime today presents a serious threat to our society. The splintered structure of American criminal law enforcement is the primary cause of law enforcement breakdown, not substantive law.

It is a startling fact that nowhere in Government does there exist a permanent force capable of unifying action of the thousands of federal, state, local and special law enforcement units all over the country. Nowhere is there even a clearing house to which police or prosecutors can turn for advice on where criminal intelligence can be found.

The remedy is to create the Attorney General's Office on Syndicated Crime, with the mission of serving as the nerve center maintaining communication between the law enforcement units, and as the cohesive force in a truly Unified Prosecutive Effort against syndicated crime.

The work of the Special Group on organized crime has established the existence of nationwide crime syndicates in the United States beyond any doubt.

While the existence of crime syndicates cannot be controverted, present criminal prosecution has yet to pierce a syndicate heart, although it sometimes convicts a few of the leaders.

Later in the report there was this discussion:

Syndicated crime has undergone great changes in the last thirty years. Indeed, the most startling developments have come only since World War II, paralleling the tremendous growth in our economy and scientific advances in the fields of communication and transportation. While government has created a new socioeconomic structure in dealing with the modern economy, it has done little to enable criminal law enforcement to deal with modern syndicated crime.

Not many years ago the most serious social threat was from crimes directed against person and property, such as burglary, kidnapping, or bank robbery. Commercial crimes such as labor, antitrust or securities law violations existed, but were not usually engaged in by syndicate members and were of relatively lesser importance.

Today, members of modern syndicates have moved into the very lucrative economic areas created by our ever growing national wealth. While doing so they have developed techniques which tend to render ineffective the ordinary methods of prosecution geared largely to crimes against the individual and property. . . .

Just as with big business, management of the syndicate operates on a very different level and often miles away from operation. This separation has two important consequences to law enforcement. First, each level operates as insulation to the higher level, since criminal law enforcement loses effect the further it strays from the specific, physical criminal act. Second, the leaders can remove themselves from the subpoena power of any particular local prosecutor. Even the most vigorous local district attorney finds it virtually impossible to investigate where the real culprits are outside his subpoena jurisdiction.

Experience has taught syndicate members to acquire the services of highly qualified attorneys and accountants. Penetration of the cloak of legitimacy created by their efforts is sometimes almost impossible, and frequently requires years of painstaking digging into documents and records.

Along with the graduation of syndicated crime into commercial areas has come an ever increasing use of the *techniques of modern public relations to deceive the public,* create the appearance of legitimacy and enable close relationships *with important public officials.* Substantial *charitable and political contributions* are the rule; membership in religious, fraternal and civic organizations a necessary part of life. The profits of criminal operations are being more and more channeled into legitimate investments in business and industry. The result is that some of the most important syndicate leaders *are men of outstanding public reputation with no criminal records, or at least none for two or more decades* [emphasis added].

The special group noted in passing "a real hunger for the Unified Prosecutive Effort against syndicated crime, particularly on the local level," and cited as evidence "the tremendous welcome and response given to the initial efforts of the Special Group." It then recommended the establishment of a small unit, the Office of Syndicated Crime, on a permanent basis within the Justice Department, which would have the responsibility of coordinating organized crime investigations and prosecutions. The report concluded:

The function of the temporary syndicated crime task force is to point the way. That way is now clear. It is to create a new and permanent force in government, providing the catalytic action and unification of effort which can bring the leaders of the criminal underworld to the bar of justice.[11]

The way may have indeed been clear, but the Eisenhower-Nixon administration had no intention of pursuing it. Wessel was later to write:

Our staff's biggest disappointment is that a recommendation made in our official report has not been adopted. We advocated the creation of a permanent task force to concentrate on criminal syndicates. . . . Strong opposition to the idea has been expressed by people who contend that crime and racketeering are primarily local problems.[12]

171

That opposition was led by John Edgar Hoover.

Ironically, perhaps, the Wessel group was to achieve vindication in 1961, when Robert Kennedy became attorney general and set up an Organized Crime and Anti-Racketeering Section within the Department of Justice. He did so in the face of strong opposition from Hoover, but as brother of the President, Kennedy had more political influence than William P. Rogers in the Eisenhower-Nixon days. Wessel had only one criticism of Kennedy—his failure to fire Hoover.[13] Rogers, Secretary of State under President Nixon, has never satisfactorily explained his reasons for disbanding the special group or his failure to implement its recommendations. No explanation is really needed, of course. The special group was formed in response to the public outcry over the Apalachin meeting. When it had served its purpose, when the public turned to other things, it was forgotten. Obviously there was no real understanding of, or interest in, the problems of syndicated crime—or, at least, not enough to make it worth defying the all-powerful Hoover.

One of the personalities to whom the public turned in 1959 was Fidel Castro. His sudden and entirely unexpected defeat of Batista captured the imagination of the public. For a brief period Castro was a popular hero. He came to New York—bringing with him some chickens and his American mistress, Ilona Marita Lorenz. The chickens had their necks wring in Castro's hotel suite, and the girl was later discarded. She fled to Miami and joined the anti-Castro rebels then training for an invasion in the wilds of the Everglades. Meanwhile, as right-wing forces put pressure on the government, Castro was driven into the arms of Russia. He had little choice, if he wanted to survive.

Why did the right wing oppose Castro while there was still opportunity to keep him friendly to this country? There were several reasons, but the most important was his attack on the national crime syndicate. He literally tossed the gangsters out of Cuba, closed their casinos, and shut down their plush brothels. Syndicate figures like Meyer Lansky lost very little of their own money—they were too smart for that—but their allies in business lost many millions. Lansky did lose, however, a gambling empire that had made millions in the past and could have been expected to make more in the future if things had worked out. Lansky himself was not one to cry over bad luck; he turned immediately to the Bahamas and began the patient intrigue that eventually established a new gambling empire even closer to the shores of Florida.[14] But the loss of Cuba rankled others—and the possibility of regaining power was not forgotten for a moment.

Gradually, thanks to the efforts of the right-wing press, public sentiment turned against Castro. He was driven steadily and surely into the arms of the Communists. Every step in that direction was hailed as proof he was a secret Communist. Soon the cries of alarm sounded throughout the land. Without saying a word to the public, the Eisenhower-Nixon administration began training Cuban refugees for a counter-revolution. The work went on quietly, behind the scenes, dependent to a large degree on the need for preparing the American people. The situation was almost ripe when the 1960 elections rolled around. Nixon, if elected, expected to carry on the program he had helped to develop under Eisenhower.

John F. Kennedy, on the other hand, was inclined to take a more tolerant view of Castro. Early in 1960 he had written about the "wild, angry, passionate course," of the Cuban revolution, and described Castro as "part of the legacy of Bolivar." Unlike the right-wingers, he had no doubt that "the brutal, bloody, and despotic dictatorship of Fulgencio Batista" had been the prime cause of Batista's downfall. Kennedy even wondered whether Castro might not have taken "a more rational course" had the Eisenhower administration not backed Batista "so long and so uncritically" and had been more receptive during Castro's visit to Washington. In October 1960 as the campaign waxed warm, Kennedy tempered his views somewhat. But he concluded a speech at Cincinnati with these words: "While we were allowing Batista to place us on the side of tyranny, we did nothing to persuade the people of Cuba and Latin America that we wanted to be on the side of freedom."[15]

Unfortunately for Cuba, and for the United States, the 1960 elections came two years too late. Had Kennedy been President when Castro achieved power on January 1, 1959,

173

the history of Cuban-American relations might have been much different, and the world might have avoided its near brush with nuclear disaster during the missile crisis of 1962. By the time Kennedy had won the office, he had been largely "locked in" to a hard position by two years of reaction on the part of Eisenhower, Nixon, and Dulles. Castro had turned to Communism, having nowhere else to go, and the stage was set for tragedy. One of Eisenhower's last official acts was to break off diplomatic relations with Cuba. It was as if the outgoing Republicans wanted to tie Kennedy's hands to make sure he could do nothing to improve relations with Castro. Behind the scenes, pushing hardest, was Nixon, and behind Nixon was the entire complex structure of big business and organized crime.

The big miscalculation at the Bay of Pigs was the underestimation of Castro and his hold on the Cuban people. Prior to 1959, the right wing had dismissed Castro as a bearded nut, refusing to believe, until the actual moment of his flight, that Batista could be overthrown. After 1959, the popular belief in right-wing circles was that Castro was a tyrant who held power only by virtue of his armed forces and that, given the slightest excuse, the Cuban people would rise against him. The ill-starred invasion by disorganized Cuban refugees was supposed to provide that excuse. The supposition was that, once news of the landing circulated, the invaders would have little to do but march in and take control.

That organized crime shared the right-wing's belief is shown by confidential police records in the Bahamas. Waiting in Nassau with a fortune in cash was a small band of syndicate leaders headed by Joe Rivers, whose real name was Silesi. In Batista's day, Rivers had worked for Lansky at the Habana Hilton. He fled Havana on January 8, 1959, but returned briefly in February when Castro allowed the casinos to reopen in a short-lived experiment to see if they could be operated without gangsters in control. When it became apparent that the mob was back in business, Castro closed the casinos for good. Rivers was forced to flee again.[16] Now he was waiting, ready to march triumphantly back into Havana and set the roulette wheels spinning again.

Castro proved more than a match for the invaders; the

Cuban people did not rise. The Cuban refugees captured by Castro were later ransomed and returned to Miami where today they still dream of victory. Most of them recognize, however, that it can come only after a third world war. Kennedy profited by the fiasco, although his administration received much criticism that might more properly have been directed at the Eisenhower-Nixon administration. When the next Cuban crisis developed, he was prepared.

Organized crime did not acknowledge defeat so readily. It had cooperated with the CIA by trying to kill Castro during the Bay of Pigs invasion, and it continued its efforts to "bump him off" after the invasion failed. A key man in the conspiracy was Johnnie Roselli, a Chicago gangster who had been convicted—and quickly paroled—in the movie-extortion case discussed earlier. Roselli knew his way around Hollywood, and around the plush casinos of Las Vegas and Havana. At the behest of the CIA, Robert Maheu, a former special agent of the FBI turned Washington public relations man, was involved in setting up some of the preliminary contacts.

In what might be called "Operation Underworld II," the conspirators—allegedly working for the CIA—tried to poison Castro. The syndicate's problem was to find someone close enough to, and trusted enough by, Castro to put the poison in the dictator's food. Once located, the poisoner would be promised a million dollars when the plot succeeded. Organized crime would pay the reward, and considered it cheap at the price. The first attempt occurred on the eve of the Bay of Pigs invasion. Castro was indeed said to be ill after the attempt, but he made a quick recovery. Another attempt to poison Castro followed. When poison failed, at least four attempts were made to land teams of assassins in Cuba armed with high-powered rifles equipped with telescopic sights. Finding volunteers in Miami was not difficult; the town was full of gangsters who had served under Batista. Some of those gangsters eventually turned to abortions, others turned to narcotics. Miami became the port of entry for a flood of hard drugs. In time the operators would be termed "the Cuban Mafia," but they got their start under Batista and Lansky.

Roselli himself personally delivered several of the assassination teams to the shore of Cuba in high-speed boats. Once a boat was shot out from under him, but the occupants were picked up by the other boat and escaped. According to syndicated columnist Jack Anderson, who disclosed part of the story in 1971, the CIA assigned two trusted operatives to the conspiracy and paid only their expenses. Roselli, on behalf of the crime syndicate, paid for everything else, including the expensive boats.[17] Cover for the syndicate's operations was provided by Cuban refugee groups, who continually plotted to overthrow Castro and at intervals even landed armed men in Cuba. Eventually, the United States cracked down on the refugees. Several weapon caches were confiscated in the Everglades and the Florida Keys. Apparently all or at least most of the men put ashore in Cuba were killed or captured. Unfortunately, the full story of organized crime's private war against Castro remains a mystery. Perhaps the CIA knows what happened, but its secrets are guarded more closely than those of the FBI.

Former FBI agent Maheu soon found another assignment when a number of Las Vegas casinos were sold to billionaire Howard Hughes. Maheu was given the job of administering the casinos while Hughes remained invisible in the penthouse of the Desert Inn, formerly the pride of the Cleveland syndicate. Despite Hughes's ownership, which was supposed to "launder" the "action," Moe Dalitz, that old rumrunner and partner of Lansky, remained behind the scenes. Dalitz had been involved in an interesting caper that had brought the casinos of Las Vegas some unwelcome attention. Through Sam Garfield, a mutual friend of Dalitz and Lansky, members of the old Cleveland syndicate entered into some complex deals with Alexander Guterma, the mysterious "mad Russian" of high finance. Among other things, Guterma convinced the gamblers that by going public they could make a pile of money and still retain control of the Desert Inn. United Hotels, Inc., was formed in April 5, 1956, and stock was sold.

The experiment didn't last long. For various reasons, among them a fear that details of a casino's operations might have to be disclosed at a stockholders' meeting, the syndicate men decided it was a bad idea and pulled back. They formed another corporation, United Resorts Hotels, Inc., and bought back all their stock. With help from Lawrence A. Wein, a New York tax expert, they turned the confusion to their advantage by finding a quite legal devise that made a dividend distribution into a capital gain. The tax savings amounted to millions.[18]

In less than a decade the device of creating publicly owned corporations to control gambling casinos came into general use. It proved to be the perfect method, in conjunction with Swiss banks and giant overseas mutual funds, of concealing the real ownership of the casinos. Various corporations such as Benguet, Parvin-Dorhmann, and Resorts International came in time to dominate the casinos of Las Vegas and the Bahamas.

Dalitz and his crew, however, found their association with Guterma to be a bit embarrassing when indictments were returned in one of Guterma's major stock swindles, the United Dye and Chemical Corporation case. Several of the gamblers were involved in the swindle and were indicted.

Several years later when Robert Kennedy's organized-crime section took a look at the Guterma situation, Roy Cohn was indicted on perjury charges. It developed that Cohn, who had become something of a wheeler-dealer on Wall Street, was deeply involved with Dalitz and his friends. The government accused him of participating in an attempt to thwart justice in the United Dye case by blocking indictments of the gamblers, and then lying about it under oath.

No purpose would be served here in attempting to detail the complicated case. If nothing more, the affair illustrates once more the relation of the right wing of American political life to organized crime. Cohn had invested in such syndicate projects as the Sunrise Hospital in Las Vegas. In 1960 he was Dalitz's guest of honor at a New Year's Eve party in Las Vegas. Like Cohn, Dalitz professes to be anti-Communist, and certainly he has every reason to wish to protect the status quo.

Cohn responded to the Federal indictment by charging he was being punished for his services to Joe McCarthy. Robert Kennedy, he said, had hated him since the McCarthy days and cherished a vendetta for him. He filed motions in the court asking for dismissal on those grounds. The court denied the motions. The first trial of the perjury case ended in a mistrial when a juror's relative died. In the second trial Cohn was acquitted. The verdict, of course, must be accepted, but Cohn's relations with gangsters remain a matter of record.

Cohn was not the only one to claim a Kennedy vendetta. Across the nation voices rose in protest as the organized-crime section of the Department of Justice launched the OCD—the Organized Crime Drive. Many veteran gangsters felt betrayed; they remembered that Joseph P. Kennedy, father of the Kennedy clan, made much money in the liquor business during Prohibition.[19] Their feelings were soon matched by those of local politicians who resented the determination of the attorney general, backed by the President, to end racial segregation. Once again the alliance between crime and politics was plainly visible.

Robert Kennedy's critics have portrayed him as a ruthless politician, motivated less by principle than a desire for power. Why such an individual would deliberately challenge organized crime with all its economic and political influence, the critics do not explain. They can't. For Robert Kennedy, his years as counsel for the so-called McClellan Committee was an education. Whatever his motive in taking the post, his probe of Dave Beck and James Hoffa of the Teamsters Union gave him new purpose. His investigators came up with proof, day after day, year after year, of massive corruption, of multimillion-dollar deals involving public officials, respectable businessmen, and notorious gangsters. As he was to write in *The Enemy Within*:

We found and duly proved that the gangsters of today work in a highly organized fashion and are far more powerful now than at any time in the history of the country. They control political figures and threaten whole communities. They have stretched their tentacles of corruption and fear into industries both large and small. They grow stronger every day.[20]

Given such personal insight, it is not surprising that Kennedy became a sincere foe of crime and corruption. In a curious way, his anger contributed to his ambition. Again and again he saw cases developed under his supervision bungled on the prosecution level. The desire for sufficient authority to control both the investigation and the prosecution was a natural one, and it led him ultimately to the job of attorney general and conflict with John Edgar Hoover.

Kennedy's first major victory in the drive against organized crime came in 1961 in Newport, Kentucky.[21] That Ohio River city once known as "Little Mexico" boasted the fanciest casinos east of Las Vegas, the meanest bust-out joints, and more brothels per capita than any city in the country. (A bust-out joint was a place where a sucker was not permitted to leave until he was cleaned of all cash. In other words, he went out "busted." If crooked dice weren't sufficient, knock-out drops were used. If, by some miracle, he managed to get outside, he was hit with a blackjack and rolled on the street.)

The Federal drive in Newport was greatly aided by developments on the state and local fronts. A reform movement led by the Newport ministerial association began in 1958. It gained strength slowly in a town that was almost equally divided between Catholic and Protestant. Political warfare on the state level eventually made it expedient for Governor Bert Combs to line up on the side of the reformers. State Attorney General John Breckinridge, who had ambitions to be governor, led the fight in 1961. Most important of all, the Catholic church put its support behind George Ratterman, a former professional football player of note, who agreed to run for sheriff on a reform ticket. A Catholic, Ratterman was able to end the community's moral stalemate, which had existed since before the Civil War. To achieve results, it was necessary for the state to appoint a special circuit judge who, in turn, appointed a special commonwealth's attorney. With these men leading the way, a special grand jury heard testimony from the ministers and ultimately indicted scores of gangsters and many of the city's top officials on conspiracy charges.

The battle's climax came when Ratterman was drugged in Cincinnati, taken across the river to the Tropicana Club in Newport, and put to bed with a strip-tease dancer whose professional name was April Flowers. Cooperative police

179

were called in, stripped off Ratterman's trousers, and arrested him. Luckily, the citizens of Newport and the surrounding suburbs proved too sophisticated. The bribe and the frame had been used too many times in the past. Instead of being shocked and disillusioned, the reformers rose in anger. Money poured in from churches all over Kentucky and Ohio to support the crusaders. The syndicate gamblers even closed all their joints in a last-minute effort to convince citizens that the town would die without them.

The Ratterman arrest was a civil rights violation. It gave the Justice Department the "handle" it needed to attack in Newport. The FBI, at Kennedy's direction, led the probe, aided immensely by other Federal agencies and local officials. The author even played a curious role in the dramatic battle. Although the Federal grand jury was ready and eager to return indictments, the author—then a *Louisville Courier-Journal* reporter—discovered that someone in Justice had put on the brakes. A decision had been made to withhold the indictments until after the local election on the excuse that to return them before the people voted would subject the Justice Department and the FBI to criticism for meddling in local politics. It seems a rather short-sighted view. If Ratterman lost the election because of the frame-up, all the indictments in the world would not have helped the reformers in Newport. The casinos would have reopened to run merrily for another four years.

With help from Federal officials who disagreed with the official decision, the author located April Flowers, the strip-tease dancer, and persuaded her to give details of the frame. She also placed herself on record as saying she feared that the delay in returning the indictments endangered her life. One day after the story appeared on the front page of the *Courier-Journal*, the Federal grand jury was recalled. Several days later it indicted two gamblers, a corrupt attorney, and three Newport police officers for violating Ratterman's civil rights. The jury also issued a rare report—the practice is frowned upon in Federal court—declaring that "the foul odors of vice and corruption hang over Campbell County [Newport] like a pall." A few days later, the citizens of Campbell County elected Ratterman sheriff. The shuttered casinos never reopened. On December 28, 1961, in his annual report to the President, Robert Kennedy was able to say: "Wagering has virtually ceased at a major gambling center, Newport, Kentucky."[21]

Thirty-six years after John Edgar Hoover boasted he had cleaned up Cincinnati and its suburbs, the job was really done—for the moment anyway—by a combination of Federal, state, and local pressure. Kennedy, not Hoover, deserves the credit.

Beaumont, Texas, was another Kennedy target. Its casinos were not as large or as plush as those of Newport, but they were many and they had operated for years. Robert Kennedy was later to speak of "the rape of Beaumont by organized crime." Once again, a citizen's revolt provided the opportunity for Federal action. Led by a former newspaperman, Patrick O'Bryan, the reform element weathered an amazing amount of corruption until a state legislative committee and the Federal government came to their rescue. As in Newport, the fact that organized crime could not exist without dishonest public officials and amoral businessmen was demonstrated beyond any doubt.[22]

Similar conditions were found in Hot Springs, Arkansas, and a score of other cities from coast to coast. In many of them, the OCS, as the organized crime section became known, simply ignored existing Federal machinery. A team of bright young lawyers, all admirers of Robert Kennedy, were assigned to various investigations across the county. As often as not, they bypassed the local United States attorney, working directly with Federal agents in gathering the evidence, and presenting it themselves to special grand juries. Theirs was also the responsibility of prosecuting the cases when they came to trial. The United States attorney was usually content to let them take the political risks and draw the anger of the politician and the big contributor. Indeed, some Democrats grumbled that Kennedy, in his zeal, was prosecuting more Democrats than Republicans.

As usual, the intelligence division of the Internal Revenue Service was extremely effective in making cases against racketeers. By following the trail of money, its agents were able to prove who got what and how little taxes were paid. As brother of the President, Robert Kennedy had more political muscle than any attorney general of the past. He used a lot of it to create, for the first time, a coordinated war on crime. As might be expected, his principal difficulty came with the FBI. In addition to his political clout, Kennedy had yet another advantage. His years as counsel to the Senate Permanent Investigating Subcommittee had given him a rare insight into the relation of crime to politics. It had also given him much information about James R. Hoffa, president of the Teamsters Union.

Like Cohn, Hoffa claimed that he was the victim of a vendetta when Kennedy organized a special section in Justice to investigate Hoffa. Known informally as the "Get Hoffa Squad," it was commanded by the very able Walter Sheridan. That Hoffa, through his control of Teamster pension funds, which were a source of loans, was deeply involved with organized crime both Kennedy and Sheridan knew. Yet, strangely enough, some so-called liberals joined with the right wing in protesting Kennedy's unrelenting pursuit of Hoffa. Apparently the nation was simply not accustomed to such dedication and drive on the part of high officials who, for the most part, rely on subordinates for their understanding of basic problems.

Back in 1957, Kennedy, then working for the Senate subcommittee, thought he had Hoffa nailed. John Cye Cheasty, a New York attorney, came to him with word that Hoffa had given him a thousand dollars in cash as a down payment to get a job with Kennedy and serve as a spy. The approach had been made by Hyman Fischbach, a Miami Beach attorney much involved with Meyer Lansky and the syndicate. His pay from Hoffa if he got the job was to be two thousand dollars a month.[23] Kennedy took Cheasty to Senator John McClellan, chairman of the committee, and McClellan called in John Edgar Hoover who, as Kennedy wrote later, "arrived within a few minutes and took complete control." Hoover's plan was for Cheasty to return to New York, inform Hoffa that he had obtained a job, and see if Hoffa would ask his "spy" to obtain documents from the committee. Cheasty was sworn in as assistant counsel to the committee at five thousand dollars a year—less than a fourth of what

Hoffa had promised to pay. Cheasty followed Hoover's directions to the letter. When Hoffa asked Cheasty for information, Kennedy supplied some documents. A rendezvous was set up for a street corner in Washington, and the information was passed.

The trap was set. A week later, on March 13, Cheasty passed more documents to Hoffa as the FBI watched, recording the transaction with hidden cameras. Hoffa was arrested. He immediately called his attorney, the same Edward Bennett Williams who had counseled Joe McCarthy. So confident was Kennedy, on the basis of Hoover's report, that he rashly promised to jump off the Capitol if Hoffa beat the rap. The "air-tight" case developed holes; witnesses changed their stories; the prosecutors neglected to ask the right questions; some facts were not presented. It was sloppy prosecution. Hoffa was acquitted. Williams jubilantly announced he would send Kennedy a parachute.

While the outcome of the case did not deter Kennedy in his determination to get Hoffa, it did impair relations between Hoover and the young counsel, the beginning of a long downhill slide. Kennedy felt that the FBI had not done its proper job of backgrounding the case to prevent the prosecutor from being surprised. Some witnesses apparently got away with perjury because the FBI had not dug up the facts that would have contradicted their testimony on cross-examination. Another 1957 Hoffa trial, this one in New York on wire-tapping charges, ended in a hung jury. In the second trial, Hoffa was acquitted. And so it went. The Department of Justice was controlled by a Republican administration, and all the prosecutors were Republicans. It was one of the facts that made Kennedy hungry for power. He wanted to be in a position to control both the original probe and the subsequent prosecution. Appointed attorney general in 1961, he got the power he wanted, and needed, both to investigate and prosecute Hoffa. He was determined that next time there would be no bungling.

When Kennedy established the special Hoffa investigation squad, it found potential cases in almost every major city. A promising one centered around Sun Valley, a Teamster housing project in central Florida, but cases offering quicker results were found in Louisville, Kentucky, and Nashville, Tennessee.

The Louisville case developed when Stoy Decker, head of a small Teamster local, was arrested for tear-gassing a non-union truck driver. State and Federal officials combined to hit him with a variety of charges, and he was sentenced to a dozen years in state and Federal prisons. Before his appeals were exhausted, Decker took all the remaining funds in his union's treasury and blew them in a gambling spree at Newport. Becoming restless after a few months in the Jefferson County jail, he decided to make a deal with the "Get Hoffa Squad." Robert Peloquin, veteran Justice Department attorney and member of Sheridan's team, was assigned to develop the case. He found an eager colleague in the local United States attorney, William Scent. The FBI provided only token cooperation until pressure from Kennedy was applied. Two special agents were assigned and soon put their future careers with the FBI in doubt by becoming dedicated members of the special squad.

Hostility between the FBI and Kennedy's men was never more apparent than on the night Decker, the star witness, suddenly became violently ill in jail. Hastily he was rushed to a hospital, and his stomach was pumped out. Peloquin asked the FBI to investigate the possibility that Decker had been poisoned. The special agent in charge of the Louisville FBI office declined to act without specific authorization from Hoover, and he had no intention of calling Hoover in the middle of the night to ask for it. Peloquin, on the other hand, had no fear of calling *his* boss. He reached Robert Kennedy at a Washington party and told him what had happened. Kennedy promptly telephoned Hoover, getting the old man out of bed. Within minutes the FBI in Louisville received orders to investigate Decker's illness.

The FBI agents were very amused when their probe disclosed that Decker—who had been given the soft job of managing the jail commissary—had whipped up some "home-brew," using dried raisins. The stuff, apparently on the order of Prohibition rot gut, made him very sick as well as very drunk. Still annoyed at Peloquin and Kennedy, the FBI Special Agent in charge took pleasure in calling the *Courier-*

184

Journal and telling the author about the "great poison mystery." Peloquin himself confirmed the story and made no apology. Decker, he said, could be the most important witness in the country if the decision were made to prosecute Hoffa on the basis of his testimony.[24]

Whether to seek indictments in Louisville or Nashville was a decision for Robert Kennedy. Aware of growing pro-Hoffa sentiment among liberals who accepted the vendetta theory, Kennedy knew he could not afford to lose another case against the Teamster president. The big problem was to decide which case offered the best chance of obtaining a conviction. There was strong competition between Justice Department attorneys assigned to the respective investigations. Each wanted the prestige of jailing Hoffa. Kennedy permitted each man to argue his case, but eventually he decided that the Nashville situation was the strongest.

Each case was different in detail. Both were extremely complicated. The Nashville case that Kennedy decided to pursue involved an alleged violation of the Taft-Hartley Law. Hoffa was accused of accepting payments from a trucking firm in return for a so-called "sweetheart contract" with the union. The 1962 trial ended in a hung jury, the jurors unable to agree on a verdict, but Hoffa's joy was short-lived. The presiding judge immediately convened a special Federal grand jury to investigate allegations that Hoffa had "fixed" the trial jury. Hoffa had walked into a trap that Kennedy promptly sprang, though it was many months before this became apparent.

Duly indicted by the Federal grand jury on jury-tampering charges, Hoffa faced a thorough Kennedy prosecution. His new trial was indeed delayed until 1964 by legal maneuvering, which succeeded only in transferring the case from Nashville to Chattanooga. But it did take place. On the twelfth day of the trial, Sheridan produced his secret weapon: a tall, red-necked man named Edward Grady Partin. The hitherto confident Hoffa took one look as Partin strode to the witness chair and turned pale. He knew what was coming. Partin, a former Teamster official at Baton Rouge, told the jury he served as a Justice Department spy during the trial in Nashville. Hoffa told him of his plans to

185

fix the jury, he said, and he arranged for Justice officials to witness a meeting on a lonely road between the husband of a woman juror and a Hoffa agent. Following Partin's direct testimony, he spent five days on the stand as Hoffa's attorneys tried unsuccessfully to break his story. The jury, which had been locked up during the trial, took less than six hours to find Hoffa guilty. An exultant Sheridan rushed from the courtroom to telephone the news to Kennedy in Washington. A few days later Judge Frank Wilson sentenced Hoffa to eight years in prison and a ten-thousand-dollar fine. "You have been convicted," said Wilson, "of having tampered with the very soul of this nation."[25]

Six weeks after his conviction in Chattanooga, Hoffa went on trial in Chicago on twenty-seven counts of mail and wire fraud and one count of conspiracy to defraud the Teamsters pension fund. Various loans from the pension fund were involved, including the Sun Valley scheme. Many of the principals in the various deals were notorious gangsters. A guilty verdict added five years to the total time Hoffa was sentenced to spend behind bars, and only the most naive could still question Kennedy's motives in the pursuit of the union official.

Appeals exhausted, Hoffa at last went to prison. It was not until June 1971, however, that Hoffa—in an obvious bid to win parole—at last relinquished control of the Teamsters Union. His handpicked successor was Frank Fitzsimmons. One of the first to congratulate Fitzsimmons on his elevation to the Teamster presidency was President Nixon, who happened to be vacationing on Key Biscayne while the union was meeting nearby at Miami Beach. Nixon drove to the hotel housing the Teamsters in a transparent effort to win the support of the powerful union. Robert Kennedy had been dead for three years. Just before Christmas, 1971, Nixon arranged for Hoffa to be released from prison on parole. Cynics assumed the move was but another effort by Nixon to win political support from Labor.

The full story of Hoffa's links with organized crime and with corrupt businessmen and politicians has not yet been told. It is a dark thread running through the fabric of American society, tying together many complex deals and explaining many strange relationships. A Federal grand jury in 1971 questioned Hoffa in connection with a nationwide probe of Meyer Lansky. Whether the cocky Hoffa revealed anything of value only time will tell.[26]

While the hunt for evidence against Hoffa was still underway, Kennedy moved on new fronts. He sponsored legislation in 1961 which, when passed, was hailed as the most important development in the Federal fight against organized crime since the passage of the so-called Lindbergh Law in 1932. It became a Federal crime to travel across state lines in aid of racketeering, to send messages across state lines in aid of racketeering, or even to send money in interstate commerce in aid of racketeering.

The FBI, which in the past had stolidly opposed legislation giving it jurisdiction in organized-crime cases, was now saddled with the new responsibility. Hoover, confronted by the most powerful attorney general in history, was too much the professional civil servant to protest. Like it or not, he was forced into the fight, and he entered it totally unprepared. Aside from the personal "hoodlum squad" in Miami, the FBI had almost no information on major gang leaders.

Years before, Hoover had called Longie Zwillman a "public enemy," but when intelligence agents probing Zwillman's taxes in 1948 sought information from the FBI about Zwillman they received a formal memorandum which stated in part: "Please be advised that a search of the records of this Bureau fails to reflect that Zwillman has ever been the subject of an investigation conducted by the Federal Bureau of Investigation." Now, however, Hoover had no choice. He had to investigate gangsters. For years he had blandly denied the existence of organized crime, of the Mafia. If his face was to be saved, some way had to be found to get him gracefully off the limb where he had perched above the battle.

La Cosa Nostra was the answer.

X

THE abortive attempt by Milton R. Wessel and his "special group" to coordinate a war on crime achieved one major breakthrough, which, ironically enough, was to be exploited later by the FBI. On October 9, 1958, the Federal Narcotics Bureau, working closely with the customs service and the special group, intercepted a letter sent by courier from Sicily. The Narcotics Bureau recognized a voice from the past. The letter came from that old Mafia trouble shooter, Nicola Gentile, who was convicted on narcotics charges in 1936 after his services in the Masseria-Maranzano war had gone unrewarded by the "young Americans" under Lucky Luciano. Gentile, as might be expected, was still unhappy in 1958, and still hoped to receive the recognition and the wealth he thought his just due.

The letter was to an old colleague, Joe Biondo. Gentile, now seventy-three years old, told Biondo: "You followed me in all things and for all things. The road you have taken by virtue of your intelligence has brought you to a superior social level so that today you are a LEADER and well regarded . . ." A recital of all the wrongs done to Gentile followed. Piously, he went on to admit that "during my lifetime I have made some errors, but as Jesus said, 'Let him who is without sin cast the first stone.' " He concluded his letter with an appeal for aid. He owed, he said, two hundred thousand lire to the Bank of Sicily. "I must get rid of this debt in order to breathe," he wrote, "and get my last daughter a job in the bank. She cannot get this position unless I pay off the debt. This really hurts my conscience so that, before I leave this life, I want to get my daughter a job."[1]

The Narcotics Bureau, which had been talking to itself about the Mafia for years, arranged to have an agent meet Gentile in Sicily and pose as an emissary from Biondo. When they met, the agent handed Gentile one half of a dollar bill and asked the old man to produce the matching half which, he said, had been sent by mail from America. Gentile, of course, knew nothing of it, but desperate to get the money he assumed the agent carried, he began talking to convince the "emissary" that he was indeed the right man. When the agent at last revealed his true identity, Gentile was terrified. He agreed to cooperate with the agent if only the incident would be kept confidential.

The Italian police were also interested in the Mafia and in Gentile's activities since jumping bond in 1936 and returning to Sicily. Gentile proceeded to write a long, book-length account of his career, beginning with his arrival in the United States and continuing into the present. The Italian police took charge of the second half of the manuscript. The special group obtained the first half, which dealt with Gentile's American career. The manuscript, written in Sicilian, was eventually filed away in the Justice Department.

When, in 1961, Robert Kennedy launched his coordinated war on crime and forced the FBI into the arena, Gentile's manuscript came to Hoover's attention. He ordered a Sicilian-born special agent to translate it into English. Upon reading it, or so say FBI sources, Hoover for the first time became convinced that yes, there was indeed a Mafia.[2] His realization of facts long accepted by the Narcotics Bureau and many others did not, of course, solve the public relations problem Hoover had created for himself by denying for so many years that there was a Mafia.

At this point it should be clearly noted that Hoover's refusal to face reality in the past was based on policy and carefully calculated. To admit the existence of a Mafia, of organized crime in any form, would have made it difficult to insist that the problem of crime control could be left to local police agencies. A nationwide criminal conspiracy would have required a nationwide Federal effort. Apparently Hoover did not want to become involved in such a drive. One can imagine that to become involved would have forced him to investigate friends, particularly his right-wing supporters who were deeply involved in business and politics. And it might have damaged his precious reputation. In 1961, however, Hoover had no choice; Kennedy had thrust him into the battle, kicking and screaming. Hoover's problem as always was self-preservation. How could he acknowledge the existence of organized crime without admitting his past failures?

While greatly enjoying Hoover's personal embarrassment, the organized crime section under Kennedy recognized that Hoover's prestige, however undeserved, could be a tremendous asset in convincing a confused public of the need for a concerted attack on crime. They reasoned that if Hoover's face could be saved so that the FBI could be committed to the battle, later would be time enough to allow the old director to retire. Circumstances, and Hoover's skill with public relations, were to frustrate this plan.

The obvious public relations gambit was to let Hoover discover a new menace, sell it to the American people, and mobilize his forces against it. That this approach was rank hypocrisy and a fraud on the public seemed unimportant at the time. The goal was to fight crime—not humiliate Hoover. As one high Justice official told this author: "Hoover could call the Mafia the YWCA if he wanted to. We didn't care. All we wanted was to get him into the fight."

Obviously, Gentile's manuscript could not be openly used. Too many people knew about it and about how it was obtained. Moreover, Gentile had referred only to the Mafia and the Honored Society. What the FBI needed was a live, convincing body who could testify. It also needed a new name for the old menace.

The organized crime section, unlike the FBI, was never under any illusion that the Mafia was all, or even the most important part, of organized crime. Gambling, the source of much of the syndicate's revenue, was largely controlled by Meyer Lansky and his associates. Most of those associates were of Jewish background, descended from East European Jews who fled from Germany and Russia around the turn of the century. Irish elements were still important in crime, as were men of other ethnic backgrounds. Basically, organized crime in the 1960s was still a "combination," and the Mafia, as such, was but a minor part of the whole. Yet, as a Justice official told this author at the time, the Mafia had certain advantages from a public-relations viewpoint, which was, of course, the viewpoint of John Edgar Hoover. It was small and relatively uncomplicated. Blood lines united many of its members since there had been considerable intermarriage between Mafia "families" in various cities. What's more, the out-of-date data supplied by Gentile was replete with tales of blood oaths, vendettas, and mumbo jumbo that might capture the imagination of the American people. A similar picture of the national crime syndicate, even if at that time it had been possible to produce one, would have been less easy to publicize. Americans were not yet ready to acknowledge that organized crime was, after all, an extension of the free-enterprise system. It seemed far better to concentrate attention on the Mafia, and hope, as the nation grew more sophisticated, to proceed from there at a later date.

Once again it was the Federal Narcotics Bureau that came to the FBI's rescue. It had arrested and convicted a minor punk named Joseph Valachi. A resumé of narcotics peddlers prepared by the Narcotics Bureau prior to Valachi's sudden fame contains this entry:

VALACHI, Joseph—Bronx, N.Y.; FBI #544

His criminal record dates from 1921 and includes entries for concealed weapons, burglary and robbery. For many years Joseph VALACHI was a member of one of the large criminal syndicates in New York City, which specialized in narcotics, labor extortion, illicit alcohol and various lucrative illegal operations. At times VALACHI was employed as a strong-arm man in enforcing this syndicate's policies. VALACHI was very active in the narcotics traffic and in the 50's supplied heroin to notorious violator John FREEMAN, who has been one of the most active Negro inter-

191

state traffickers of heroin in the United States. In 1960, as a result of an investigation conducted by the Bureau of Narcotics, VALACHI was sentenced at the Eastern District of New York to 15 years imprisonment for violation of the Federal Narcotic [cq] laws. This sentence was in regard to his involvement in the narcotic traffic with John FREEMAN's son and other individuals. While in Federal prison, VALACHI killed an inmate and subsequently was sentenced to life imprisonment.[3]

Facing a lifetime in prison, Valachi was ready to make any deal that might improve his lot. His story began with an effort to explain the murder he had committed in prison. It was really self-defense, he explained. The dead man had been an agent of Vito Genovese, who was in the same prison, and had been trying to kill Valachi. Valachi soon improvised an even more elaborate plot. Genovese was in reality the "boss of all the bosses" of the Mafia, and was running that organization from his prison cell. He hated and feared Valachi, so, ergo, he had arranged to have him murdered after giving him "the kiss of death." Valachi appeared talkative indeed.

The Narcotics Bureau reported Valachi's willingness to talk to the organized crime section, and someone had a bright idea. Here possibly was the live body they needed to get Hoover off the hook. The FBI was notified, and an Irish agent who had considerable difficulty understanding Valachi's accent was sent to interview the prospect. Since Valachi was, by his own admission, only a "soldier" in the Mafia, his experience was confined almost exclusively to the New York-New Jersey area. The FBI decided it was necessary to supplement his education, and the Gentile manuscript, translated into English, was supplied to him.

One of the most interesting ways to review the evolution of the La Cosa Nostra image is by quoting from John Edgar Hoover's comments in the FBI *Law Enforcement Bulletin*, a monthly publication distributed to law-enforcement agencies.

On February 1, 1960, with the election of John Kennedy still only a possibility, Hoover wrote:

192

America has the law enforcement tools with which to do the job; we need but to use them together and with more vigor than ever before. It is encouraging that this country's citizens and governing bodies are becoming more and more concerned over organized crime . . .

[This was after Wessel's special group had made its report.]

. . . and interested in providing methods of successfully fighting it. But some, in their zeal to achieve this objective, have called for federal domination over the investigation and prosecution of racketeers. Nothing could be more harmful to the tradition of American law enforcement.

The jibe at Wessel's recommendation is unmistakable. Hoover was faithfully following his old line that crime was the province of local law enforcement.

By August 1, 1961, things had changed. Robert Kennedy was attorney general and a coordinated war on crime had been launched. On that date, also in the *Law Enforcement Bulletin*, Hoover wrote: "America is not a vengeful land, it is not a cruel land; but certainly something must be done to make it an internally peaceful land. Crime in 1960 rose 12 percent over the previous year." This note of urgency, this suggestion of required change, this admission that past methods had failed, were new to Hoover and must reflect the changed attitude of his superiors.

By January 1962, Hoover was boasting of progress: "By the exchange of valuable criminal intelligence information, the FBI and other Federal, State and local agencies are successfully penetrating the innermost sanctums of the criminal deity." As yet Hoover's enemy had no name, but he had, for the first time, acknowledged the existence of a criminal organization.

By September 1963, Hoover was more specific. He wrote:

In recent weeks, nationwide attention has been focused on the inner workings of a sinister criminal syndicate known as "La Cosa Nostra." This federation of professional racketeers is a strong arm of organized crime in America. Its illicit operations span the country from coast to coast, netting its criminal hierarchy hundreds of thousand of dollars daily.

193

Note that at this point Hoover is satisfied to call La Cosa Nostra "a strong arm of organized crime." Not yet has it become all of organized crime. In the same article Hoover goes on to boast: "Information furnished to the FBI since June, 1962, by a federal prisoner, a member of 'La Cosa Nostra' since 1930, has corroborated and embellished the facts developed by the FBI as early as 1961 which disclosed the make-up of this gang-land horde." This is, of course, a guarded reference to the Gentile manuscript, which came into the FBI's possession in 1961. That Valachi—the Federal prisoner—had "embellished" the facts cannot be doubted.

In this connection, the testimony of Thomas W. O'Brien, a detective in the central investigation bureau of the New York City Police Department, is worth noting. O'Brien testified in 1968 before the New York Joint Legislative Committee on Crime about the five "La Cosa Nostra" families of New York referred to by Valachi. He stated:

Twenty years prior to Valachi's testimony, we were well aware of these five families. We were on top of them constantly. In fact, I believe when he testified, we knew more about the organization than he did himself, and we knew more of the members. *But he served his purpose* (emphasis added).

This is startling testimony when the reputation of the FBI is considered, and there was more. Detective O'Brien noted that he was temporarily assigned to the McClellan Committee—the old McCarthy Committee—before which Valachi testified in 1963. In his words:

I also, during the course of my assignment in Washington, helped prepare the charts of the families which Mr. Valachi testified to at the hearings. And, incidentally, most of the material that was testified to by Mr. Valachi was prepared by our Central Intelligence Bureau.

Deputy Inspector Louis Cottrell, another New York officer, confirmed O'Brien's claims. He told the legislative committee on crime:

Through the use of electronic surveillance, the Central Intelligence Bureau had definitely established the order of structure

194

of organized crime and identified those involved in the so-called criminal families and their interrelationships long before Valachi took the stand. Valachi really confirmed what was long since in our files.

Thus, for all the world to see, Hoover was boasting that Valachi "elaborated and embellished" facts known to the FBI since 1961, while New York detectives were swearing that they had had the same facts, and more, for twenty years. Yet, as usual, and this time as planned, the FBI got all the praise for exposing the "new" menace. Gentile was never mentioned, and the public was not told of the work of the Federal Narcotics Bureau and the now-forgotten special group, which found Valachi and persuaded him to talk. So complete was the FBI's control of the situation that a mistake by the Irish agent who interviewed Valachi was directly incorporated into the La Cosa Nostra legend: the rank of "capo-regime" was created and appeared on official charts. The press used it for years to describe the official next in rank to the capo—the boss of the family. Detective O'Brien put it this way: "I understand from Valachi that actually what he meant was capo decina, or head of ten, but this here got confused with capo-regime." Gentile had indeed used the term "capo decina," noting that Al Capone had achieved that status in Chicago, but nowhere did he use the word, "capo-regime." In all likelihood, Valachi had not done his homework with the Gentile manuscript and managed to confuse the Irish FBI agent. For some time the FBI followed the erroneous nomenclature, even getting it used by the President's Commission on Law Enforcement in its official report. Only recently has the term been dropped and "capo decina" substituted. No explanation was given for the change.

The origin of the name Hoover espoused, La Cosa Nostra, is another story. Gentile never used it, referring always to the organization as the Mafia and/or the Honored Society. But for the purposes of FBI public relations, it was essential that a new name be used. Ironically, it was in the transcripts of illegal wiretap conversations that Hoover found what he needed. In some conversations tapped by the FBI in the New York area, the words "cosa nostra" appeared. They were code words, nothing more. Just as bootleggers in telephone conversations referred to their liquor as "stuff" or "white," Mafia leaders used substitute words when talking about their secret organization. "Cosa nostra" meant, literally, "Our thing," and it was convenient slang. But it was too informal for the FBI, which dressed it up. "La Cosa Nostra" sounded much more impressive, even if it meant "The Our Thing." At any rate, the term was put into the mouth of Joe Valachi.

After the McClellan Committee hearings, La Cosa Nostra was the talk of the nation. The hearings in 1963 were televised and proved to be the best crime show since Frank Costello testified before Estes Kefauver in 1951. Handsome in a bluff way, Valachi's garbled English and obvious lack of education fitted the public's conception of a gangster. Few could follow his complicated account of the Masseria-Maranzano war, but to achieve his purpose Valachi didn't have to make sense. The appearance of reality was all that was wanted. As Detective O'Brien testified later: "We felt by producing Valachi, seeing that he was willing to testify, producing him and letting the general public see him, they would get an idea of organized crime."[4] They got an idea, all right, but it was not the correct idea. And the end results were a disaster.

Following the murder of President John Kennedy and the subsequent resignation of Attorney General Kennedy, John Edgar Hoover was able to perpetuate his own image of organized crime. Everything that conflicted with the FBI's vision of La Cosa Nostra—recent as it was—was ignored or twisted to fit. Public attention was shifted to men with Italian names, and the real leaders of organized crime were left undisturbed. The press, ready to print anything, so long as Hoover and the FBI vouched for it, fell in line and magnified the hoax. Police agencies, having little information of their own and, in any case, unwilling to contradict the FBI, joined the chorus. It was so easy to blame the mythical La Cosa Nostra for everything—particularly easy when contrasted to the job of penetrating the insulation with which such men as Lansky were protected.

Nevertheless, a few voices were raised in dissent. Virgil Peterson, executive director of the venerable Chicago Crime Commission—a man who had been fighting the syndicate for decades—made this comment in his 1963 report on crime:

Following Valachi's testimony, organized crime in the United States was widely depicted as being under the rule of La Cosa Nostra with its secret initiation rites including bloodletting. Such a version is a highly oversimplified and unrealistic picture of organized crime as it actually exists. Known facts clearly refute the validity of any effort to reduce organized crime to any nationality or ethnic group. . . . Based on the public testimony of Valachi, it would be a grave error to accept an oversimplified version of organized crime in America as being under the control of a single secret organization which he alone has described as La Cosa Nostra. To date the greatest significance of the Valachi testimony has been its tremendous impact on the public.

But Peterson was ignored. The lies, half-truths, and flights of imagination continued. Typical was the report that a huge price had been placed on Valachi's head. The author happened to be visiting an office in the Justice Department on the day that tale started. A reporter called, looking for a new angle. He wondered if La Cosa Nostra wouldn't put out a reward for Valachi's murder. He was told only that it was possible. After some speculation about the size of the price, the conversation ended. Next day, however, the reporter had a front-page story declaring that La Cosa Nostra had—no qualifications mentioned—offered a hundred-thousand-dollar bounty. Every other newspaper and the wire services picked it up. The conjecture became a standard "fact" to include in every Valachi story. No one ever supplied any details about who offered the reward, but the story was swallowed by the reading public without question.

Actually, Valachi's testimony hurt no one, however much it distorted the truth. Unlike the confession of Abe "Kid Twist" Reles, which broke up Murder, Inc., and sent men to the electric chair, no one was indicted because of Valachi. Some members of the Mafia may have been annoyed by the heat, but non-Italian syndicate men like Lansky, Dalitz, Eddie McGrath, Sam Garfield, Hymie Martin, and thousands of others enjoyed the charade. No one had any real desire to have Valachi knocked off, and some even considered he had performed a real service by diverting public wrath into a very narrow channel.

The FBI, of course, not only fooled the public, it fooled itself. Hoover's special agents in the field knew very well that their reports had to conform to the official line, even in the so-called "logs" of tapped conversations. If such logs are to be believed, New Jersey hoods in 1961 referred to Mafia lieutenants as "capo-regime," but by 1965—after someone in the FBI had realized the error—the same hoods switched to "capo decina."

More than terminology was changed. Facts were ignored. Those same New Jersey tapes contained references to Meyer Lansky and "the Jews" that conflicted with the official view that La Cosa Nostra ruled organized crime. A conversation recorded on April 23, 1962, between Ray DeCarlo and "Pussy" Russo, two minor-league hoods, will illustrate. The two men were discussing Jerry Catena, a New Jersey Mafia boss:

RAY: JERRY's got an income bigger than anybody around—except MEYER LANSKY.

RUSSO: That MEYER! Who's got MEYER?

RAY: Nobody's got MEYER; he's like a horse.

RUSSO: . . . JIMMY BLUE EYES.

RAY: Well him and Jerry own that—Jimmy always had 10 per cent of that Green Acres, 10 per cent of La Boheme Club, 10 per cent of Colonial Inn. I guess he has big pieces in Vegas with them too, this Jimmy. MEYER *owns more in Vegas than anybody—than all of ours put together. He's got a piece of every joint in Vegas.* They were over in New York about a week ago, I hear, JERRY and MEYER, and CHUCK KUSIN (ph) [the FBI uses the symbol (ph) to indicate a name spelled phonetically], and BLUE EYES. They were cutting up the pie from that joint out there—the joint they're robbing all the money out of. What's the name of it? [Emphasis added.]

RUSSO: The Flamingo.

RAY: Flamingo, that's it. HARRY JAMES took 6 per cent of it. I was going to take 3 per cent off HARRY but JERRY said "Don't do nothing with him because the joint is being robbed."[5]

Vincent "Jimmy Blue Eyes" Alo was for decades a close personal friend of Lansky, and his official liaison man with the Mafia. The clubs mentioned by DeCarlo were part of Lansky's old gambling empire in Broward County, Florida, that closed following the Kefauver hearings of 1950.

The fact that the FBI could hear such conversations indicating Lansky owned more in Las Vegas than all the Mafia holdings combined, and yet insist that La Cosa Nostra ruled crime is but one example of the hypocrisy involved in the entire gimmick created to save Hoover's face.

This conversation, and subsequent developments, show something else. The references to Lansky and Alo "cutting up the pie" from the Flamingo was good, hard intelligence. On record in 1962 Lansky had nothing to do with the Flamingo or any other Las Vegas casino. Yet the FBI did not act on the new information. Hoover still had done nothing nine years later when, in 1971, the intelligence division of the Internal Revenue Service presented evidence to a Federal grand jury in Las Vegas and secured indictments, which are still pending, against Lansky and the former official owners of the Flamingo, Morris Lansburg and Sam Cohen. The indictments charged them with illegally "skimming" more than thirty-six million dollars from the Flamingo over a period of ten years. Clearly, the Mafia had nothing to do with the Flamingo deal. Consequently, Hoover and the FBI weren't interested. How much more Lansky received for his "piece of every joint in Vegas" may never be known, but the official IRS estimate of his personal fortune places the total at three hundred million dollars and may yet prove to be an understatement.

There were other wiretapped conversations that should have shattered the FBI official line that attributed control of organized crime to La Cosa Nostra. For example, an entry in the FBI "log" for August 13, 1963:

DECARLO deplored the fact that the Jews wield so much influence in Las Vegas, giving the Italians only a few crumbs. DECARLO feels that this position should be reversed if necessary. He cited the Chicago Mob as one which functions properly and cannot be bought "for a ham sandwich."

An earlier conversation on May 5, 1961, given in full in an FBI report, contains a fascinating discussion of the relations

199

between Jews and Italians. Ray DeCarlo (R), "Tony Boy" Boiardo (T), and (C) are talking:

T: Remember I croaked that little Jew?

R: Yeah. HARRY.

T: Yeah, the little one.

R: Little HAROLD.

T: He told me how he wanted to help out. Sent word to JERRY.

R: Yeah, you see, if you want to kill a Jew, you're supposed to let the Jews know. When WILLIE [Moretti] killed CHARLIE the Jew—Oh, there was a helluva beef.

T: Yeah?

R: Oh yeah. CHARLIE the Jew was supplying all their guns and ammunition to Israel at the time. And the Jews knew what the hell depended on it.

C (Last Name Unknown): There's a guy helping our country helping the Jews over there. How come you kill him without an okay?

T: Yeah, I said to JERRY, how important is this guy? That LANSKY is a stool pigeon for the FBI—they're working on sugar . . .

Unhappily, most Mafia punks weren't too articulate to begin with, and the FBI's illegal tape recorders sometimes picked up other noises that garbled what was said. However, this particular conversation would indicate that the all-powerful La Cosa Nostra was not free to kill a Jew without getting permission from the Jews. When on occasion a hot-blooded son of the Honored Society cut loose anyway, "there was a helluva beef."

Another conversation a few days later indicated that the Mafia also had problems dominating Negroes as well as Jews. The discussion took place in DeCarlo's office on May 9, 1961, as several visitors waited for the boss to arrive:

SI: Niggers!

LUCKY: Oh, niggers? There's nigger bookmakers in Newark?

SI: They got more business than the white guys.

LUCKY: No kidding! How do they let them go?

SI: They were there for the last thirty years or more that I know of.

LUCKY: Even when LONGIE [ABNER ZWILLMAN] and them had it?

SI: Yeah.

LUCKY: Is that right? And nobody can cut in on 'em either, eh?

SI: No—you can't even get near them. They got the law and everything. All they do is holler cop. You know what one nigger said to a guy that was trying to cut in to him? He said, "You might have the law on your side—the State and everything else—but I got the press." He'd go to the newspapers.

But always the Mafia's attention returned to the Jews. On August 16, 1961, this gem was reported:

JOE: You know, what I can't understand—it don't make sense—you never hear of Jews under investigation.

RAY: All the investigators are Jews.

In 1961 DeCarlo became very interested in joining the Masons. A conversation recorded on October 17, 1961, gives insight into Mafia organization, past and present. At this early date, of course, no one, including the FBI, had ever heard of La Cosa Nostra. The FBI special agent listening in noted that the "group had been discussing several of their acquaintances who have recently joined the Masonic Order," and went on to record this subsequent conversation:

RAY: In two, three, more years time we'll get everybody in. We'll have two secret organizations. This is the Mafia-Mason Lodge.

[*Laughter*]

BENNY: You might get an order that all you Masons—youse better drop it or get out.

RAY: That's all right with me.

FRANK: How you gonna drop it? Once a Mason, always . . .

RAY: Always a Mason. Same as this thing. Once you're in this thing, you're always in it. You can put aside—same way

201

with the Masons. They can't do like the Masons. They can't take your card away from you.

FRANK: No card. They just can't . . .

RAY: Listen, you got plenty of Masons in the mob today. I can name about ten myself . . . There's ten I know and that's only in our crew. How about Cleveland, Chicago and different other places?

FRANK: I think you got more of the—the majority's here in New York.

RAY: It's easier out of town.

FRANK: I don't think they go for it out of town.

RAY: They go for the benefits you get out of it. They know very well that almost every judge and every prosecutor is a Mason.

FRANK: No. I'm talking about like here, New Orleans. Now they don't stand for that.

RAY: Well, they're all greasers down there. They're all greenhorns. What have they got there? JOE PORETTO and his kid are about the only Americanized guys. I don't know if CARLOS is Americanized. Is he? I know the kid is—JOEY is. JOE PORETTO is a pretty Americanized guy. Did you meet JOE PORETTO?

FRANK: Yeh.

RAY: Most of them guys are all dyed-in-the-wool, you know, greenies. The old mustache mob.

Then the boys discussed the old days. To them, as to more respectable citizens of middle age, the old days look good—in retrospect.

FRED: In the old days they did it the right way.

RAY: You bet your life. Today they're talked about like everybody knows. You never read nothing in the paper about it years ago. Today, everybody—every newspaper reporter . . .

FRANK: But at that time there was always a lot of trouble, you know.

RAY: Today you got an American mob, a Polack mob, a Jew mob, and Irish mob—they all know about this thing.

FRED: They had Jew mobs then.

RAY: I mean they didn't know about it. Maybe MEYER [LANSKY] knew about it but the rest of the mob didn't.

FRED: That's right.

RAY: That's right. Today they all know. All the Irish know, the Polacks know, everybody knows. The newspapers know. MORTIMER, he writes books! He wrote a book. Told how you get stabbed, how you take the oath, and everything.

FRED: I'll tell you one thing. The old ways, the regime, they really run it. The new guys don't run it.

RAY: That's right. It was secretive.

FRED: Forget about JOE MUCCERIA (ph) and them guys, huh? You had to do something.

RAY: Another thing is they shouldn't let nobody in this unless he croaked a couple of people. Today you got a million guys in here that never broke an egg. Just because you can make a little money . . .

[*All talk at once*]

FRED: But they're making a lot of mistakes.

BENNY: I don't think they're going to make any more mistakes.

FRED: No, it's all done now.

For the FBI, "it" was just beginning. Ignoring the current picture of "it"—the Mafia—as described, the FBI went back to the old days and resurrected the ancient Mafia. Luciano and Lansky had "Americanized" it thirty years before, but that fact was ignored by the press agents of John Edgar Hoover. The existence of other ethnic elements in crime—the Irish, the Jews, the "Polacks," was also ignored. The FBI hypocrisy is pointed up by the testimony in New York of Detective O'Brien before the state legislative crime committee. After noting that the late "Trigger Mike" Coppola was a lieutenant in the Genovese "family" of the Mafia, O'Brien stated: "One of Mike's top men was Max Eder who is Jewish. In fact, Eder is right now down in Miami running the organization down there for them." Eder operates a linen shop in the plush Fontainebleau Hotel, but he can usually be found in the cardroom, where the "action" is heavy during the

203

season. O'Brien added that "out in Chicago you have a Syrian group." In Harlem, he said, "there is a colored gentleman up there who is actually a lieutenant of the organization." For good measure, he added: "The Irish have run the docks for years and years and they are part of the organization."

It is clear that the organization O'Brien was talking about was the national crime syndicate, composed of all ethnic groups, but having contributed to the La Cosa Nostra build-up, O'Brien was not prepared to admit it. He did admit that after five years of emphasis on La Cosa Nostra, "they are becoming stronger." His "they" has to mean the syndicate. Why stronger? Because over the years the FBI sat on its tape recorders, ignoring everything that didn't fit the official line, collecting just a few nuggets amid vast amounts of trivia. For example, the "bug" on Sam de Cavalcante did reveal that Sam and Harriet, his secretary, were having an affair. More than one FBI report of the day's activities ended in this fashion:

> Sam alone in the office . . . Harriet in outer office.
> Harriet comes into the office.
> hanky-panky

It was all material for John Edgar Hoover's files. How much it contributed to the war on crime, only he can say.

In 1967 the President's Commission on Law Enforcement and Administration of Justice made Hoover's concept of La Cosa Nostra official. Few noticed, however, that it based its conclusions on Hoover's testimony. The Commission said in its final report:

> Today the core of organized crime in the United States consists of 24 groups operating as criminal cartels in large cities across the Nation. Their membership is exclusively Italian, they are in frequent communication with each other and their smooth functioning is insured by a national body of overseers. To date, *only the Federal Bureau of Investigation has been able to document fully the national scope of these groups, and FBI intelligence indicates that the organization as a whole has changed its name from the Mafia to La Cosa Nostra* [emphasis added].[6]

The Commission then proceeded to quote John Edgar Hoover saying exactly the same thing.

Hoover's prestige was never better demonstrated—and the fight against organized crime never served so poorly.

XI

*W*HEN in 1961 Robert Kennedy ordered the FBI into action against organized crime, John Edgar Hoover knew he had to move swiftly to compensate for and conceal his past neglect. The obvious answer was to use wiretaps and electronic "bugs" on a massive scale. That such devices were strictly illegal except in cases involving national security was of no concern to Hoover. As a high Justice Department official told the author: "The FBI had experienced great success with bugs and wiretaps against the Reds, so it was decided to use the same tools against organized crime."

Even today the extent of the FBI's illegal activity in the 1960s isn't fully recognized. As fast as gangsters were identified, teams of agents began what was euphemistically referred to as "electronic surveillance." From the plush casinos of Las Vegas and the posh hotels of Miami Beach to the meanest back room in New Jersey, the Bureau's eavesdroppers went to work. There was only one known exception—Hoover refused to tap the Las Vegas casinos controlled by his good friend Del Webb. Webb built the Flamingo for Lansky and Siegel, and later controlled the Thunderbird after Lansky's secret interest in the hotel was exposed. Nevertheless,

206

Hoover considered him a friend, and Hoover's friends were strictly immune.

The FBI teams kept written "logs" of all conversations monitored. Occasionally, when a conversation was of particular interest, a full transcript was prepared. The magnetic tapes were then erased and used again, destroying the prima facie evidence of an illegal tap or bug. Each bug or tap had its code number, and all logs and other reports referred to that number as if it represented a live informer. The spectacle of a respected Federal agency, dedicated to law and order, deliberately violating the law day after day, year after year, and going to elaborate extremes to disguise its activity, is shocking. Yet so pristine was Hoover's image that ultimate—if only partial—disclosure produced only a ripple of protest—and that only when some civil rights leaders such as Dr. Martin Luther King was the object of the FBI's attentions.

The King episode was unique in many respects. In 1963 President Kennedy was basing his plans for racial progress on Dr. King's prestige as a civil rights leader. This was naturally displeasing to Hoover—as a native Washingtonian he was Deep South in spirit—and to his right-wing friends. Almost as if to sabotage the President's program, Hoover warned that King was associated with "hard-core, controlled Communists." He demanded the right to "bug" King to get more information. Reluctantly, Robert Kennedy agreed, in order —so say his friends—to disprove Hoover's allegations. And indeed over the next few years it did become apparent that Hoover failed to find any proof. Frustrated, Hoover began calling Dr. King a "moral degenerate," meaning, apparently, what other FBI reports called "hanky-panky." The smear came into the open in 1968 when FBI officials offered Washington journalists transcripts of tape recordings made in a hotel room allegedly occupied by Dr. King. If John Edgar Hoover could not find a Red under the bed he could at least comment on private activity in the bed.

In the vast majority of cases, of course, Hoover had no "national security reasons" to legalize his electronic activity, so he proceeded without authorization. And, as might be expected, he did not offer transcripts of the tapes to the press.

207

For some of those conversations concerned the FBI and, if made public, would have disastrously damaged the G-Man legend. For example, on March 14, 1963, the bug in Ray DeCarlo's office picked up this exchange:

RAY: PUSSY told me the FBI wanted to get on his payroll down in Florida. I said, "PUSSY, let me tell you something . . ."

JOE: Ho ho.

RAY: ". . . they'll take your money. They'll report it. Then at the end of the year when you don't put that in your income tax—what you gave them—they've got you for income tax. They only take with the boss's okay."

JOE: Why should he let them know what he's doing?

RAY: They know what he's doing. They even told him what he's doing down there. He's got the county down there nice. The county guy fixed it—how to collect the money. He's the guy that sent the FBI to him. He said, "They want to get on the payroll. . . ."

Did Russo exaggerate? As countless other intercepted conversations made clear, the county referred to was Dade—home of Miami and Miami Beach. At the time it boasted the largest and most corrupt sheriff's department in Florida, if not the nation. Graft was well organized. The county had its own bag man, who collected from the crooks and passed the loot on to officials, and the major cities had theirs as well. All the rackets paid fixed amounts for protection at regular intervals. The FBI knew about these payments since many of the lesser crooks were paid informers for the FBI who devoted much of their time to thinking up tales to embarrass their rivals. In private conversations with the author, several hoods identified various FBI agents as being on the payroll of other crooks. Confirmation, in part, came from an FBI supervisor, who explained that the agents had to take money from the crooks in order to gain their confidence and get information. Norman Ollestad, a former FBI special agent, tried to describe the bizarre conditions in the Miami office of the FBI in his book *Inside the FBI!* and while, if anything, he was guilty of understatement, his account seemed incredible to many brainwashed critics.[1]

208

Any law-enforcement officer or agency operating in south Florida is subjected to fantastic pressures. The pressure at the FBI office is worst of all because over the years John Edgar Hoover has become friendly with many of the area's powerful business and political figures. Any special-agent-in-charge in Miami has to know Hoover's friends and how to please them. If he is to avoid transfer to some FBI "Siberia," he has to accept the fact that many friends of Hoover's friends are important figures in the socioeconomic structure the crime syndicate has built along the Gold Coast. They are not to be disturbed. A similar problem confronts the rank-and-file special agent. When, in 1966 a young "G-Man" assigned to go through the motions of watching Meyer Lansky began to take his job seriously and develop good informers, he was abruptly transferred to a rural area of Georgia. His successor on the Lansky assignment was an older man who knew the score. When he retired a few years later he accepted a job with a Bahamian gambling casino originally developed by Lansky.

A particularly clear illustration of the involved nature of relationships in south Florida unfolded in 1965 when Lewis S. Rosenstiel and some of his friends followed the example of Roy Cohn and agreed to testify before the Senate subcommittee chaired by Senator Edward Long of Missouri.[2] Senator Long professed to be investigating "invasions of privacy," but he proved selective in his choice of targets and witnesses. Much ado was made about a handful of wiretaps operated against gangsters by the intelligence division of the Internal Revenue Service, though not one word was said about the FBI's extensive activities in the same field. Most of the witnesses were anti-Kennedy, and anti-IRS. Since even before Kennedy the IRS had been the most effective agency against the syndicate, some witnesses, among them Cohn, claimed that any investigation of them was, in effect, an unwarranted invasion of privacy. Cohn charged he had been hauled before a Federal grand jury, asked four thousand, five hundred and eighty-one questions, and then indicted for perjury. Rosenstiel more simply stated that he had, while investigating a "leak" in his organization, found an "electronic bug" in his Miami Beach mansion. Rosenstiel reported the device to the

FBI, of course, and also to Dade State Attorney Richard E. Gerstein whose *"reputation for vigorous enforcement of law within his jurisdiction is well known"* (emphasis added).

Louis Nichols, then working for Rosenstiel, and Gerstein —the tall, balding prosecutor known in Miami as "Bad Eye" —took up the tale. Nichols, who was still close to Hoover, blandly urged that all wiretapping be prohibited. Gerstein was asked by Senator Long about reports that there were an estimated ten thousand bugs and taps in the Greater Miami area. Solemnly, Gerstein acknowledged that the problem was a serious one within his jurisdiction. A few months later the Long Committee continued its hearings in Miami and established that the IRS actually had four taps on gangsters' phones in the area. Who had the remaining nine thousand, nine hundred and ninety-six, neither Long nor Gerstein bothered to inquire. The FBI did not have to inquire—it knew about most of them. Long's attack on the IRS demonstrated his friendships and indicated his presumption that the FBI could be counted on to play it safe.

The complexity of relationships involving criminals, businessmen, and politicians, and the hypocrisy of the FBI under Hoover are all well illustrated by the saga of MM877-C*— code number for the electronic bug installed by the FBI in the Miami Beach office of attorney Alvin Ira Malnik.[3] The bug was planted in June, 1963, after Richard E. Jaffe, a special agent of IRS intelligence, tipped the FBI that young Malnik was deeply involved with organized crime figures in the Bahamas and Las Vegas. Shortly after graduating from the University of Miami Law School, Malnik became a shareholder in and a director of the Bank of World Commerce in Nassau. Officers and stockholders included such syndicate figures as "Nig" Devine, Eddie Levinson, and the mysterious John Pullman, Lansky's international money mover. The bank was a "laundromat," the first of several established in the Bahamas. It permitted gangters to deposit their loot under banking laws similar to those of Switzerland, laws guaranteeing strict secrecy. The gangsters got their deposits back as needed in the form of "loans," either to individuals or to syndicate-controlled companies. Thanks to modern business methods, the syndicate had more money than it knew how to handle as millions poured in from gambling, narcotics, and a thousand other rackets. Before that money could be used, particularly in legitimate business operations, it had to be "cleaned up"—given a legal source behind which the IRS could not probe. Although Swiss banks have performed this function for years, the Bank of World Commerce had the added advantage of being convenient to Florida. It was easier to make a deposit. The importance of Malnik's bank was shown by the interest in it displayed by Vincent "Jimmy Blue Eyes" Alo, Lansky's liaison man with the Mafia. Eventually Alo would go to Federal prison rather than tell a grand jury about another Malnik venture.

Malnik's principal concern at the time the FBI's "bug" was installed seemed to be the protection of State Attorney Gerstein—the man whose reputation for law enforcement Rosenstiel praised. Gerstein had invested with two local businessmen, L. F. Popell and Jay Weiss, in a stock promotion deal which also involved Malnik.[4] The *Miami News* had been digging into the smelly case and was threatening to expose Gerstein. The FBI was handling the case most tenderly because Weiss was a Schenley liquor distributor powerful enough to have Louis Nichols testify in his behalf when he got into trouble with the State Beverage Department.[5] Weiss was a frequent visitor on Rosenstiel's yacht, and was a personal friend of both Gerstein and Malnik. Popell, on the other hand, had powerful friends elsewhere—in the Mary Carter Paint Company—friends who were on good terms with such people as Charles "Bebe" Rebozo and Richard M. Nixon. One of Mary Carter's stockholders was that old gangbuster Thomas E. Dewey. In time, Mary Carter would operate a plush gambling casino in Nassau harbor. Meanwhile, it came to Popell's rescue with a hundred-thousand-dollar loan —a loan Malnik was overheard to say was illegal under Florida law.

Also involved in trying to protect state attorney Gerstein was Hyman Fischbach, the attorney who had tried to place a Hoffa spy on Robert Kennedy's staff several years earlier. The FBI log on MM877-C* for July 15, 1963, quotes Malnik as saying he might "throw some ice on the GERSTEIN matter" by having Fischbach notify "the *Miami News* that we consider the material so far printed libelous." Malnik did call Fischbach, the log shows, and after relaying the suggestion about the newspaper, he added with some urgency: "Between you and me there are a couple of judges in town that have had windfall property. It would be a real ball buster if this reporter ever went all the way with it."

Later in the day Malnik briefed Popell on the story Gerstein was supposed to tell if asked by the press about a plane ticket to New York Popell had bought for Gerstein. After clarifying details for Popell, Malnik double-checked with Gerstein: "Just say it was a social trip and actually you offered to pay it back at the time but he said, 'Well, you can pick up the tabs in New York and we'll adjust it later.'" Which is exactly what Gerstein did later tell the press when asked about the ticket. Popell naturally confirmed his story. Encouraged, Malnik decided to counter the unfavorable *News* investigation by getting some good stories in the rival *Miami Herald*. He called reporter James Buchanan to his office and tried to prove that all the malicious tales about Popell and Gerstein originated with disgruntled exemployees and business rivals. He had asked the FBI to investigate, Malnik said, since the publicity threatened to hurt the value of all stock in L. F. Popell, Inc. To prove this assertion, Malnik called FBI Special Agent John Lenihan and—as other FBI agents listened with their illegal "ears"—talked to the agent in general terms about the case. Although Buchanan didn't know his conversation was being recorded, he was a veteran reporter. The FBI listeners reported that if Malnik's apparent chummy relations with the FBI impressed him, he gave no audible sign. Nevertheless, as soon as Buchanan left, Malnik was heard to make a long distance call and boast that "any report by the *Herald* would be favorable."

A little later Gerstein called. The FBI log noted: "AM [Malnik] mentions 'real good' meeting with Buchanan. AM says Buchanan was unaware of the conv. AM had with Gerstein last night." Eighteen minutes after Malnik's conversation with Dade County's chief law-enforcement officer, the FBI log records:

212

AM mentions that Popell has given gratis stock to some Pastors, Actresses, Jockies Hartack and Schoemaker, and other well known persons. AM compares Popell's office to a house of prostitution with the secretaries wearing sun glasses and having poodles in the office. Calls the environment of the office "highly unusual." Fischbach says that Popell could be charged with sodomy and AM says Popell is the kind of guy that likes to watch 4 women perform with each other. AM anticipates having things straightened out by Mon., and Popell making them some money over the weekend. (Doesn't say how)

The friendly relations existing between Gerstein and Malnik were never better illustrated than on July 24, 1963, when the FBI log contained this report of a call from Malnik to the state attorney:

Hi Dick, thank you. How are you? . . . Now that I'm back I'll find out . . . What can he say? It's a nice spot, I think we ought to buy a piece. . . . I think that it is a hell of a deal. Why don't you invest "twenty large ones" with it? . . . Really, it's like playing crap . . . I think that they are all a gimmick. . . . We'll let you in at 1½ times our cost; we got to take the promotional aspect out of it. . . . Well, we're going to merge, we—L. F. Popell. . . . more stock. . . . Really? . . . Why don't you come on down? . . . Oh yeah. . . . Are you at home now? . . . Oh, you're in the office. . . . I have an extra apartment there you are most welcome to use. . . . I may be afraid on the apartment . . . Well, it came back with a little higher price; I think I'll get it down to 2,400 . . . OK . . . OK, I will . . . Yeah . . . OK, all right, Dick.

Contrast this approach to a key public official with the one implied in a conversation recorded in New Jersey some six months later. The FBI log gives this account of a conversation between Ray DeCarlo and Pussy Russo: on January 24, 1964:

d: I've got some guys to meet in Hoboken later. They claim they got a real O.K. The president of a bank, he's going to take a piece; he'll pay for our expenses to come down there to talk everything over.
r: On what?

D: They got an OK for a game.

R: (Inaudible) . . . I paid the Attorney General myself.

D: Who's the Attorney General?

R: GURNSTEIN (ph).

D: (Inaudible)

R: GURNSTEIN is the Attorney General. The federal attorney general is something else. Now as far as the 79th Street, Hialeah and Opa-Locka the only thing we ain't got is . . . (inaudible)

D: Who?

R: G-Men.

D: You don't need them. They got nothing to do with crap games.

R: I got everybody else and I ain't worrying about nobody.

D: That's why I want you to listen to these guys tonight.

Russo's remarks about 79th Street, Hialeah and Opa-Locka leave no doubt it was to Dade County, Florida, that he referred.

The importance of these episodes is in the contrast they offer between the old way—the Mafia way—of bribing a public official, and the sophisticated methods of the syndicate. Malnik offered Gerstein a stock deal—a perfectly legitimate arrangement. Russo boasted he had paid Gerstein directly—an illegal act if true. In the years to come Gerstein admitted he made money from Malnik's stock deals—and his reputation did not suffer. Had he admitted accepting a bribe from Russo—or anyone else—his political career would have been finished.

At the time of this writing Richard Gerstein is still Dade state attorney although the political grapevine has it that he plans to run for Congress in 1972. His situation well illustrates the possibilities for blackmail originating in the FBI's illegal activities. Suppose Gerstein is elected to Congress. That the FBI, which heard his dealings with Malnik and Russo's boasts, will have a friend and supporter in Representative Gerstein seems obvious. Under the circumstances, Gerstein can't afford to step on John Edgar Hoover's toes. That many other public officials are in the same boat also seems obvious. Here, perhaps, is the secret of Hoover's power and the real danger to our political system.

For the FBI the sometimes tedious task of supervising MM877-C* was somewhat mitigated by a bizarre drama that occurred shortly after the bug was installed. It continued for months and proved that the FBI's illegal activity offered blackmail possibilities to wiretap victims as well as John Edgar Hoover. Page three of the FBI log for July 25, 1963, gives this running account of the opening:

4:18 P.M., incoming call—Unk male places a call to Helen and asks for A.M. UM is advised AM has gone to Nassau.

6:00—Trash pickup.

7:30—Cleaning noises.

10:06—incoming call—Not answered.

10:48—Movements in office.

10:50—Voices heard and then all quiet.

11:12—AM Go out back: maybe we can catch them on the lot. AM and another man [probably Jay Weiss] leave the office.

11:42—AM and JW return with a third man, possibly the building guard. Unk. man says that he will make a report in his books. JW insists on searching some other room before they leave.

11:45—AM says if the guy didn't finish he will probably come back sometime about 3 A.M. when he is out of town.

11:49—AM mentions he might call Dick [probably Richard Gerstein].

11:57—outgoing call—AM [Alvin Malnik]—As I was walking in someone ran out with a bunch of wires . . . I would like to get it checked out . . . If it is bugged I want to find it . . . A guy came walking out of the next office but I didn't question him. . . . AM said they got the guard to let them in the office next door but they found very little there. . . . a typewriter desk and a file cabinet. . . . The guy that got away is not the same one that was in the office. . . . AM asks the man to come over there.

JW states he followed one guy down the street but he had not seen him up in the office. He said he didn't ask him for any identification but did ask him if he had been up in the law office and the man told him that he had been up in an insurance office and that he had not seen anyone while he was up there.

12:16 A.M.—AM and JW discussed what a break they had returned to the office. JW described it as a miracle . . . a divine accident.

12:21—AM and JW move apparently into another part of the office probably searching the office.

12:22—Unit shorted.

The FBI agents listening to Malnik's reaction were disappointed when their equipment failed. For no known reason, by morning the tap was working again. Thereafter, like a soap-opera serial on television, the episode was discussed again and again. Malnik made the mistake of assuming he had permanently interrupted an effort to bug his office. He felt entirely free to discuss the affair, not realizing that the FBI's electronic device had been installed much earlier and had been reactivated. The FBI was thus able to follow Malnik's investigation step by step as gradually he learned the identity of the FBI intruder and made plans to use the episode to gain immunity from Federal prosecution.

The subject of immunity first came up about a week later on August 3, 1963, when Malnik conferred with Jay Weiss and Jake Kossman, the noted criminal attorney who had defended such men as James Hoffa and "Trigger Mike" Coppola. Kossman's first reaction was to Malnik's failure to catch the intruder. "You're alerted to these things," he said. "You got a warning." Upon learning that Malnik had secured the license number of the car used by the nocturnal visitor, Kossman was more cheerful. According to the log: "JAKE: Right now, I think what you got to do is to write a letter to this—which maybe, which maybe will prevent them from processing a case against you." The discussion continued. The two attorneys tried to figure out why Malnik was a target. Malnik noted: "They see me one day in Vegas with a group; they see the same or a different group contacting me in New York . . . They probably figure that I'm being groomed for something . . ."

Kossman didn't agree. "I would tend to think they think you're a courier. I've seen confidential reports that's coming out the last few months and they take every courier there is—right on there they say such and such . . ."

During the next few days Malnik exercised caution. The FBI log noted that on some telephone calls he whispered. On August 6, 1963, however, when a call came in from John Pullman, Lansky's money mover in Toronto, super caution was in order. Malnik told him, "I've been dying to talk to you, Jack . . . I'm going downstairs and call you back . . . five minutes, Jack."

Exactly when the Royal Canadian Police started bugging Pullman's room in the Royal York Hotel in Toronto isn't a matter of public record. Although the subject of this particular call remains a mystery, over the years the Canadian police intercepted both sides of several Malnik-Pullman conversations. One, in 1966, included this exchange:

PULLMAN: Al. Got something very, very interesting.

MALNIK: Really?

PULLMAN: But you never heard anything like it.

MALNIK: Boy, I need something. . . .

PULLMAN: Listen. I want to ask you something. You know, how'd you like to have a crap game going on the Champs Elysees?

MALNIK: Oh. You're kidding me.

PULLMAN: I'm not.

MALNIK: I'd move tomorrow.

PULLMAN: I am not.

MALNIK: And how!

PULLMAN: You hear what I'm saying?

MALNIK: It would be the greatest thing in the world.

PULLMAN: I got a chance to get a license on a restaurant right on the Champs Elysees.

MALNIK: With a game?

PULLMAN: With everything.

MALNIK: Fantastic!

PULLMAN: The restaurant is there. Everything is there.

MALNIK: Fantastic.

217

PULLMAN: I must talk to you.

MALNIK: Jack, I'll call you Sunday morning. There's some probability I'll come up there as soon as I can.[6]

In other conversations Pullman and Malnik talked often of "the little guy"—Lansky—who was troubled with ulcers, and of the money Pullman was holding for him in his own name.

To return, however, to 1963 and MM877-C*. Listening FBI agents heard obscure references to big deals in the Bahamas and in Las Vegas. Malnik expected to make millions. That possibility was very much in mind on August 13, 1963, when Kossman called. Malnik's side of the conversation went like this:

Hi ya, Jakie, are you in town? . . . No . . . I don't know, I have never heard of him. . . . Did he name you? . . . Did he really? . . . Well, that's what I just told you . . . How do I know? . . . I don't know. I never heard of VO-LA-CHI . . .

In parenthesis, the monitoring FBI agent inserted, "Probably Valachi."

That and only that was Malnik's reaction when the news broke about Joe Valachi singing his celebrated song of La Cosa Nostra. Malnik, like the real leaders of organized crime, had never heard of Valachi and was completely unconcerned. He changed the subject and made no further mention of Valachi as long as the FBI bug continued to operate. Malnik had financial matters on his mind that were more important than anything Valachi might say. He told Kossman:

I'm going to buy you out for about $2\frac{1}{2}$ million in cash . . . I like to give it to you in cash so you don't have to report it on your taxes . . . Well, I've got six suitcases here . . . I have to do a lot of counting . . . Why? . . . The best protection I got . . . Better than President Kennedy has . . . deep around him, everybody knows, and the ones around me, nobody knows. . . . OK, I'll see you tomorrow. . . .

Although Malnik had six suitcases of cash in his office, he could laugh at Kossman's fears about security. It was syndicate cash; the syndicate would protect it.

218

Kossman came to Malnik's office the next day, and there was a review of Malnik's continuing investigation of the FBI. Victor Powell, long since identified as the FBI agent who had entered Malnik's office, was mentioned in a whisper. The FBI log notes grimly: "It's possible that JK advises AM to 'bump' Powell." But the next few words clarified the situation:

JK: You're not going to kill him are you?
AM: I'm going to have the Causa Nostra . . . [laughing]

Seven years passed before the "Malnik tapes" became public. The FBI, perhaps frustrated by its knowledge that Malnik "had the goods" on special agent Powell, did nothing with the information it collected. The intelligence division of IRS—the agency which in the spirit of Robert Kennedy's coordinated war on crime first told the FBI about Malnik—was left to make a tax case against the young attorney. When the case came to trial in 1970, Malnik's attorneys claimed the prosecution's evidence was "tainted" by the FBI's illegal activity seven years earlier. Acting on defense motions that stemmed from Kossman's and Malnik's planning for immunity, the judge forced the FBI to produce its logs and admit its eavesdropping. Although it turned out that nothing the FBI heard had anything to do with the tax case, Malnik's attorneys were so astounded to learn the illegal tape recorders had continued to roll even after agent Powell was almost trapped, that they neglected to move that the FBI logs be ordered sealed by the court.[7] Ultimately, after two trials, Malnik won a directed verdict of innocence, but his dealings with syndicate figures and local officials had become a public record.[8]

Because of future events, one conversation in Malnik's office, on August 12, 1963, is worth noting. His visitor was Jesse Weiss, who operated a stone-crab restaurant on Miami Beach and whose friendship with John Edgar Hoover was such that a word to the Director about the off-duty cop at the restaurant door was enough to get that officer into the FBI Police Academy. According to the FBI log:

AM and JW begin discussion of law enforcement and methods used . . . then AM mentions FBI and Dir. Hoover—

JW: But Al, you don't see anything in the paper about him; It's all BOBBY KENNEDY.

AM: That's all; nothing about him.

JW: They're taking the play away from him.

AM: HOOVER is a lost . . .

JW: Cause.

AM: A lost cause, that's all; a lost cause.

The FBI log continued:

AM: Well, does HOOVER realize this great transformation that's happening within his own organization?

JW: I spoke to him two weeks ago—I was in Washington before he went to California—he goes out to California every year—he goes to SCRIPPS Clinic in LA JOLLA—couple—goes out there every year—6 weeks ago . . . [inaud] . . . it's like he . . . he told me the same thing . . . shucks, the Bureau is shot, what the hell, he says, but what can I do, he says; the Attorney General is the boss of the Bureau, he runs it . . . dare you to defy it.

It is ironic that such men as Jesse Weiss and Alvin Malnik should attempt to blame Robert Kennedy for Hoover's illegal acts. Perhaps they recognized that had it not been for Kennedy, Hoover would never have launched a probe of organized crime.

The belief in the summer of 1963 that Hoover was "a lost cause" was a realistic appraisal of the situation. The Justice Department building in Washington was alive with rumors about Hoover's impending departure. Members of the organized-crime section were gleeful at the prospect and enjoyed passing on the latest Hoover-Kennedy confrontation story: Hoover tapping the Attorney General's phone only to hear Kennedy say that Hoover "is just too damned old"; Kennedy appearing unannounced in Hoover's private office to find the old man taking his afternoon nap; Kennedy calling Hoover to his office in defiance of the tradition that the Attorney General always visited the Director. Only political considerations prevented Hoover's immediate dismissal. It was thought best to let the veteran depart with honor. On January 1, 1965, he would be seventy, the age of mandatory retirement. What's more, the second-term campaign of 1964 would be past. Let Hoover remain until then. At that time he could step down and receive the tributes of a brainwashed nation. No one would be hurt politically.

There can be no doubt that this was the plan. White House aides have confirmed that when President Kennedy was told that Hoover could be retained past the age of retirement if a Presidential proclamation waiving the statutory requirement, was issued, he stated flatly: "We are not going to have such a proclamation."[9] Fate intervened. In 1932 the sudden and mysterious death of Senator Walsh saved Hoover's job; the murder of President Kennedy on November 22, 1963, saved it once again.

Fifteen minutes after the shooting in Dallas, Hoover called Robert Kennedy at his home, where the attorney general was having lunch with Robert Morgenthau, the United States attorney from New York. For two days Kennedy had been holding conferences on organized crime, and the sessions were scheduled to resume after lunch. "I have news for you," said Hoover, his voice without expression. "The President's been shot."

Kennedy paused, then asked if it was serious.

"I think it is serious," said Hoover. "I am endeavoring to get details. I'll call you back when I find out more."

Eighteen minutes later he called back. "The President's dead," he said, and hung up.[10]

Robert Kennedy remained attorney general for nine months, but John Edgar Hoover never walked down the hall to offer his condolences. With John Kennedy dead and another man in the White House, Robert Kennedy was suddenly, in the words of James Hoffa, "just another lawyer." Hoover obviously felt no compassion for the man who had planned his dismissal.

It is ironic to note that Hoover ordered his men into action that sad November of 1963, on the assumption that the sniper in Dallas had violated Federal law. Following the murder of an FBI agent thirty-seven years before, Hoover had pushed through a law making it a Federal crime to kill *his* men. Despite the fact that every Secret Service chief since 1902 had urged Congress to do the same thing for the President, it had not been done. Needless to say, had Hoover advocated such a law, thereby giving the President the same protection as a FBI agent, it would have passed. In 1963 Hoover was apparently unaware of the omission.

The Warren Commission, assigned to investigate the assassination, soon found evidence that the FBI, despite the millions given it over the years for internal security, had fallen down on the job. The FBI did have a file on Oswald —after all the man had moved to Russia once upon a time— but it did not know that Oswald had attempted to kill General Edwin Walker. The FBI *did* know that Oswald was working in the Texas Book Depository on the route of the President's motorcade, but it did not see fit to inform the Secret Service.

Hoover, as usual, defended the failure of his agency by denying it had failed. He told the Warren Commission: "There was nothing up to the time of the assassination that gave any indication that this man was a dangerous character who might do harm to the President or to the Vice-President." Just as, one might note, there was noting to indicate that the Russians were going to steal atomic bomb secrets until after they had stolen them.

The Warren Commission found Hoover's statements a little hard to swallow. For once, the Director was unable to force his views upon a Presidential commission, although the commission was not as harsh in its judgment as it might well have been. After noting the FBI's excuses, the Commission stated:

The Commission believes, however, that the FBI took an unduly restrictive view of its responsibilities in preventive intelligence work prior to the assassination. The Commission appreciates the large volume of cases handled by the FBI (636,371 investigative matters during fiscal year 1963). There were no Secret Service criteria which specifically required the referral of Oswald's case to the Secret Service; nor was there any requirement to report the names of defectors. However, there was much material in the hands of the FBI about Oswald: the knowledge of his defection, his arrogance and hostility to the United States, his pro-Castro tendencies, his lies when interrogated by the FBI, his trip to Mexico where he was in contact with Soviet authorities, his presence in the School Book Depository job and its location along the route of the motorcade. All this does seem to amount to enough to have induced an alert agency, such as the FBI, possessed of this information, to list Oswald as a potential threat to the safety of the President. This conclusion may be tinged with hindsight, but it (is) stated primarily to direct the thoughts of those responsible for the future safety of our Presidents to the need for a more imaginative and less narrow interpretation of their responsibilities.

It is the conclusion of the Commission that, even in the absence of Secret Service criteria which specifically required the referral of such a case as Oswald's to the Secret Service, a more alert and carefully considered treatment of the Oswald Case by the Bureau might have brought about such a referral. Had such a review been undertaken by the FBI, there might conceivably have been additional investigation of the Oswald case between November 5 and November 22 . . .[11]

Contrast the indifference shown by the FBI in Dallas prior to the assassination with the concern shown by Hoover a few days later when General Charles de Gaulle arrived in Washington for the funeral of the President. Warnings were heard that the distinguished visitor might be assassinated. The FBI got into the act. It had no facts—far more had been in its files in Dallas—but, officially, "the Director" was "disturbed." Sargent Shriver, brother-in-law of the dead President, was annoyed when told of Hoover's concern. "That's just ridiculous," he said. "We're *all* concerned. You don't have to be the Director of the FBI to know it's going to be dangerous— even the White House doorman knows that. It's a ploy, so that if anybody gets shot the Director can say, 'I told you so.' It'd be a different story if he'd turned up hard proof that some famous gangster had taken an apartment on Connecticut Avenue, or if the best agent in the OGPU had checked in at the Washington National. Then I'd have to do a double-take. But this is just a self-serving device."

Le grand Charles was even more blunt. Shown Hoover's report, he puckered his lips and said: "Pfft."[12]

Hoover could afford to ignore the sneers. They were a small price to pay for being rid of the Kennedys. Lyndon Johnson, the new President, was a creature of Texas politics and very close to Hoover's wealthy friends. His campaign manager when he won his Senate seat was John B. Connally, Jr., Connally was employed for years by Sid Richardson, co-owner with Clint Murchison of the La Jolla hotel where Hoover spent so many happy days on the cuff. Connally had lobbied for a natural-gas bill worth millions to Richardson, and he had received hundreds of thousands from Richardson's estate while serving as governor of Texas. President Johnson considered Connally almost a brother, telling him in 1964: "I think you're the only man who ever made me cry."[13]

John Edgar Hoover had other links to the new President, but his friendship with Connally was enough to assure him the freedom he wanted. Connally's importance in the conservative scheme of things became even more apparent in 1971 when President Nixon named him secretary of the treasury. Immediately, a boom began to replace Vice-President Agnew with Connally on the Republican ticket in 1972. Republican or Democrat—it didn't matter to Connally any more than it mattered to Hoover. Labels meant nothing —power was all that counted. And in the post-Kennedy era, both men had plenty of it.

With his immediate future taken care of, it was time for John Edgar Hoover to give thought to his place in history. That old public relations expert, Louis B. Nichols, had a bright idea borrowed from the past. Roy Cohn, the aging boy wonder of the McCarthy days, thought it a great idea. He joined forces with Nichols to sell the concept to Lewis B. Rosenstiel. Why not resurrect the J. Edgar Hoover Foundation, endow it with Schenley stock, and let it sing the praises of Hoover for decades to come? Back in the forties, exbootlegger Joe Fusco had the same idea and set up the Joseph L. Fusco Foundation. Its objective: "Charity."

Years before, after his first wife died, the Schenley chairman had created the Dorothy H. and Lewis S. Rosenstiel Foundation in the pattern of successful businessmen—and the nation's top gangsters. As a tax saving gimmick a foundation had immense advantages, especially if the donor retained control of its funds. Rosenstiel retained control, and over the years the foundation had given very little of its money away. Yet to honor Hoover, he agreed to make sizable contributions—from one foundation to another.

The Hoover foundation was incorporated on June 10, 1965. It immediately applied to the Internal Revenue Service for tax-exempt status and listed as its purpose the following:

1. To safeguard the heritage and freedom of the United States of America, to promote good citizenship through an appreciation of its form of government and to perpetuate the ideals and purposes to which the Honorable J. Edgar Hoover has dedicated his life.

2. To combat communism or any other ideology or doctrine which shall be opposed to the principles set forth in The Constitution of the United States of America or the rule of law.

The foundation also declared its intention "to act in conjunction with Freedoms Foundation, a not-for-profit corporation organized under the laws of Pennsylvania, so long as said corporation shall be entitled to exemption from Federal Income Tax."[14]

Don Belding and Kenneth D. Wells had decided to form Freedoms Foundation at a meeting in Wells's kitchen in 1948. Wells was an executive of the Union Oil Company of California. He became the Foundation's first president. First winners of Freedoms Foundation awards were Senator Robert A. Taft, George E. Sokolsky, and Harold Gray. The latter was the author of the comic strip *Little Orphan Annie*. Daddy Warbucks, Annie's wandering stepfather, has for many decades upheld the virtues of free enterprise and been an active fighter against Communism. Later, Al Capp, the creator of *L'il Abner*, another comic strip, received the award. Capp has been a strong supporter of right-wing administrations and, in recent years, a stern critic of college liberals. Officials of Freedoms Foundation have included such right-wing personalities as the Reverend Billy Hargis, founder of the Christian Crusade; Howard "Bo" Callaway, a segregationist; Tom P. Brady, associate justice of the Mississippi Supreme Court; and Dean Clarence A. Manion of the

John Birch Society. One would have to look a long time before finding a better representation of right-wing sentiments and outright prejudice. A J. Edgar Hoover Library is in a basement room at the Freedoms Foundation Center at Valley Forge, Pennsylvania. It boasts a color painting of Hoover and is stocked with books about the FBI—most of them paid for by Lewis S. Rosenstiel.

The J. Edgar Hoover Foundation began modestly enough. It got its tax-exempt status on October 28, 1965, some six months earlier than is usual. Nichols, Hoover's former assistant and now Rosenstiel's man, was president. C. D. "Deke" de Loach, for years the number-three man in the FBI, was secretary. William G. Simon, former special agent in charge at Los Angeles, was vice president, N. J. L. Pieper, a colleague of Nichols in the FBI, was treasurer. Patricia Corcoran, Nichols' assistant at Schenley, was assistant treasurer. The only officer not with either Schenley or the FBI, was Robert F. Sagle, a director. Sagle, a Washington attorney, was a close friend of Nichols.

To get the Hoover foundation rolling, the American Jewish League Against Communism—still alive under President Roy Cohn—gave five hundred dollars. Proving how good deeds can redound to the benefit of the giver, the Rosenstiel Foundation gave the League five thousand dollars in 1966 and another five thousand in 1967. Rosenstiel's foundation gave the Hoover Foundation Schenley stock worth $35,000, in 1965; stock worth $6,500 in 1966; and stock worth $53,350 in 1967. But in the big year, 1968, two separate gifts of stock, one worth $705,625, and the other worth $713,067.91, were made.[15]

It was 1968 before any public mention was made of the existence of the J. Edgar Hoover Foundation, and when the news broke who should have the "scoop" but that old drum beater, Hoover's friend Walter Winchell. Writing discreetly, Winchell said:

The John Edgar Hoover Foundation, the existence of which has never before been made public, is the recipient of a New Yorker's $1 million in securities. He does not want his name publicized. The foundation's president and guiding light is Lou

226

Nichols—with the FBI 24 years until retirement. He was assistant to the director.

Winchell added the curious assurance that "all donors contributed voluntarily" to the foundation, and he quoted Nichols as saying the foundation "is educational in concept. It will combat Communism and related subjects and promote Americanism."

Nichols provided additional information in 1971. In a prepared statement he declared:

> I have always had a compelling urge to do something to perpetuate Mr. Hoover's name and honor him during his lifetime. I went to him in 1965 and obtained his permission to set up the J. Edgar Hoover Foundation . . . I have never deviated from my belief that Mr. Hoover is the finest public servant of the 20th Century and it is my hope that he will continue in his post as long as he wishes.
>
> The contribution of the Dorothy H. and Lewis Rosenstiel Foundation in the amount of a million dollars worth of Glen Alden 6% 20-year Subordinated Debentures was made after the Glen Alden acquisition of the Schenley Company in 1968. *Mr. Rosenstiel announced the J. Edgar Hoover Foundation gift to Mr. Hoover in my presence* [emphasis added].[16]

On June 1, 1969, Rosenstiel got public credit for his gifts. *Washington Post* reporter Maxine Cheshire gave details including the involvement of Roy M. Cohn, and noted:

> Cohn caught Hoover's eye when the FBI director became impressed with the younger man's devotion to anti-Communist activities. Hoover, according to a former Justice Department source who knows both men well, showered Cohn with compliments and notes and photographs.

Reporter Cheshire also mentioned the chummy relationship of Cohn and Rosenstiel:

> Cohn and Rosenstiel have been like father and son. One source who knows them says that Cohn refers to Rosenstiel as "Commander in Chief." The two routinely salute each other on sight.
>
> "I never believed that until I saw it with my own eyes at an Al Smith memorial dinner," says the source. "I spotted Rosenstiel

looking around the room. He scanned every table until he saw Cohn and caught his eye. Then Cohn stood and Rosenstiel stood and they saluted right there in front of everyone."

Perhaps proving that politics does make for strange bedfellows.

XII

*T*HE boys in the backroom of Ray De-
Carlo's New Jersey office discussed on May 5, 1963, the "de-
sirability of obtaining property on Grand Bahama Island,
B.W.I.," as the FBI log for the day put it. The log continued:

> In a jocular manner DECARLO said he has always been excluded
> from Las Vegas because of his reputation, and now he will prob-
> ably be kept out of this deal which he predicted would be even
> bigger than Las Vegas. He said, "I hear Meyer Lansky has this
> guy—this Lou Chesley."

Not only did the FBI get Louis Chesler's name wrong, it
managed to ignore the role of Lansky. Despite information
from a dozen sources, it continued to insist that gambling in
the Bahamas was controlled by La Cosa Nostra with everyone from Angelo Bruno of Philadelphia to Sam "Mooney"
Giancana of Chicago being listed as the boss. More than
three years later the FBI still didn't know what was going on
just a few miles off the coast of Florida. A memo dated
"T/8/8/66" proves it. Addressed to Fred M. Vinson, Jr.,
assistant attorney general, criminal division, Department of

229

Justice, the memo was signed by William G. Hundley, chief, organized crime and racketeering section:

On August 5, 1966, Bob Peloquin received a telephone call from Harry Glazer, Bahamas Desk Officer, State Department. Glazer stated that he had received a communication from the Consul General in Nassau to the effect that on Saturday evening, July 30, the Consul went to dinner at the home of Sir Stafford Sands, Vice Premier of the Bahamas.

While at the party, which was composed of approximately 12 people, the Consul General was introduced to Frederick Frohbost, FBI SAC, Miami. Frohbost informed the Consul General that he and his wife had been in town for the past three days on a "combination social and business" trip.

During discussion with Frohbost, indications were given by Frohbost that he was greatly impressed by Sir Stafford Sands and found him to be a very charming and knowledgeable politician. Frohbost indicated to the Consul General that the FBI was going to become more active in the Bahamas due to the many problems that are present in that area.

The Consul General stated that he was amazed as to the lack of knowledge of the Bahamas problem on the part of Frohbost. He stated that Frohbost asked the Consul General to come to Miami and brief him on the problem. The Consul General indicated concern as to whether he should accept such invitation in that "apparently nobody else had bothered informing Frohbost of what the Department problems were in Nassau."

The Consul General expressed extreme displeasure over the fact that Frohbost came to Nassau and spent 3 days apparently on business without informing the Consul General's office of his presence. A suggested memo to the Director of the FBI is attached.[1]

The memo, which eventually went to Hoover, signed by Vinson, was captioned, "Sir Stafford Sands, Vice Premier, Bahamas," and it contained this statement: "The records of this Division contain information indicating that *Sir Stafford Sands is a highly corrupt politician in the pay of the gambling interests in the Bahamas*"[2] (emphasis added).

Ironically, the local police agencies of the Bahamas had been relying on the FBI for information about the horde of American gangsters that descended on the islands even before the first casino on Grand Bahama opened in January,

1964. There was a reason for the FBI's pathetic efforts to blame La Cosa Nostra for the new gambling empire. In its files, largely as a result of its illegal electronic activity, was ample information about Mafia figures, but there was less than nothing about the Jewish gamblers associated with Lansky. Moreover, under Hoover's stern, self-protective discipline, field agents didn't dare seek information about non-Mafia figures. And, as we have seen, they ignored it when they happened upon it. Yet Lansky was so important that the FBI eventually had to label him a "non-member associate" of LCN or, alternately, "the hired brains" of LCN. Although the terms themselves are absurd, this mythology enabled the FBI to acknowledge Lansky's importance while continuing to hunt for the LCN leaders it believed had hired Lansky's brains. They were never found. Undisturbed by the FBI, Lansky was able to build his new empire at the height of the hue and cry about La Cosa Nostra.

In the Bahamas the process that had begun with the introduction of bootleg cash into the island's economy, reached its logical climax, and the shape of future developments along economic-political lines became as clear as the gin-clear waters of the Caribbean. The modern history of the Bahamas began in 1946 when a former Wall Street "operator," Wallace Groves, after serving a term in Federal prison for mail fraud, began building anew in the islands. Along the way Groves became friendly with Stafford Sands, the so-called "doyen" of the Bay Street boys—that small group of white businessmen who for generations had controlled the political and economic life of the Crown colony.[3]

From conversations between Sands and Groves there emerged an idea for a free port on Grand Bahama, a lonely, thinly populated island that had seen little "action" since Prohibition days when it was one of many storage areas for rum smugglers. In the twenties Lansky had visited Grand Bahama as part of the Bugs and Meyer mob's job of expediting the flow of liquor to Rum Row off New York. Nassau had been the principal port for the illegal liquor trade, but even tiny Bimini had its share. The fourth Mrs. Rosenstiel testified in 1970 of a honeymoon cruise to Bimini in 1956. Along for the ride was Joe Linsey, Schenley distributor in Boston and an exbootlegger. Mrs. Rosenstiel gave this account:

I was upstairs having breakfast in the drawing room of the yacht, and Mr. Linsey and his brother-in-law, Dave Yaffe, were looking out of the porthole. And Mr. Rosenstiel came upstairs and they greeted him with—they always address him as the Supreme Commander—and they said, "Good morning, Supreme Commander." And he said, "Well, boys, what are you doing looking out of the porthole?" And Linsey said, "It's a little different, Supreme Commander, than when we were looking for the patrol boats."[4]

In 1955 Stafford Sands drafted and got enacted into law the Hawksbill Creek Act, which, in effect, turned over most of Grand Bahama Island to Groves to be developed as a free port. The city of Freeport was built. Thanks to such men as Daniel Ludwig and Charles Allen, known as the "richest man on Wall Street," millions were invested in the development. Freeport was not successful, and by 1960 the entire project faced ruin. Lansky came to the rescue. Driven out of Havana by Castro in 1959, Lansky wanted a new, off-shore location for his gambling empire. For decades he had considered the Bahamas, where years before Sands had sponsored legislation setting up legal machinery to grant "exceptions" to the laws against gambling. Sands had made an effort to utilize that legislation in 1946, after Lansky's first retreat from Havana, but Lansky decided to develop casinos in Florida instead. Now, fourteen years later, Lansky agreed that the time for the Bahamas had come.

Sands later admitted that Lansky in 1960 offered him two million dollars to be deposited in Swiss banks if Sands would give him exclusive gambling rights in the Bahamas. The portly Sands piously insisted he turned down the offer. Lansky was apparently undeterred, for a short time later Louis Chesler, previously described as the guy Meyer Lansky "had," appeared on Grand Bahama with a new proposal for Sands. And years later it was proved that Sands received *at least* one million, eight hundred thousand dollars in "legal fees" for establishing gambling on Grand Bahama. There was solid information that he got twice that much.[5] Chesler's proposal was to change from industrial development to an economy based on tourism. Groves agreed. Central to Chesler's scheme was the construction of a resort hotel, the Lucayan Beach, which was to be completed by January 1, 1964. In the official plans for the hotel, space was reserved for a "handball court." Lansky, of course, planned to convert the handball court into a casino.

The scale of the corruption in the Bahamas became public knowledge only after Allan Witwer made his celebrated deal for his never-to-be-published book and United States Attorney Robert Morgenthau—in 1966, still fighting the battle begun under Robert Kennedy—got his hands on the supporting documents. The resulting public scandal led to the overthrow in 1967 of the Bay Street boys by the black majority. Sir Stafford Sands, the official whom FBI agent Frohbost found so charming, took his millions and fled to Spain "in the best tradition of a deposed dictator."[6]

There was more than met the eye in the Bahamas' "quiet revolution." Lansky, having learned in Cuba the folly of basing a gambling empire solely on the power of an unpopular dictator, played a discreet but significant role in the developments. Efficiently, step by step, he cut all his public or obvious ties to the Bahamas gambling operations while, at the same time, making sure that tax revenues from the gambling became an essential part of the Bahamian government's budget. Consequently, when the blacks took office in 1967, they had pledged not to end the island's gambling, but to use the taxes received for the public good rather than private profit. This development put gambling on a solid basis in the Bahamas—and that was Lansky's goal.

Meanwhile, in 1963, the Mary Carter Paint Company was permitted to build a housing development on Grand Bahama, which was still tightly controlled by Groves. The paint company had a curious connection with the L. F. Popell, Inc., stock promotion mentioned earlier. It loaned money to Popell's company which, as FBI agents listening to their "bug" in Alvin Malnik's office heard Malnik boast, was uncollectable since it was illegal under Florida law. When, despite his manipulations, Popell's company went bankrupt, Mary Carter cushioned the blow by buying the company's assets at auction, then leasing them back to Popell, who formed a new company.

In 1966, after its housing development on Grand Bahama was underway, Mary Carter worked out a deal with Groves that provided for joint ownership and operation of a new casino on what is now called Paradise Island in Nassau Bay. Plans required the developers of the casino to build a bridge from Nassau to the smaller island, a project Sir Stafford Sands had blocked in the past when it was proposed by less influential persons such as Huntington Hartford. Robert Peloquin, veteran member of the organized-crime section of the Justice Department, reviewed the complicated deal in great detail in an official memorandum. Well aware that Lansky, through Lou Chesler, had been involved in the Sands-Groves tourist casinos developed on Grand Bahama, even though Lansky's name appeared nowhere officially or on record, Peloquin concluded that the new partnership of Groves, Sands, and the Mary Carter Paint Company was but a more elaborate version of the original. His memo concluded with these words: "The atmosphere seems ripe for a Lansky skim."[7]

A little more than a year later, however, the Bay Street boys were defeated; Sands was out of office, and Groves was discredited in the public eye. Some changes were not only necessary but desirable. Groves allowed his interest in Paradise Island to be bought out by his partner, Mary Carter, and he retired to Grand Bahama and a secondary role in future developments. The Paradise Island Casino, with its vast hotel complex, would be built and owned entirely by Mary Carter. Thus anyone who had previously agreed with Peloquin could now assume—if he really wanted to—that all links to Lansky had been cut. Ironically, Peloquin would be one of the first to make that assumption.

Vital to an understanding of what had, and would, happen, is the knowledge that an important stockholder in Mary Carter from the beginning of its Bahamian adventures was that old gang buster, Thomas E. Dewey. After giving up his own Presidential ambitions, Dewey had been a prime mover in the career of Richard M. Nixon. Both Dewey and Nixon were strong friends and supporters of John Edgar Hoover,

234

despite the fact that Nixon had been rejected when, after graduating from Duke Law School, he applied for a job as a special agent of the FBI. The underworld whispered that the Mary Carter Paint Company won casino rights in Nassau at the expense of Groves only because Lansky owed Dewey a debt for paroling Luciano from prison.[8] There was irony in the fact that in 1971 Murray Gurfein, Dewey's former assistant who met with Lansky to arrange Luciano's cooperation in "Operation Underworld," was appointed a Federal judge by President Nixon.

The next stage in the intriguing corporate saga was for Mary Carter to sell its paint division and change its name to Resorts International. Shortly thereafter, Resorts International, Inc., retained the services of Robert Peloquin and William G. Hundley, former chief of the organized crime section of the Justice Department. Under President Johnson, the war on crime had bogged down. With John Edgar Hoover directing a crusade against La Cosa Nostra, many young men in Justice and in the intelligence division of IRS began to look after their personal interests. Under Attorney General Ramsey Clark, the "strike-force" technique had been devised, requiring the cooperation of various Federal agencies on the local level. Hoover, who detested Clark—he remembered his father—refused to let the FBI cooperate, thus limiting the effectiveness of the strike forces. Many of the bright men quit, among them Peloquin and Hundley. The murder of Robert Kennedy in 1968 was for many who stayed on the final blow. A long, dark night seemed to be settling over the nation and the excrusaders knew they might be old men before it lifted.

Hundley and Peloquin were hired by Resorts International officially to keep the Paradise Island casino "clean." Nevertheless, it appears that the resort's standards were relaxed. The manager of the casino was Eddie Cellini, the brother of the notorious Dino Cellini who had played an active role as Lansky's lieutenant in setting up the first casino on Grand Bahama. Eddie Cellini had credentials in his own right. A native of Steubenville, Ohio, he had cut his teeth in the illegal gambling joints of that city and graduated with honors from the plush casinos of Newport, Kentucky.

He was working in the even more plush Riviera in Havana, a Lansky casino, when Castro took power. Returning to Newport, he served as a collector for the bust-out joint known as the Tropicana Club—the place where George Ratterman was framed with stripper April Flowers. Eventually he was indicted in Newport. Charges were dropped, and he moved to the Bahamas.[9] Although this author gave Peloquin information about Cellini, he was nevertheless retained as manager of the Paradise Island casino for a full year. Eventually he was transferred to Miami after receiving too much press publicity. In the spring of 1968, as Robert Kennedy returned to the political wars, Peloquin was asked by the casino company that employed him to work against Kennedy on Richard Nixon's behalf. He declined. Mary Carter-Resorts International strongly supported Nixon, even making its yacht available to the Nixon forces for use at the Republican convention in Miami Beach. Nixon had attended the gala opening of the Paradise Island Casino in January 1968, and now, Resorts International could recognize a natural ally for the future.

Another Nixon ally, and part of the pattern for the future, was Louis B. Nichols. Nichols has told of meeting Nixon shortly after his nomination.[10] "Lou," said Nixon, "we want to use you for a special assignment." John Mitchell, the future attorney general, filled in the details. Nichols was to set up an organization to guard against "vote frauds." It was called "Operation Integrity," and, if Nichols is to be believed, it was responsible for Illinois going Republican. "For once," said Nichols, "Illinois had not been stolen." The Illinois vote made Nixon's victory decisive.

Nixon's election assured John Edgar Hoover's continued tenure. Organized gambling continued to flourish. It had grown from the dingy back rooms of saloons into regional and then international gambling centers, and had already proved respectable enough to "go public." Resorts International offered its stock on the American Stock Exchange. In 1968 Groves led his Grand Bahama casinos into a complicated deal with Benguet Consolidated, and thus found his way to the New York Stock Exchange. Other "public corporations" such as Lum's, which began as a hot-dog stand on

236

Miami Beach, bought Las Vegas casinos. The biggest shift of all involved the mysterious billionaire Howard Hughes, who bought out the Cleveland syndicate's holdings in Las Vegas and acquired other casinos there as well.

In Las Vegas, where wealth was worshiped above all else, Hughes was uniquely beyond moral or social values. So vast was his fortune, ordinary standards did not apply. Even though he remained invisible, he was regarded with awe by everyone from the governor down. From his penthouse headquarters atop the Desert Inn, Hughes passed orders to Robert Maheu, the ex-FBI agent who had cooperated with the mob in the conspiracy to kill Castro.

Maheu, protected by Hughes's magic, worked closely with Moe Dalitz, former first-among-equals of the Cleveland syndicate and personal friend of Meyer Lansky, in the day-by-day operation of the Hughes-owned casinos. The casinos were legally owned by the Hughes Tool Company, the flagship of the flotilla of corporations controlled by Hughes, the same Hughes Tool Company that years before loaned two hundred and five thousand dollars to Richard Nixon's brother in a curious transaction that caused Nixon some embarrassment in his 1960 and 1962 campaigns. "I was never asked to do anything by the Hughes Tool Company and never did anything for them," Nixon said on October 1, 1962.[11] Events since then, however, have linked Nixon friends in Las Vegas with Nixon friends in the Bahamas.

Hughes kept one Las Vegas casino, the Silver Slipper, in his own name, enabling him to use its funds without showing the money's disposition on corporate books. In this fashion Hughes in 1968 was able to divert one hundred thousand dollars from gambling revenues to Nixon's campaign. According to Maheu, Hughes's modest goal was to permit Nixon to win the Presidency "under our sponsorship and supervision."

The courier who delivered the hundred thousand from Maheu to Nixon's friend Bebe Rebozo, was Richard G. Danner, a former FBI agent. Danner, after leaving the FBI, had been installed as city manager of Miami in the corrupt 1940s when the syndicate controlled the town. A dispute developed between two factions in the police department.

When Danner sided with one faction, the other tried to frame him by sending two men to Newport, Kentucky, to get them arrested in a brothel. Friendly Newport police—as corrupt as their counterparts in Miami—released the two men when they identified themselves as the mayor and city manager of the Magic City. A blackmail attempt followed, forcing the syndicate to intervene. In a midnight confrontation in a gravel pit, the Newport cops admitted that Danner and the mayor were not the men they arrested in Newport. Nevertheless, Danner, soon quit public service, and he was available in 1952 to accompany Nixon and Dana C. Smith on that famous gambling jaunt to Havana. When Hughes began buying Nevada casinos, Danner reappeared as the manager of one of them. Because he remained friendly with Nixon and Rebozo, he was a logical choice to transport the gambling money that Hughes hoped would help elect the next President of the United States.

At about the same time Hughes was moving into Las Vegas, Resorts International, operators of the new casino at Nassau (like Hughes, contributors to Nixon's victory) advanced two million dollars to Peloquin and Hundley to form International Intelligence, Ltd., better known as Intertel. Hundley soon abandoned an active role as eyebrows were raised in law-enforcement circles around the world. Peloquin remained active and enlisted a number of disillusioned Justice and Treasury officials, including William Kolar, chief of the Intelligence Division of IRS. Ironically, Peloquin was able to recruit a nephew of John Edgar Hoover in a gambit that vastly impressed the *Toronto Telegram*. In a long and favorable article about Intertel, the newspaper naively concluded that ugly rumors about the organization had to be unfounded because, otherwise, the omniscient and omnipotent Hoover would not have permitted his nephew to accept the job.[12]

The image of purity Intertel sought to create was vital to the purposes of its parent company, Resorts International. While the avowed purpose of Intertel was to help any and all private companies resist the black hand of the Mafia, in practice it seemed chiefly concerned with aiding corporations owning, or planning to own, gambling casinos. When legislation was enacted to permit gambling casinos in Quebec Province, Intertel opened offices in Canada. Officials there said both Benguet Consolidated and Resorts International had been "dickering" for future casino rights whenever the legislation was to be implemented. Intertel cited its experience on Paradise Island as proof that casino gambling could be kept clean. When someone mentioned Eddie Cellini, Peloquin blandly denied Cellini had any direct links with organized crime.[13]

Drives to legalize casino gambling were flourishing in Miami Beach, and were reported in New York and a dozen other states. The big argument in favor of legalization was that Intertel with its staff of experts provided the guarantees needed that organized crime could be kept out. In 1970, when legal gambling was proposed in New Jersey, Resorts International secured options on prime resort property, and representatives of both Intertel and Resorts International appeared before a legislative committee in 1971 to testify how easy it was to keep Lansky and the syndicate out of casinos. The pressure on city and state officials to find new and painless sources of revenue fostered the urge to legalize gambling. New York took the first step by permitting off-track betting, basing its actions on the dual excuse that it would cripple the mob while diverting its profits to the state. Similar arguments had been heard when the state introduced the lottery—which proved to be a big disappointment: revenues were far below expectation. New York's bookies remained in business.

Intertel's views about clean gambling conflicted sharply with those of the Kefauver Committee outlined in its third interim report in 1951, which stated: "It is the *nature* of the business of gambling and not its legality or illegality, that makes it so attractive and lucrative for gangsters and hoodlums." The committee also derided the notion that were gambling to be legalized

the crooks and the cheats will retire from the field and leave the operations of the handbooks, policy wheels and gaming rooms to honest and upstanding businessmen, and . . . public officials, who have previously been persuaded to ignore or affirmatively aid illegal gambling operations, will automatically prove incorruptible when entrusted with responsibility for controlling these same operations through a licensing system.

What finally took the bloom off the flowering cactus was not distrust of Intertel's abilities, but the Nixon recession, which began shortly after Nixon took office and rapidly gained strength. Corporations whose revenues were based on gambling led the retreat of the stock market, making it obvious that when Americans had to tighten their belts gambling casinos and exotic resorts would suffer first. This fact of economic life in 1970 specifically helped defeat the drive for legal casinos in Miami Beach. Exponents of legalization had argued that the area needed casinos to compete with the Bahamas. When tourism dropped sharply on the off-shore islands, that argument lost much of its effect.

Intertel's biggest coup came at 8:10 P.M., Las Vegas time, on November 25, 1970. A station wagon, a sedan, and a closed van backed up to the entrance to Distinctive Apparel at the Desert Inn. Distinctive Apparel was the exclusive clothing store formerly known as "Goldwater's of Nevada," the Goldwaters being the family of a well-known Arizona politician. A filing cabinet and other items were taken from the clothing store and loaded in the van. Suitcases were put in the station wagon. Simultaneously, five limousines bearing California plates shot off conspicuously toward McCarren Field south of Las Vegas. A few minutes later the mysterious Howard Hughes appeared, climbed into the van, and the little caravan headed for Nellis Air Force Base northeast of Las Vegas where a Lockheed JetStar waited. At 9:24 P.M. the plane took off. The crew of the JetStar had its orders: "Your life depends upon you not looking to the rear. Who's aboard that plane is none of your business."[14] They did know they were bound for the Bahamas and Paradise Island. Arriving in Nassau after midnight, the JetStar was met by two panel trucks from the Britannia Beach Hotel, one of several hotels on Paradise Island. Security men under the supervision of Jim Golden loaded the baggage, and Hughes, into the trucks.

Golden was a former Secret Service agent assigned to the White House detail until 1957, when he was assigned as one of two agents guarding the then Vice-President Nixon. Golden accompanied Nixon on his travels to Russia and to Central America. When John Kennedy was elected in 1960, Golden quit to work for private enterprise, ending up with the Lockheed Aircraft Corporation. In April 1968, Lockheed granted him a leave of absence to travel with Candidate Nixon as staff security chief. His campaign work brought him into close contact with Resorts International, and, after Nixon's victory, Golden was hired as deputy director of security on Paradise Island. There he was known as "Nixon's man." Golden's appointment did nothing to squash rumors that Nixon, like Thomas Dewey, owned a "piece" of Paradise, rumors that had been steadily circulating for months. When the black leaders of the new Bahamian government abruptly canceled an announced hike in casino taxes, which they had promised in their election campaign, local newspapers reported the retreat was due entirely to pressure from the White House. Allegedly a telephone call from an unnamed person in the White House persuaded the government leaders that a huge tax increase was unjustified. Apparently there was no objection to a smaller tax increase which was approved without explanation. Friction continued, however, and by 1971 the Bahamas government was openly looking ahead to political independence from England and financial independence from American investors. The possibility that a future upheaval in the Bahamas might close all casinos there became all too real and perhaps spurred Resorts International in its world-wide search for other locations for casino operations.

The capable Golden whisked Hughes to the Britannia Beach Hotel where he was installed in a ninth-floor penthouse. A complete week passed before the *Las Vegas Sun* headlined a story: "Howard Hughes Vanishes." Hank Greenspun, the publisher of the newspaper, was a former press agent for Moe Dalitz and Bugsy Siegel. Greenspun was close to Maheu, and, in effect supported the old ways of Las Vegas, which had continued more or less unchanged while Hughes occupied the Desert Inn penthouse. Maheu had been paid well for his services to Hughes: five hundred and twenty thousand dollars a year, plus expenses. He has since

241

admitted that Dalitz, the old rumrunner, was "very helpful" to him in Las Vegas, although he insisted that "many contacts I made with Mr. Dalitz were made at the specific suggestion of Mr. Hughes, wherein Mr. Hughes wanted the benefit of his thinking."[15]

Maheu's value was apparently ended, for on December 4, 1970, he was fired. His associate security chief, Jack Cooper, was also fired. It was announced that Hughes had retained Intertel to handle all security matters for him in Las Vegas.

The announcement created chaos. Clark County officials, aware of Intertel's direct connection with Resorts International, ordered Hughes's representatives to get the Intertel men out of Las Vegas. Maheu agreed that Intertel should go. But from Nassau by telephone the invisible Hughes convinced Nevada authorities that the action of his representatives, not Maheu's, reflected his wishes. Intertel was indeed in. Shortly thereafter, Jim Golden left Paradise Island to work for Intertel in Las Vegas, where once again he was known as "Nixon's man." The *Las Vegas Sun* published a series of articles by Allen Witwer charging that Intertel was the "secret police" of the syndicate.[16] Intertel officials, while scorning Witwer, still found it necessary to deny formally that their organization had kidnaped Hughes and was holding him captive on Paradise Island on behalf of Resorts International. No one could or did deny that a power struggle for control of Las Vegas was under way. Maheu filed a fifty-million-dollar damage suit against Hughes and won the right to take a deposition from his former employer. The court ruled that if the bashful billionaire did not appear for the deposition, "judgment by default will be taken against you." As of this writing, the issue is unresolved.

Organized crime, like any other business, was adjusting to new situations—social, economic and political—as the final third of the century got into gear. Its methods and procedures had reached an evolutionary stage that was almost incomprehensible to minds far more sophisticated than John Edgar Hoover's. Casino gambling had moved from the back rooms of Prohibition speakeasies into international resort complexes during Hoover's tenure as Director of the FBI. And, while Hoover showed no intention of surrendering power, the syndicate ganglords began the delicate business of transferring their authority to younger hands.

Meyer Lansky, the sixty-eight-year-old chairman of the board of organized crime, disappeared from his plush apartment in Miami Beach in the summer of 1970, and reappeared in Israel with every intention of staying. He obviously had been tipped off that IRS intelligence was ready to seek an indictment against him in connection with the skimming of funds from the Flamingo in Las Vegas—the deal the FBI learned about in 1962 and ignored. In Israel, Lansky also had friends in high places. The indictment was returned in 1971, listing not only Lansky but Morris Lansburgh and Sam Cohen, the official owners of the Flamingo during the period covered by the indictment. The two hotelmen also owned the Eden Roc and some other hotels on Miami Beach and leased the King's Inn on Grand Bahama from Daniel K. Ludwig.

In the months that followed the indictment, which is still pending, evidence mounted that the Nixon administration had no desire to bring Lansky back for trial. The indifference of the Justice Department was manifested as Attorney General John Mitchell noted that the offense with which Lansky was charged was not covered by the United States's extradition treaty with Israel. Perhaps not, but with Israel's life depending on good relations with the United States, not too much persuasion would have been necessary to get Israel to boot Lansky out. Nixon and Mitchell apparently chose to ignore the fact that Lansky, if permitted to live undisturbed in Israel, could boss international gambling from there as easily as from his home in Florida.

The Nixon administration's attitude toward Lansky in Israel was consistent with its action in New York where Hoover's protégé, and Rosenstiel's attorney, Roy Cohn, flexed his muscles. Cohn had made sure he would have influence in the Nixon administration by convening a luncheon meeting prior to the 1968 elections. A number of wealthy New Yorkers attended. Louis Nichols was there, representing Candidate Nixon, as was Maurice Stans who would become Nixon's secretary of commerce. Cohn wanted one thing from the next President—assurance that Manuel Cohen, chairman of the Securities and Exchange Commission, and Robert Morgenthau, United States attorney for the southern district of New York, would be removed from office.[17] The two men had annoyed Cohn by investigating his complex business affairs.

The assurance Cohn desired was given on behalf of Nixon by Nichols and Stans so Cohn's luncheon guests happily contributed more than forty thousand dollars to the Nixon-Agnew campaign. Seven months later Cohen was fired. Getting rid of Morgenthau, who refused to follow tradition and resign, took a little longer. In the interval, Cohn came to trial on the first of two new indictments secured by Morgenthau. The right-wing press supported Cohn. Columnist William F. Buckley, Jr., wondered if Morgenthau suffered from a "devil fixation" because of his pursuit of the elusive Cohn. It was not mentioned that Buckley in 1966 had been given the "George M. Sokolsky Memorial Award" by the American Jewish League Against Communism, Roy M. Cohn president. Others who received the honor were Senator Everett Dirksen, who had helped Cohn in an Illinois banking venture, and Rosenstiel, Cohn's most important client.

Prior to his trial, Cohn secured an affidavit from an exconvict, Milton Pollack, which accused Morgenthau's office of offering him a pardon if he would in turn help Morgenthau "in inveigling Roy Cohn into some transaction that would result in his prosecution."[18] Three special agents of the New York FBI office joined Morgenthau's staff in signing affidavits refuting Pollock's charges. The denials were filed with the court and, in due time, Cohn got copies. He turned his copies over to Nichols, who marched into the FBI office in Washington and demanded the three special agents be censured. John Edgar Hoover promptly complied. Each agent was given a letter of censure and thirty days to report to a new post—away from New York. Morgenthau was enraged and complained to the FBI. Hoover reacted again—the three agents were told they had only thirty-six hours to report to their new posts. What effect this demonstration of Cohn's influence had on prospective witnesses is not known. When the first case came to trial—Cohn did a brilliant job of defending himself—it ended in an acquittal. Before the second indictment could be brought before a jury, Morgenthau was fired as United States attorney by the Nixon administration. The case seemed lost in legal limbo until September 27, 1971, when trial began with the announcement that six of the ten charges were being dropped. What's more, it was disclosed, the key witness who previously had pleaded guilty, was too ill to testify. No one was surprised, therefore, when six weeks later a jury required only an hour to acquit Cohn once again.

Prior to firing Morgenthau—dubbed the most effective United States attorney in the nation by a Republican study group—the Justice Department set up what it called a "super strike force" in New York City. (Under Nixon, Hoover permitted the FBI to take part—officially, anyway—in the strike-force concept.) The new group of crime fighters proved as gossipy as a ladies' bridge club. Writers and reporters were told of big plans to crush the La Cosa Nostra "families" in Manhattan. Assurances were given that even non-Mafia gangsters would be investigated "if we can tie them into one of the Mafia families." Supposedly there was just one problem—before the big drive could begin. The super strike force had to gain access to Morgenthau's files. Morgenthau, who had in fact convicted Mafia and syndicate bosses indiscriminately, was portrayed as stubbornly refusing to cooperate. Writers—this author was one of them—were repeatedly told that Morgenthau had to go, that he was blocking the way. Eventually he was fired outright. Ironically, very little has since been heard from the super strike force, with or without Morgenthau.

Roy Cohn, meanwhile, was busy trying to protect Rosenstiel's reputation. On the very day that Nichols testified before the New York Joint Legislative Committee, March 11, 1971, reporters discovered Nichols conferring with Cohn at a nearby restaurant during the lunch break. When Nichols returned after lunch he explained that he just happened to run into Cohn, who just happened to be waiting out a "hung jury." In a bit of an understatement, Nichols confessed: "I have a friendly relationship with him."

At one time Rosenstiel and Cohn shared a dream that Nichols would succeed Hoover as FBI director, but Hoover clung tenaciously to his job. Nichols, too, was growing older, and his chances faded with every month that passed. Rosenstiel retired and disposed of his interest in Schenley in a mysterious if profitable deal, but his retirement was marred in 1971 when details of his efforts to free himself from the fourth Mrs. Rosenstiel made the front page of the *New York Times*. Benjamin A. Javits, brother of New York Senator Jacob Javits, represented Rosenstiel in his troubles with his wife. It was a complex story. Javits had attempted to void Rosenstiel's marriage by attempting to nullify Mrs. Rosenstiel's divorce from her first husband in Mexico. If, indeed, Susan Rosenstiel was still legally married to Felix Kaufmann, then obviously her marriage to Rosenstiel was invalid. The nullification has been obtained, but on appeal Mrs. Rosenstiel won a landmark decision upholding the validity of Mexican divorces. The decision delighted thousands of New Yorkers who had followed the same route to freedom. In effect, the courts ruled that Rosenstiel was married to his fourth wife even if, in the interim, he had married again.

During the course of the case, Benjamin Javits was charged with "attempting to perpetrate a fraud upon the courts of Mexico and the United States by paying moneys to Mexican public officials and another Mexican national in order to improperly obtain and subsequently defend a nullification of a Mexican divorce decree . . ." He was suspended for three years from the practice of law by the New York courts.[19] The decision to suspend Javits was not unanimous. In a minority opinion, Justice James B. M. McNally dissented, and said Javits should be disbarred. He noted:

Respondent's client was anxious for results. His own testimony shows the client, Lewis S. Rosenstiel, said in substance that money was no object to get rid of his fourth wife. The respondent testified that Rosenstiel told him "it doesn't make any difference. I will spend five million dollars, ten million dollars, whatever it is. Spend it, get it done."[20]

Javits, as Rosenstiel's attorney, was succeeded by—who else?— Roy M. Cohn.

Later on, the fourth Mrs. Rosenstiel testified in executive session before the New York legislative committee on crime in 1970. After spending months checking her allegations, the committee was preparing to hear her in public session early in 1971. Preliminary witnesses testified publicly that Rosenstiel, during Prohibition, had been in league with Lansky to sell bootleg liquor. But before a hearing for Mrs. Rosenstiel could be scheduled, District Attorney Frank Hogan brought perjury charges against her in a completely unrelated civil case. Hogan accused Mrs. Rosenstiel of lying in a pretrial deposition. Her attorneys called the action unprecedented, and the *Village Voice* said bluntly: "What this situation looks like is that Hogan wants to shut Mrs. Rosenstiel up or at least damage her credibility before her testimony before the Joint Legislative Committee." Hogan was a long-time friend of Rosenstiel and was especially close to Thomas Dewey, who had served as Rosenstiel's counsel for many years. Whatever Hogan's motives, Mrs. Rosenstiel's scheduled appearance before the legislative committee was canceled. Months later, by arrangement, she pleaded guilty to one count of "attempted perjury" and was fined five hundred dollars. The other charges of perjury were dropped.

Rosenstiel retired to his Miami Beach mansion while expensive public relations firms in New York bombarded the nation's press with flattering stories about how the retired "giant of industry" planned to fight the narcotics problem by getting young people to contribute a penny a day to a special fund and thus become "involved." The old man also went to Representative Wright Patman, chairman of the House Committee on Banking and Currency, with a plan to fight crime by changing the color of the nation's currency. The scheme, known to the committee staff as "the pink money plan," was based on the assumption that gangsters still kept their unreported cash in tin boxes buried in their back yards. Rosenstiel supposedly believed that by changing the color of the currency at frequent intervals, and calling in all the old money, the gangsters would have to choose between giving up their profits or facing income-tax raps.[21]

Of course, Rosenstiel's plan completely ignored the sophisticated nature of syndicate financing. The big shots of crime had their money in foreign banks or in blue-chip stocks. Changing the color of the currency might hurt some minor punks, but it would do nothing to the big-time gangsters. Patman, then busy trying to achieve some controls over money flowing to Swiss banks, listened politely and brushed Rosenstiel off.

Like Rosenstiel, John Edgar Hoover, who was seventy-four when Nixon took office, sometimes appeared to be something more than slightly senile. His old ability to adjust agilely to new situations and new personalities, began to fail him. Doggedly he stuck by his guns, firing away at old enemies, apparently unable to comprehend the twists and turns of policy as that most expedient of men, Richard Nixon, shaped and reshaped his game plan for his Administration and the 1972 elections. For example, while Nixon climbed to power, it had been politically useful to help build a wall around Red China. As late as 1962, in his book *Six Crises,* Nixon had written:

Admitting Red China to the United Nations would be a mockery of the provision of the Charter which limits its membership to "peace-loving nations" . . . it would give respectability to the Communist regime which would immensely increase its power and prestige in Asia, and probably irreparably weaken the non-Communist governments in that area.

Nine years later Nixon was President. Good politics dictated a shift of policy. Misreading the shifting wind and the realities, Hoover told a House Appropriations Committee, "The potent threat to our national security posed by Red China still exists . . . the United States is Communist China's No. 1 enemy. . . ." A few weeks after this message from Hoover, Nixon announced his plans to visit "the People's Republic of China" and called for admission of that government to the United Nations. The FBI Director made no public comment, but the FBI's plans to publish Hoover's testimony were canceled for "budget reasons."

Under the circumstances it was not surprising that a nationally syndicated news feature included this rather bleak capsule description of John Edgar Hoover in 1971:

At 76, the nation's leading crime fighter is described by those close to him as "increasingly arbitrary and irritable." He is

248

nervous when eating in strange restaurants, rides slumped down in the corner of his bullet-proof Cadillac, with a hat propped in the rear window as a decoy for assassins, and consults a Washington psychiatrist over a nightmare in which people chase him.[22]

A vicious attack on a dead man has been typical of Hoover's outbursts in recent years. The smear of Dr. Martin Luther King, the civil rights leader murdered in 1968, annoyed many liberals far more than Hoover's shortcomings in the field of law enforcement. Despite the indignation his irrational actions aroused, events soon proved it was much safer for John Edgar Hoover to attack dead men than live ones. Hoover's treatment of special agent John F. Shaw (discussed earlier) created an uproar and shocked some of Hoover's most staunch supporters. A married agent, Shaw had impressive academic qualifications and was one of three special agents selected for advanced study at John Jay College of Law in New York City. A Marine veteran with seven years in the FBI, Shaw was one of those all too few bright young men who over the years have lived up to the FBI legend. When his professor, Abraham S. Blumberg, suggested Hoover had been too long in power Shaw was intrigued and decided to research the subject in an attempt to defend his boss. In September 1970, he wrote his findings, which were mostly flattering, in a long letter to Professor Blumberg. He concluded with a request that the letter be kept "in complete confidence." On September 15 he naively turned the letter over to the secretarial pool at the New York FBI office for final typing. He got the finished letter but the rough draft was torn up and placed in the wastebasket. Some of the secretaries talked, however, and within minutes ten special agents were sifting through the wastebasket, putting together the jigsaw pieces of the long letter. The agents were able to reconstruct eight pages. Among other things Shaw had written to Blumberg: "We are not simply rooted in tradition. We're stuck in it up to our eyeballs. And it all revolves around one key figure—the life and exploits of J. Edgar Hoover."

When Shaw refused to turn over the entire letter, he was suspended. Four days later, Hoover transferred him to Butte, Montana, considered a special "Siberia" by the FBI. Hoover in a personal letter to Shaw criticized him not only for writing the letter but for failing to report Blumberg's criticisms. "Your derelictions are inexcusable," said Hoover. Hoover also demanded that John Jay College fire Professor Blumberg and ordered that fifteen agents attending the college withdraw until the college officials obeyed. The officials refused, and more than a thousand students petitioned Attorney General Mitchell to investigate the entire incident and return the agents to classes.[23]

Rather than accept the transfer, Shaw resigned. His wife was seriously ill. The American Civil Liberties Union filed suit on Shaw's behalf, charging that his civil rights had been violated. Attorney General Mitchell's reaction was to use the suit as a pretext for withholding information about the case. Months passed. Mrs. Shaw died of cancer, and her husband publicly regretted that she could not have been spared "the mental anguish which this controversy brought to her bedside." Finally, in June 1971, John Edgar Hoover backed down. The suit was compromised. Hoover agreed to expunge his prejudicial remarks from Shaw's personnel records —remarks that, given the awe in which Hoover is held by police agencies, effectively prevented Shaw from finding new employment in his field. Hoover also agreed to give Shaw thirteen thousand dollars in back pay.[24] ACLU attorneys noted that it was the first time in Hoover's forty-six years as FBI director, that he had been forced to reverse himself in a disciplinary matter. Better than anything else, the Shaw case indicated that Hoover's days of power were nearing an end.

The Shaw episode was one of several mentioned on April 26, 1971, when Representative Hale Boggs loosed the most bitter, the most devastating attack in the history of the Congressional Record against the man who, until a short time before, had been immune to criticism. Boggs, after discussing the theft of documents from the office of an FBI safe in Pennsylvania and Hoover's ludicrous attempts to force the Xerox Corporation to help him find the person who copied and purloined the secret files, concluded:

In no country in the world could a director of a nation's secret police escape censure and removal for what is happening now.

The offices of the Bureau have been burglarized and the files of the Bureau have become common knowledge.

The system of informers has turned on its master and is filling the stream of public dialogue with disclosures and revelations which only serve to undermine the Bureau's future and further effectiveness. The agents of the Bureau are demoralized and in fear of the pettiness and wrath of the man under whom they work. The standards for recruitment are falling. These are all symptoms of internal disarray and decay which would be acceptable in no other organization, public or private.

Facing this, as we and the Nation must, it is no reassurance to read and hear, as we do, that the White House and the Department of Justice know that changes must be made but that they are fearful of acting in what is clearly the national interest.

Has the power of one man become so great that the American system is in paralysis before him?

That question can only be answered by the President himself.[25]

Afterword

*T*HE career of Albert Francis Sinatra well illustrates the amoral nature of our society and the hypocrisy of John Edgar Hoover and his friends. As an entertainer, Sinatra had his ups and downs before achieving, in the 1950's, a unique position in American life. Despite the whispers of gangster influence that accompanied his rise, by 1960 he seemed untouchable. A Democrat, he supported John F. Kennedy and, together with his "rat pack," which included a Kennedy brother-in-law, had been an honored guest at pre-inaugural festivities.

Shortly after he became attorney general, Robert Kennedy decided that the rumors about Sinatra should be investigated. Dougald D. MacMillan, later to head the Federal strike force in Miami, was the Justice Department attorney assigned. His report, dated April 3, 1962, linked Sinatra to a score of syndicate gangsters in Miami Beach, New York, and Las Vegas. Close ties with Joseph Fischetti, a cousin of Al Capone, were described. Sam Mooney Giancana, an important Mafia figure in Chicago, was listed as a Sinatra pal, and his partner in the Cal-Neva Casino at Lake Tahoe. Johnnie Roselli, the ex-Chicago hood, then cooperating with the CIA in an attempt to murder Fidel Castro, was mentioned, as was the notorious Jimmy Blue Eyes who, allegedly had given Sinatra seven percent of the Sands Hotel in Las Vegas. MacMillan's long report concluded:

> Sinatra has had a long and wide association with hoodlums and racketeers which seems to be continuing. The nature of Sinatra's work may, on occasion, bring him into contact with underworld figures but this cannot account for his friendship and/or financial involvement with such people as Joe Fischetti and Rocco Fischetti, Paul Emilie D'Amato, John Formosa, and Sam Giancana, all of whom appear on our list of racketeers. No other entertainer appears to be mentioned nearly so frequently in connection with racketeers.

Robert Kennedy, after receiving this report, quietly cut all ties with Sinatra. Pending Federal investigations, Sinatra received a green light. The Sinatra-Giancana partnership in the Cal-Neva Casino became public knowledge, and Nevada officials forced both men to sell their interests. The murder of President Kennedy saved what was left of Sinatra's reputation. During the administration of President Johnson, Sinatra retained his friendship with leading Democrats. In 1968 Sinatra was scheduled to entertain at a Democratic fund-raising gala in Miami Beach when the *Wall Street Journal* revealed the existence of MacMillan's unfavorable report. The Democrat's gala was shifted from Sinatra's favorite hotel, the Fontainebleau, and Sinatra's appearance was canceled.

Undaunted, Sinatra began courting the Republicans. Soon he was being entertained by President Nixon in the White House and by Ambassador Walter Annenberg in London. In 1971 Vice-President Spiro Agnew left the wedding of the President's daughter Tricia to fly to Los Angeles to attend Sinatra's "farewell" performance there. Agnew was Sinatra's weekend house guest. John Edgar Hoover certainly had access to ample information about Sinatra, but Hoover—who could wax pious over the alleged security risks posed by Dr. Martin Luther King—apparently saw no harm in an associate of gangsters becoming a buddy of the President and Vice-President of the United States.

The American gangster began as a bootlegger, supplying

those wet goods demanded by a rebellious public. He moved into illegal gambling, catering once again to the weaknesses of the citizens and their system of laws. Along the way he invested his illicit millions to achieve economic and political influence as John Edgar Hoover diverted public attention with his crusades against punks and pinks. The gray area between crime and business and politics deepened and widened until in the 1970s it is impossible to say where one ends and the other begins. But we can say that a new cycle is beginning. Frustrated young men, impatient with the slow pace of reform, unimpressed with the hypocrisy of our leaders, are already seeking shortcuts to the fast buck. As they become more free in their enterprise than the law allows, as power is transferred to a new generation of sophisticated executives unhampered by criminal records or public association with syndicate figures, a new syndicate may be born. Its growth will depend upon how intelligently the nation meets such social problems as the control of narcotics, but that it will grow is inevitable so long as greed motivates mankind. The process is taking place today, although it may be thirty years before the public learns the details. As economic opportunities are found in space, men will conspire to make greater profits, and crime syndicates will be born beyond the stars.

To recognize the realities of human nature is not to say that man could not have done better in the past and cannot do better in the future. Essential to man's progress, however, is his understanding. As long as greedy politicians can keep him in ignorance, just so long will he lack understanding. A study of the continuing alliance of crime, business, and politics is vital, and the place to concentrate such a study is with the career of John Edgar Hoover.

For a half century John Edgar Hoover, unique among Americans, had the power to destroy the infamous syndicates of organized crime. He failed to use it. Instead, as crime grew into the nation's biggest business, Hoover used his power to enhance his reputation and that of the FBI. Sworn to defend the country, he was unable to distinguish its true enemies. Posing as a moral leader, he helped create a generation of cynics. Under the guise of fighting subversion, he encouraged those on the Right who distrusted democracy. Perhaps his greatest disservice has been to confuse the American people about the real nature of organized crime. Instead of admitting it was an economic problem, he described it as a moral issue and assured the public that it did not pay. It did, handsomely, and largely because of him.

John Edgar Hoover, the man, is now relatively unimportant. So are his efforts to build monuments to himself and his attempts to dictate the selection of his successor. It is the Hoover legend, with all its pious claptrap, that remains a barrier to the hope of progress. Given the truth, the American people can be relied upon to make the right decisions. Where Hoover is concerned, the truth, long overdue, is beginning to be known.

Notes

Introduction

1. *Congressional Record*, vol. 117, 1 February 1971.
2. J. Edgar Hoover, *Masters of Deceit* (New York: Henry Holt & Co., 1958).
3. Leo Huberman and Paul M. Sweezy, "The Roots and Prospects of McCarthyism," *Monthly Review*, January 1954.

Chapter I

1. Allan Nevins and Henry Steele Commager, *A Pocket History of the United States* (New York: Washington Square Press, 1942).
2. Max Lowenthal, *The Federal Bureau of Investigation* (New York: William Sloane Associates, 1950).
3. Jack Alexander, "Profiles: The Director, II," *The New Yorker*, 2 October 1937.
4. *Ibid.*
5. Lowenthal, *op.cit.*
6. *Ibid.*
7. Don Whitehead, *The F.B.I. Story* (New York: Random House, 1956).
8. J. Edgar Hoover, *op.cit.*
9. *Senate Document No. 153*, 66th Congress, 1st Session, 1919, "Investigation Activities of the Department of Justice: Letter

From the Attorney General," (Washington: Government Printing Office, 1919).

10. Lowenthal, *op.cit.*
11. *Congressional Record*, vol. 64.
12. Lowenthal, *op.cit.*
13. *Congressional Record, op.cit.*
14. Whitehead, *op.cit.*
15. William Allen White, *Autobiography* (New York: Macmillan Co., 1946).

Chapter II

1. *New York Times*, 11 August 1922.
2. Harry M. Daugherty, *Inside Story of the Harding Tragedy* (New York: The Churchill Co., 1932).
3. *House Appropriations Committee*, "Hearings on Department of Justice Appropriations" (1923).
4. *Ibid.*
5. White, *op.cit.*, p. 619.
6. Herbert Hoover, *The Memoirs of Herbert Hoover* (New York: Macmillan Co., 1952), p. 49.
7. Samuel Hopkins Adams, *Incredible Era* (New York: Capricorn Books, 1939), p. 308.
8. Francis Russell, *The Shadow of Blooming Grove* (New York: McGraw-Hill, 1968), p. 570.
9. Daugherty, *op.cit.*
10. Whitehead, *op.cit.*
11. Andrew Sinclair, *The Available Man* (New York: Macmillan Co., 1965).
12. Allan Nevins and Frank Ernest Hill, *Ford—Expansion and Challenge* (New York: Charles Scribner's Sons, 1957).
13. White, *op.cit.*
14. Herbert Hoover, *op.cit.*
15. Adams, *op.cit.*
16. *Ibid.*
17. Herbert Hoover, *op.cit.*
18. Lowenthal, *op.cit.*
19. Whitehead, *op.cit.*
20. Alpheus Thomas Mason, *Harlan Fiske Stone* (New York: Viking Press, 1956).
21. *Ibid.*
22. Herbert Hoover, *op.cit.*

23. Harold L. Ickes, *The Secret Diary of Harold L. Ickes, 1933–36* (New York: Simon and Schuster, 1953).
24. Blair Coan, *The Red Web* (Chicago: Northwest Publishing Co., 1925).
25. Burton K. Wheeler with Paul F. Healy, *Yankee From the West* (New York: Doubleday & Co., 1962).
26. *Senate Hearings: Select Committee on Investigation of the Attorney General* (Washington: Government Printing Office, 1924).

Chapter III

1. Mason, *op.cit.*
2. *New York Times*, 11 May 1924.
3. Mason, *op.cit.*
4. Wheeler, *op.cit.*
5. *Literary Digest* (24 January 1925) pp. 44–46.
6. James Phelan, "Hoover of the F.B.I.," *Saturday Evening Post*, 25 September 1965.
7. Confidential files of the Internal Revenue Service, Intelligence Division.
8. Whitehead, *op.cit.*
9. Unpublished Ford Foundation study, "An Attack of Virtue," University of Louisville Library.
10. *Ibid.*
11. New York Joint Legislative Committee on Crime, Nichols's Statement, 1971.
12. *Ibid.*
13. Personal statement to the author.
14. Files of New York Joint Legislative Committee on Crime.
15. Nicola Gentile, unpublished manuscript in F.B.I. files.
16. See Hank Messick, *Secret File* (New York: G. P. Putnam's Sons, 1969).
17. Whitehead, *op.cit.*
18. All details of the Lindbergh kidnaping are taken from the files of the Intelligence Unit, Internal Revenue Service.
19. Herbert Hoover, *op.cit.*
20. Files of Intelligence Unit, Internal Revenue Service.
21. *Ibid.*
22. Hank Messick, *Lansky* (New York: G.P. Putnam's Sons, 1971).

Chapter IV

1. Wheeler, *op.cit.*
2. *New York Times,* 1 March 1933.
3. *Ibid.,* 3 March 1933.
4. William Seagle, "The American National Police," *Harper's,* November, 1934.
5. Lowenthal, *op.cit.*
6. Howard McLellan, "Shoot to Kill," *Harper's,* January, 1936.
7. Alvin Karpis with Bill Trent, *The Alvin Karpis Story* (New York: Coward, McCann & Geohegan, 1971).
8. Quentin Reynolds, "Death in Headlines," *Collier's,* 13 August 1938.
9. Fred J. Cook, *The F.B.I. Nobody Knows* (New York: Macmillan Co., 1964).
10. Richard O'Connor, *The First Hurrah* (New York: G.P. Putnam's Sons, 1970), p. 282.
11. *United States vs. John Torrio, et al.,* Federal Court, N.Y. (1939).
12. Confidential files of the Intelligence Division, Internal Revenue Service.
13. *Ibid.*
14. John Morton Blum, *The Morgenthau Diaries* (Boston: Houghton, Mifflin Co., 1959).
15. *House Judiciary Committee, Hearings Before Special Subcommittee to Investigate Department of Justice,* 2nd session, 82nd Congress (1952) "Chelf Subcommittee."
16. *Special Committee to Investigate Organized Crime in Interstate Commerce, Hearings,* Part 5, 2nd Session, 81st Congress (1950) "Kefauver Committee."
17. *Ibid.*

Chapter V

1. Ramsey Clark, *Crime in America* (New York: Simon and Schuster, 1970).
2. Gentile, *op.cit.*
3. For details, see Messick, *Lansky, op.cit.*
4. Confidential files of the Intelligence Division, Internal Revenue Service.
5. See Messick, *Lansky, op.cit.*

6. Burton B. Turkus and Sid Feder, *Murder, Inc.* (New York: Farrar, Straus & Cudahy, 1951).
7. Harry J. Anslinger, *The Murderers* (New York: Farrar, Straus & Cudahy, 1961).
8. *Ibid.*
9. See Messick, *Syndicate in the Sun* (New York: Macmillan Co., 1968).
10. Robert E. Sherwood, *Roosevelt and Hopkins* (New York: Harper & Brothers, 1948).
11. Francis B. Biddle, *In Brief Authority* (New York: Doubleday & Co., 1962).
12. Max Freedman, ed., *Roosevelt and Frankfurter* (Boston: Little, Brown & Co., 1967).
13. In 1971, Lansky disclosed from Israel that Frank Costello was also consulted as part of Operation Underworld.
14. For details see Messick, *Lansky, op.cit.*
15. Biddle, *op.cit.*
16. Arthur H. Samish and Bob Thomas, *The Secret Boss of California* (New York: Crown Publishers, Inc., 1971).
17. Estes Kefauver, *Crime in America* (New York: Greenwood Press, 1951).
18. "The Big Wine Deal," *Fortune*, September 1943.
19. Samish, *op.cit.*
20. See Messick, *Secret File, op.cit.*
21. *New York Times*, 28 March 1957.
22. See Hank Messick, *The Silent Syndicate* (New York: Macmillan Co., 1967).
23. Author's files.
24. See Messick, *Secret File, op.cit.*

Chapter VI

1. James MacGregor Burns, *Roosevelt: The Soldier of Freedom* (New York: Harcourt Brace Jovanovitch, Inc., 1970).
2. Edward J. Flynn, *You're the Boss* (New York: Viking Press, 1947).
3. See Messick, *Lansky, op.cit.*
4. Jules Abels, *The Truman Scandals* (Chicago: Henry Regnery Co., 1956).
5. See Hank Messick, *Syndicate Wife* (New York: Macmillan Co., 1968).
6. "King Subcommittee," *Investigation of Department of Justice*, 1st Session, 82nd Congress (1952).

7. *House Judiciary Committee, op.cit.*
8. Messick, *Lansky, op.cit.*
9. *Cleveland Plain Dealer,* 8 November 1959.
10. Messick, *The Silent Syndicate, op.cit.*
11. *Ibid.*
12. "The Governor and the Mobster," *Life,* 2 May 1969.
13. "Letters to the Editors," *Life,* 20 May 1969.
14. "King Subcommittee," *op.cit.*
15. Cook, *op.cit.*
16. Whitehead, *op.cit.*
17. Richard M. Nixon, *Six Crises* (New York: Doubleday & Co., 1962).
18. Joseph Keeley, *The China Lobby Man* (New York: Arlington House, 1969).
19. *Ibid.*
20. Hank Messick, *Syndicate Abroad* (New York: Macmillan Co., 1969).
21. "Chelf Subcommittee," *op.cit.*
22. Roy Cohn, *McCarthy* (New York: New American Library, 1968).
23. *Ibid.*
24. Jack Anderson and Ronald W. May, *McCarthy: The Man, the Senator, the "Ism"* (Boston: Beacon Press, 1952).
25. Cohn, *op.cit.*

Chapter VII

1. Anderson and May, *op.cit.*
2. *Business Week,* 2 October 1958.
3. Keeley, *op.cit.*
4. *Miami Herald,* 12 August 1971.
5. *New York Times,* 13 February 1938.
6. "Dangerous Thoughts," *The Nation,* 27 January 1951.
7. *Congressional Record,* 1 September 1950.
8. *New York Post,* 7 September 1950.
9. All references to the "Kefauver Committee" testimony are taken from transcripts of the Special Committee to Investigate Organized Crime in Interstate Commerce, 2nd Session, 81st Congress (1950).
10. Dwight D. Eisenhower, *Mandate for Change* (New York: Doubleday & Co., 1963).
11. Cohn, *op.cit.*
12. "Chelf Subcommittee," *op.cit.*

13. Cook, *op.cit.*
14. "Kefauver Committee," *op.cit.*
15. Norman Ollestad, *Inside the F.B.I.* (New York: Lyle Stuart, Inc., 1967).
16. "Kefauver Committee," Part One, *op.cit.*
17. Cohn, *op.cit.*
18. *New York Herald Tribune,* 18 November 1953.

Chapter VIII

1. Nina Totenberg, "Hoover: Life and Times of a 76 Year Old Cop," *National Observer,* 12 April 1971.
2. Theodore H. White, "Texas: Land of Wealth and Fear," *The Reporter,* 25 May 1954.
3. *Hearings Before the Committee on Rules and Administration,* U.S. Senate, Part 10, 1st and 2nd Sessions, 88th Congress (1964) "Bobby Baker Hearings."
4. Sheilah Graham, "A Gallery of Holt Authors," *Fortune,* December 1959.
5. "Kefauver Committee," Part 18, *op.cit.*
6. See Messick, *Syndicate Abroad, op.cit.*
7. *Miami Herald,* 8 April 1971.
8. Allen Witwer, unpublished statement in author's files.
9. *Las Vegas Sun,* 22 March 1971.
10. *Miami Herald,* 8 April 1971.
11. Files of New York Joint Legislative Committee on Crime.
12. *Ibid.*
13. *Miami Herald, Tropic Magazine,* 2 May 1971.
14. See Messick, *Lansky, op.cit.*
15. Cohn, *op.cit.*
16. *Ibid.*
17. Arthur V. Watkins, *Enough Rope* (Englewood Cliffs: Prentice-Hall, Inc., 1969).
18. *Ibid.*
19. Files of New York Joint Legislative Committee on Crime.
20. Watkins, *op.cit.*
21. *Ibid.*
22. Eisenhower, *op.cit.*
23. *Ibid.*
24. Cohn, *op.cit.*

Chapter IX

1. Cohn, *op.cit.*
2. Messick, *Secret File, op.cit.*
3. *New York Times*, 8 August 1939.
4. Files of New York Joint Legislative Committee on Crime.
5. *Ibid.*
6. *Ibid.*
7. *Ibid.*
8. *Congressional Record*, 5 August 1958.
9. Messick, *Lansky, op.cit.*
10. Milton R. Wessel with Stanley Frank, "How We Bagged the Mafia," *Saturday Evening Post*, 16 July 1960.
11. *Annual Report to The Attorney General of the United States*, 10 February 1959. Unpublished.
12. Wessel and Frank, *loc.cit.*, 23 July 1960.
13. Statement to the author.
14. See Messick, *Syndicate Abroad, op.cit.*
15. Arthur M. Schlesinger, Jr., *A Thousand Days* (Boston: Houghton Mifflin Co., 1965).
16. F.B.I. files.
17. *Miami Herald*, 18 January 1971.
18. See Messick, *The Silent Syndicate, op.cit.*
19. Richard J. Whelan, *The Founding Father* (New York: New American Library, 1964).
20. Robert Kennedy, *The Enemy Within* (New York: Harper & Brothers, 1960).
21. For full story of Newport, see Messick, *Syndicate Wife, op.cit.*
22. Unpublished Ford Foundation study, *op.cit.*
23. Kennedy, *op.cit.*
24. Files of the *Courier-Journal*, Louisville, Ky.
25. *New York Journal American*, 12 March 1964.
26. *New York Times*, 10 June 1971.

Chapter X

1. Wessel and Frank, *loc.cit.*, 16 July 1960.
2. Gentile, *op.cit.*
3. Files of U.S. Bureau of Narcotics and Dangerous Drugs.
4. Files of New York Joint Legislative Committee on Crime.
5. All taped conversations pertaining to New Jersey are taken

from official transcripts made part of the Federal Court record at trials in New Jersey.

6. President's Commission on Law Enforcement and Administration of Justice, *The Challenge of Crime in a Free Society* (Washington: U.S. Government Printing Office, 1967).

Chapter XI

1. Ollestad, *op.cit.*
2. Hearings Before the Subcommittee on Administrative Practice and Procedure of the Committee on the Judiciary, United States Senate, 2nd Session, 89th Congress (1965). "Long Subcommittee."
3. *United States vs. Malnik*, U.S. Federal Court, Miami (1970).
4. See Messick, *Syndicate in the Sun, op.cit.*
5. *Hearings*, Florida Beverage Department, 6 January 1968.
6. Files of the Royal Canadian Police.
7. The author attended the hearing.
8. The author was subpoenaed as a Federal witness, but did not testify when Malnik produced no character witnesses.
9. Drew Pearson and Jack Anderson, "The Last Days of J. Edgar Hoover," *True*, January 1969.
10. William Manchester, *The Death of a President* (New York: Harper and Row, 1967).
11. *Report of the President's Commission on the Assassination of President John F. Kennedy* (Washington: U.S. Government Printing Office, 1964).
12. Manchester, *op.cit.*
13. Ronnie Dugger, "John Connally: Nixon's New Quarterback," *Atlantic*, July 1971.
14. Files of the Internal Revenue Service.
15. *Ibid.*
16. Files of New York Joint Legislative Committee on Crime.

Chapter XII

1. Files of the Justice Department.
2. *Ibid.*
3. The documented history of Bahamas gambling is given in *Syndicate Abroad*.
4. Files of New York Joint Legislative Committee on Crime.
5. Messick, *Syndicate Abroad, op.cit.*, and *Report of the Com-*

mission of Inquiry into the Operation of the Business of Casinos in Freeport and in Nassau (London: Her Majesty's Stationery Office, 1967).

6. Files of the *Bahama Observer*.
7. Files of the Justice Department.
8. See Messick, *Lansky, op.cit.*
9. Messick, *Syndicate Wife, op.cit.*
10. Louis B. Nichols, "The Battle Against Vote Fraud," *Reader's Digest,* July, 1969.
11. Nixon, *op.cit.*
12. *Toronto Telegram,* 4 June 1971, p. 19.
13. Intertel's reply to *Las Vegas Sun* articles, privately circulated, 1971.
14. Benjamin F. Schemmer, "What Happend to Howard Hughes," *Look,* 1 June 1971.
15. *Ibid.*
16. *Las Vegas Sun,* 21 March through 2 April 1971.
17. William Lambert, "The Hotshot One-Man Roy Cohn Lobby," *Life,* 5 September 1969.
18. *Ibid.*
19. *New York Law Journal,* 6 January 1971.
20. *Ibid.*
21. Files of House Banking and Currency Committee, 1969.
22. *Miami Herald, Tropic Magazine,* 17 April 1971.
23. *Congressional Record,* 1 February 1971.
24. *Miami Herald,* 18 June 1971.
25. *Congressional Record,* 22 April 1971.

Index

Index

270

271